TRANSITION

Transition *was founded more than*
thirty years ago in Uganda by the late
Rajat Neogy and quickly established
itself as a leading forum for intellectual
debate. The first series of issues
developed a reputation for tough-minded,
far-reaching criticism, both cultural
and political, and this new series carries
on the tradition.

AN INTERNATIONAL REVIEW

Contents

ISSUE

69

V6N1

SPRING

1996

Cover photo of
Rajat Neogy reading
Transition **32, 1967**
© *John Goldblatt.*
Courtesy of
Barbara Lapcek Neogy.

RAJAT NEOGY REMEMBERED

Paul Theroux

We made our introductions through our work and met in person later, which is the right sequence for writers to get acquainted. Rajat's magazine had recently begun in Uganda; I was writing poetry and fiction in Malawi. Africa was a small place then—or so it seemed, because it was one place, where writers were eagerly signaling to each other: Chinua Achebe and Wole Soyinka and Chris Okigbo and Ulli Beier from Nigeria, Cameron Duodo from Ghana, Dennis Brutus and Nadine Gordimer and others from South Africa, Ezekiel Mphahlele and Ngugi from Kenya, David Rubadiri and I from Malawi, and yet others in the Sudan, Ethiopia, Zambia, Tanzania. Nearly all these signals were directed toward Uganda, where Rajat edited them for publication in *Transition*.

It is hard to imagine a little magazine that was so generally influential on such a vast continent, but that is what happened with Transition. Rajat began his magazine at just the right time, and it became a rallying point throughout the 1960s. It helped that Rajat was a local boy, with Africa inside him as well as the experience of a British university. It all showed in the way he spoke, moving from Swahili to Hindi to English. Kampala then was a small green city, and Uganda was prosperous and full of distinguished people: in 1966, Chinua Achebe, V. S. Naipaul, Ali Mazrui, Ezekiel Mphahlele, the anthropologists at Makerere. Rajat had lived through Uganda's later colonial years, through its independence and hopeful years; he was also to experience its disintegration and terror.

He was brave, he was forthright and funny, he was a tease; he had tremendous confidence, not the ranting and fearful bravado that was common among some Ugandans, but a stylish poise that was both intellectual and social. He was handsome, clever, and young. He used all his gifts. He traveled across Africa, and to London and New York. His magazine mattered. He liked me, he published my work—he was the first publisher of my work—and I felt lucky to know him.

One of his strangest requests of me—but typical Rajat—was that I agree to sign a paper saying that I had committed adultery with his Swedish wife, Lotte. This was 1965. Adultery was grounds for divorce in Uganda, and it had to be proven. "I wouldn't ask this of anyone else," he said. "I am asking you because you're my friend." Well, that was true, but Kampala was such a small place that I did not want to be known in this town as a "co-respondent," the legal term for the adulterous party. Rajat said that he had excellent contacts at the printers of the Uganda *Argus*—also the printers of *Transition*—so he would see to it that my name would not appear in the Court column, where divorces and criminal convictions and bankruptcies were listed, once a week in very small print.

Although I had never laid a hand on the woman, I agreed to be named as co-respondent and said that I had slept with her on three occasions. I was soon served with papers. I was warned by Rajat's attorney that this was illegal—connivance, in fact. In court, the magistrate said, "This Theroux chap, isn't he supposed to be a friend of yours?" Rajat admitted this was so. Magistrate: "Some friend!"

In spite of Rajat's promises, my name appeared in the Argus, and afterward when I showed up at parties, people—expatriates or leathery ex-colonials—smiled at me knowingly. At the age of twenty-four, I had my first experience of celebrity. It was also one of the happiest periods of my life. I fell in love. Rajat ap-

proved of the woman, Anne Castle. He was a witness at our wedding—his elegant signature on our marriage certificate. Rajat married two more times and fathered seven children, who are now scattered around the world.

In those years, because we were friends, because we were in Africa, I saw him every day. (I had started out as a Lecturer at Makerere; a few years later, because of the rapid departures of expatriates, I was Acting Head of the Adult Studies Centre. "We have no one else in the pipeline," the chancellor, Y. K. Lule,

**Rajat Neogy:
born, Kampala,
Uganda, 1938;
died San Francisco,
California,
3 December 1995**

© *Camera Press*

said.) Rajat's natural element was at a large table—City Bar on Kampala Road was one; the Staff Bar at Makerere was another; and an austere vegetarian restaurant, Hindu Lodge. He sat, he talked, he teased, he encouraged; he then went back to his office and worked on his magazine. We all assumed that Uganda would just get better. Naipaul disagreed. The politicians were clearly opportunists and crooks, he said: "This country will turn back into jungle."

We did not really know what would happen. You never do. But it got worse, many of us left. Rajat stayed and got thrown into jail for sedition—criticizing the Ugandan government, something he had been doing for years. His detention in prison might have broken him. Or was it disillusionment? It was revealed that for some years the magazine had been partly funded by the CIA, the grubby money dispensed by the clean hands of the Congress for Cultural Free-

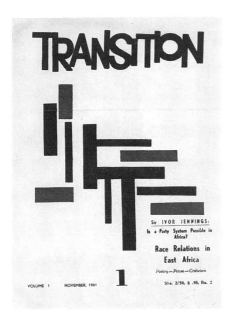

dom. (*Encounter* magazine, in England, was another recipient.) He brought *Transition* to Ghana in 1970 and edited it for two years. He then went to the United States, and he just about vanished. I saw him once: he looked frail, unsteady, and he had no interest in pursuing conversation. He was found dead a month ago in the San Francisco hotel that had been his home for a number of years. He was fifty-seven. After he left Africa, he was not the same. But when I knew him, thirty years ago in Africa, he was brilliant and his friendship meant everything to me.

THE DAY I STOPPED RAJAT NEOGY BECOMING A MUSLIM

Ali A. Mazrui

Rajat Neogy had returned to Uganda for a visit after the fall of President Milton Obote in 1971. It was a Friday morning when Rajat walked into my office on Makerere Hill. In the course of the conversation he asked if I was coming to Kibuli mosque for Friday prayers. I was startled. Rajat was raised Hindu, and his adulthood was totally secular. Where did the mosque come into it?

He abruptly said he would see me at prayers. And as he was walking out of my office, he said, "It is a submission, not a conversion!" It was then that it dawned on me, almost with a shock, that he planned to join the Islamic faith that day!

I was even more shocked when I detected in myself a compelling desire to stop him. I of all people, descended from a long line of devout Muslim *ulemaa*, son of the late Chief Kadhi of Kenya—why did I want to close the doors of Islam against Rajat as a new supplicant?

There was no time to reason why. I rushed to the Kibuli mosque. Rajat was waiting for me outside. The Friday prayers were about to begin. We hurried in together.

After the prayers Buganda's Prince Badru Kakungulu, who was serving as the imam at the mosque, stood up to inquire if Professor Mazrui was in the congregation. When I confirmed, the imam asked me to move to the front of the mosque. That was the moment I realized that Rajat had made advance preparations for his public conversion.

I whispered urgently to Rajat at my side that this was not the right way to take such a momentous step. As we walked toward Prince Badru, Rajat fortunately whispered the reassuring words, "I will do whatever you say."

When Imam Badru handed the microphone to Rajat, expecting him to request the rituals of conversion, I snatched it away. I explained that Rajat had suffered in Uganda under the regime of Milton Obote and that Rajat considered me the friend who had risked the most to stand by him. Now that Obote was gone and Rajat was back in Uganda, he

Ali Mazrui and Rajat Neogy in 1971

had decided to join his old friend, Ali Mazrui, in a prayer of thanksgiving at our mosque. I therefore called upon the congregation to pray for Rajat and me in this new post-Obote era. Prince Badru was greatly perplexed, but the congregation swallowed my whole story quite happily.

I later convinced Rajat that even if he wanted to convert, it did not have to be in the presence of hundreds of worshipers. A private conversion, I argued, had greater solemnity. In reality I also felt that a private conversion would be easier to retract if he had a change of heart. Subsequently, Rajat did convert privately to Islam.

Why was this complex character suddenly so intrigued by Islam? Was it because Bangladesh was born in 1971—at a time when Rajat was losing his African roots? Bangladesh was a Muslim country. Was this young Bengali (originally Hindu) seeking a new identity in the wake of his dis-Africanization by Milton Obote?

Or was Rajat attracted by Islam's doctrinal austerity? As he struggled to overcome his alcoholism, did he see Islam as a sanctuary of sobriety?

Or was Rajat influenced by the fact that the forces that had overthrown Mil-

ton Obote in January 1971 were Muslim-led? It is true that political Islam under Idi Amin in Uganda quickly turned sour. But Idi Amin had helped to destroy the best years of Milton Obote, just as Milton Obote had helped to destroy the best years of Rajat Neogy. Had this been a third factor behind Rajat's flirtation with Islam?

Or, finally, egocentric though it may sound, was Rajat influenced by me? Apart from his exceptionally strong wife, Barbara, none of Rajat's other friends in Uganda had stood up for him the way I had. I had risked my freedom, my Ugandan career, and conceivably my life to protest his detention. In Parliament at the time, President Obote threatened to detain me or throw me out of the country.

Islam as Bengali identity, Islam as sobriety, Islam as a political ally in Uganda, Islam as friendship. That itinerant soul called Rajat Neogy was constantly in transition. (This pun is fully intended!)

In all probability, Rajat Neogy was looking for a reconciliation between a culture of freedom and a culture of submission. His fascination with Islam was part of this dialectic of anguish, part of his restless soul.

MEMORIES OF RAJAT

Wole Soyinka

How many white hairs ago was it that a bunch of explorers of Africa's New Age fought an epic battle through the unruly borders of the then-Leopoldville, on to Bujumbura, finally crashing through the more reassuring and welcoming immigration post of Kampala to land, the following day, on the terrace of a young Asian, beardless and strikingly handsome? A strange mixture of vulnerability and self-possession, he shyly offered a pianist's hand to the wild invaders— Christopher Okigbo, Kofi Awoonor, J. P. Clark, myself and others–from the western part of the same continent.

He was not primarily a writer, artist, or radio or theatrical producer, unlike most of the creative brigade that had traveled here from Nigeria, Ghana, and elsewhere for the first postcolonial encounter of African writers. He was a special breed, a budding literary editor— or more accurately, a literary innovator —and he was engaged in piecing together a unique journal that would both nurture and serve African literature, art,

and politics. Our visit was both a courtesy call and a literary initiation, on both sides.

We were an irreverent lot from West Africa, full of uncharted energy and creative impatience. By contrast, Rajat's composure appeared to be expressive of that midwife chore of bringing a new entity to life, and in an improvised crib. His office was the open-air porch in front of the house, his work desk the practical surface of a broad plank laid across two columns of stacked bricks, and his implements—a pair of scissors, a jar of paste, a brush, markers, dummies, galley proofs all over the table, cover designs and cartoons (this was, after all, decades before desk top publishing), a chart of fonts, an editor's ruler, etc., etc. As we raised our beer glasses on that hot Ugandan afternoon, we poured a silent libation to the birth of a journal that would itself become an expression of our own nature—brazen, eclectic, and boldly adventurous.

It has been countless clumps of white

hairs since that day: many martyrdoms, triumphs, and agonies. Rajat Neogy is the latest in the line of our prematurely devoured creative generation that began with the poet Christopher Okigbo and has extended to others like Ben Kadadwa, Okot p'Bitek, and most recently Ken Saro-Wiwa. Even though Rajat's demise was painfully drawn out, like Okot p'Bitek's, it began with his incarceration at the hands of the most depraved of Africa's predators. The scars that resulted never truly healed. As a former sojourner in like places, I sensed this space of loss, of lostness, each time we interacted, even at his most energetic, innovative, or simply convivial, and no matter the occasion or place—Paris, London, but especially in Accra. Something had snapped in Rajat's sensitive soul, like one who had looked into the heart of evil and found the harmony of existence permanently untuned.

We became quite close in Accra. He was setting up a new home for his journal, and I was teaching in the university at Legon—that was before I took over the editorship. And the image of him that continues to linger in my mind? Rajat pulling out his rolled-up goatskin prayer mat acquired during his encounter with Islam, soon after his release from prison. He had brought it with him from Uganda, the hide of the very ram that was sacrificed at his conversion ceremony by the Chief Imam of Kampala, no less. It was a phase I never truly understood, especially as he would impishly remind me that he belonged to the Brahmin caste whenever I asked him

Wole Soyinka and Rajat Neogy

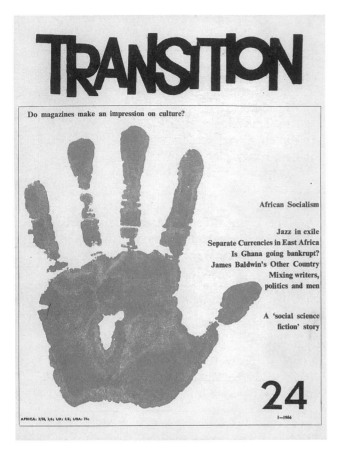

Transition 24
(1966)

© *Transition Ltd.*

what a glass of whiskey was doing in the hands of a devout Muslim. Was it not *El Amin* that he adopted as his Muslim name? Nothing but what savored of the princely would satisfy Rajat; it simply complemented his being, the aura of his presence.

Then the sibilant "Beast!" from his now-bearded lips. "Beast" was Rajat's intimate accolade, a mark of approval/ acceptance/affection, a private language that raised the eyebrows of many a stranger who did not understand that for Rajat, "beast" was a distinguishing mark of nobility within the merely animal kingdom. His favorite piece of music at the time, displacing his Indo-jazz recordings, was Bob Dylan's "Blowin in the Wind," and he drove me to distraction with it, leaving the record on the automatic player, repeating itself late into the night while he sat gazing into the darkness and communing only with his drink. Often I simply slipped away without any leave-taking. The first callers in the morning would find Rajat fast asleep in the chair, and that music still running on and on . . . in what cosmic winds did Rajat take flight night after night, and in quest of, or recovery of, what, I sometimes wondered?

It is an immense consolation that *Transition* was eventually resurrected, and that Rajat did live to witness its fourth coming. There is a beautiful, though sad, symmetry to it all, that after so much meandering by both, Rajat and his life achievement were ultimately united in one spot, and that his creation has endured to bear witness to his vision, and stand as his epitaph.

FOR POLITE REACTIONARIES

Too shy to join the militia? Try The Atlantic Monthly

Charles Sugnet

What does it mean when a respectable 100-year-old magazine that prides itself on being published from Boylston Street in Boston's patrician Back Bay runs a cover story headlined "Dan Quayle Was Right"? Certainly, one answer is that *The Atlantic Monthly* was trying to be shocking for sound commercial reasons—and there *is* a pattern of alarming cover stories over the last few years, including "The Crisis of Public Order," "The Code of the Streets," and the mother of all scary stories, Robert Kaplan's "The Coming Anarchy," a lurid argument that the end of the world has already begun in West Africa and will soon overtake everyone—even white people in Back Bay. Generating months of letters to the editor and several prominent rebuttals, Kaplan's article demonstrated that a little sensationalism is always good for a magazine's circulation.

With more than 450,000 readers, *The Atlantic* is twice the size of its more leftish (and usually more interesting) fraternal twin, *Harpers,* and its circulation has

sagged very little in a period when many magazines are in trouble. Strangely, the percentage of female subscribers is up slightly, in spite (or because?) of the magazine's editorial affection for the "backlash" against feminism. But a survey of recent *Atlantic* issues suggests something more than sensationalism: changes at *The Atlantic* cater to the anxieties of a class that has hitherto always been able to take its position for granted. *Atlantic* readers still play golf and tennis (some of them are nostalgic for wooden tennis rackets). They make comfortable incomes in the $60,000-plus bracket, but judging by the ads, they're more likely to drive a Taurus or even a Chrysler van than a BMW or a Porsche. They're Anglophiles who like to vacation in cozy B&Bs and perhaps take day hikes along Hadrian's Wall in the north of England. They're still willing to pay for a Waterman pen to distinguish themselves from the Bic crowd, and they're interested in the extra leg room you get by traveling business class on Northwest/KLM. They still believe

Guess who's coming to dinner

© *The Atlantic Monthly Company*

ROY BLOUNT: IN PRAISE OF PAULINE KAEL / JEFFERSON AND RELIGION

The Atlantic Monthly

DECEMBER 1994

MUST IT BE THE REST AGAINST THE WEST?

BY MATTHEW CONNELLY AND PAUL KENNEDY

Whether it's racist fantasy or realistic concern, it's a question that won't go away: As population and misery increase, will the wretched of the earth overwhelm the Western paradise?

HOME SWEET HOME

DAN QUAYLE WAS RIGHT

fter decades of public dispute about so-called family diversity, the evidence from social-science research is coming in: The dissolution of two-parent families, though it may benefit the adults involved, is harmful to many children, and dramatically undermines our society

there is a powerful American "we" that they belong to, and this first-person plural recurs frequently in *The Atlantic*— as in, "The population bomb . . . should we disarm it?" (February 1993), or "A new threat to our security" (February 1994), or "We have fled our cities. We have permitted the spread of wastelands ruled by merciless killers." (July 1995). But this "we" is increasingly embattled from the outside, and there's growing confusion about who has the rights of membership.

Atlantic readers' sense of WASP entitlement has been profoundly shaken by the seismic shifts of decolonization, feminism, and the globalization of the economy. The long-standing fears of ghetto criminals were bad enough, but at least familiar. But what's a white person to do when "Female Circumcision Comes to America" (October 1995), and when public intellectuals are "suddenly back. And they're black" (March 1995)? They're frightened of the "Third World," at home and abroad, which in all its guises

threatens their privilege, but they're also oh-so-fascinated with what Joseph Conrad called "the horror" of it. The magazine boasts that almost 90 percent of its readers have been to college, and 75 percent have graduated. They want to think of themselves as rational and moderate, so the magazine makes its living by simultaneously frightening them *and* reassuring them that its articles are based on the latest "evidence from social science research." Each issue devotes a page, headed "745 Boylston Street," to describing the contributors, who often have heavy academic (Yale, Stanford) or quasi-academic (Institute for American Values, Olin Institute for Strategic Studies) credentials. Evocation of national patriarchs like Lincoln and Jefferson reinforces this aura of moderate wisdom. (See "How Lincoln Might Have Dealt with Abortion," September 1995, and "Jefferson and Religious Freedom," December 1994.) As a friend of mine in the advertising business puts it, *The Atlantic* wants to be "an opinion-leader publication, not a lifestyle sheet." Hence a certain solemnity is required, even in recounting the most lurid fictions.

The West Against the Rest

Perhaps the clearest statement of *The Atlantic* reader's position is the illustration for the December 1994 cover story, "Must It Be the Rest Against the West?" by historian Paul Kennedy (*Rise and Fall of the Great Powers*) and his Yale graduate student Matthew Connelly. The illustration shows a single white male American of middle age (the inevitable representative of "the West"), barbecuing on the concrete patio of his sixties-style rambler. There is the inevitable dog, the inevitable white picket fence, and the black bowl of the Weber grill with several wienies sizzling on it. (Perhaps, after all, the solitary man has loved ones somewhere off camera who will consume a few of these carcinogenic treats, thereby helping him postpone his—inevitable?—coronary attack.) Otherwise the backyard has a sterile and empty look to it; the static figures of man and dog lack energy and are out of relation to each other. The man, with his long face, large ears, greased-down hair, and tacky striped polo shirt, looks neither handsome nor happy. He casts a baleful, anxious glance toward the picket fence. Over the top of it, one can see the massed faces of the so-called Third World. Black and brown and yellow, wearing turbans, fezzes, and veils, they press for entrance to the empty yard, though it's hard to believe they really want to eat those hot dogs.

The illustration anchors the reader firmly inside the backyard, looking out from what passes for "the West" at the faces of "the Rest." Clearly it has not occurred to the illustrator that any of those faces might overlap with the "we" that reads *The Atlantic Monthly*. On the other hand, it's difficult to imagine that Mr. Great American Barbecue reads much of anything, either. Such a lowbrow representation of the West seems to give the game away: would George Will or Bill Bennett admit that this guy is the noble cultural descendant of Aristotle, Locke, and Jefferson? Probably not, but the article's subtitle describes without irony his backyard getaway as heaven on earth: "Whether it's racist fantasy or realistic concern, it's a question that won't go away: As population and misery increase,

will the wretched of the earth overwhelm the Western paradise?"

The accompanying article offers no critique of the "developed" way of life, assuming indeed that the "Western paradise" is perfect and everyone wants in. The idea that there might be, for example, Malians who are attached to their land and culture and do not wish to emigrate in spite of Mali's low per capita income as measured by Western banking institutions seems unthinkable. Nor does the piece contain a glimmer of recogni-

The rapid reciprocation between the sensational and the boring is a common feature of *Atlantic* writing

tion that "development" and "underdevelopment" are reciprocal, that there might be a causal connection between the wealth of the West and the poverty of the wretched. And the article does not waste much energy on compassion for those outside the picket fence, who are

IS THERE A SCIENCE OF SUCCESS? / THE SHOCK-ART FALLACY

The Atlantic Monthly

FEBRUARY 1994

THE COMING ANARCHY: NATIONS BREAK UP UNDER THE
TIDAL FLOW OF REFUGEES FROM ENVIRONMENTAL AND
SOCIAL DISASTER. AS BORDERS CRUMBLE, ANOTHER
TYPE OF BOUNDARY IS ERECTED—A WALL OF DISEASE.
WARS ARE FOUGHT OVER SCARCE RESOURCES, ESPE-
CIALLY WATER, AND WAR ITSELF BECOMES CONTIN-
UOUS WITH CRIME, AS ARMED BANDS OF STATELESS
MARAUDERS CLASH WITH THE PRIVATE SECURITY FOR-
CES OF THE ELITES. A PREVIEW OF THE FIRST DECADES OF
THE TWENTY-FIRST CENTURY. BY ROBERT D. KAPLAN

*Both © The Atlantic
Monthly Company*

presented as repulsive and threatening. What it does do is devote five full pages to an account of Jean Raspail's racist, paranoid, apocalyptic novel, *The Camp of the Saints* (1973). Raspail describes the invasion of Europe by boatloads of hungry refugees from Calcutta and elsewhere in terms worthy of Conrad or Céline: "All the kinky-haired, swarthy-skinned, long-despised phantoms: all the teeming ants toiling for the white man's comfort." The invaders appear as an undifferentiated mass of thousands of "brown and black . . . fleshless Gandhi-arms."

Why are two respectable historians from Yale discussing poverty and immigration through this third-rate imitation of Conrad's nightmares? Where are the numbers about actual immigration patterns, the reasoned consideration of the various existing barriers to mass migration, and the scholarship on immigrant contributions to the cultures and economies of Europe and North America?

Including a section titled "The Doom of the White Race," they assume, like the cover illustration, that "the West" is uniformly white, and that racial categories are stable natural entities. Where, I wonder, would an African American reader of *The Atlantic* (and surely there must be a few) position herself? In the backyard with Mr. Barbecue? Or outside the picket fence? With "The West"? Or "The Rest"?

Having summarized Raspail's novel, the authors hasten to put a little distance between themselves and its racism, but at the same time they try to substantiate Raspail by adducing examples of nonfictional refugees who have traveled comparably long distances in recent years. Then, having raised the alarm in the most lurid way, they conclude with a series of practical suggestions that are so staid and commonsensical as to be almost banal: rich countries should make good on their pledges to contribute 0.7 percent of their GNP to development aid; no more expensive vanity projects for poor countries; better UN peacekeeping arrangements; better availability of contraception; use of Cold War scientific talent to solve development problems, etc. This rapid reciprocation between the sensational and the boring seems to be a common feature of *Atlantic* writing. Emblematically, as we shall see, the purpose of these sensible recommendations is not so much to promote social justice or aid those in distress as it is to protect the privileged West against mass immigration and the delicate ethical dilemma that would be presented by the need to slaughter immigrants en masse—a dilemma explored in Raspail's book.

In the last analysis, it seems, unsurpris-

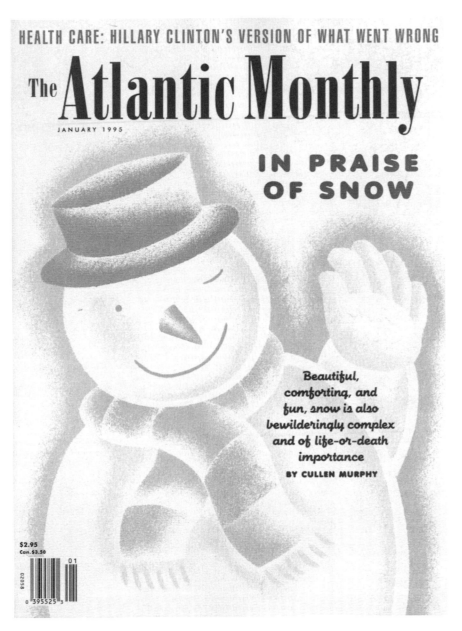

ingly, that the lonely little man is the inheritor, not of Aristotle, Locke, or Jefferson, but of Malthus. Right after Connelly and Kennedy's lukewarm recommendations comes the cold water of Virginia Abernethy's "Optimism and Overpopulation." Abernethy suggests that "encounters with scarcity that are being forced upon literally billions of people by the limits of their environment" will finally lead to "reproductive restraint." Abernethy believes, against the consensus of the demographic profession, that misguidedly generous development help and foreign aid have created various local population explosions. She doesn't

speculate about whether there has in fact been a net flow of resources *to* the rich countries, nor does she specify whether debt repayment to banks in New York and London constitutes part of what she means by the natural "limits of [the] environment." But she does make it clear that a little starvation will thin out the congestion behind the picket fence and ease the mental strain on Mr. Barbecue, who has enough on his mind just thinking about South Central L.A.

The Grand Hotel Abyss

Because of the way its contents are arranged, *The Atlantic* almost always features a bucolic travel article just before a horror story about lawlessness in the ghetto or anarchy in Africa. First comes a piece about an expensive, comfortable place where an *Atlantic* reader would actually go; then the interesting, passion-filled, and frightening details about a place such readers would never consider going to, and which is, in fact, just as unreal, just as much a collection of old tropes, as the charming little towns and perfect B&Bs in the travel literature. Curiously, the safe and comfortable places

are often sanitized tourist spots within the dangerous "Third World," so that the magazine creates two contradictory images of the same zone, one entirely under white metropolitan control, and the other terrifyingly and intriguingly out of control.

In the December 1994 issue, Kennedy, Connelly, and Abernethy's thoughts on the West and the Rest were immediately preceded by a piece about winter vacations in Mexico, which turned on a very *Atlantic* dilemma: how to hang out on the beach and still salve your conscience with "a vacation steeped in culture and history." According to Barbara Wallraff, who wrote the Mexico article, the answer is to go to Oaxaca for culture and history, then on to the beaches around Puerto Escondido. You will be uncomfortably close to Chiapas, "that troubled place," but not to worry—Oaxaca is "heavily Indian," but it's "generally middle-class and prosperous," with "nothing even faintly threatening." Improbably, the people and the social relations in Oaxaca remind her of Norman Rockwell's version of America.

"In beach towns," opines Wallraff,

"choosing a hotel has special importance. Pick the wrong one and you'll feel resentful and trapped." The people jammed against the picket fence would certainly agree. But Walraff warns against the minimum-price rooms at the Hotel Camino Real Oaxaca—at $150 a night, they're "noisy and airless," so it's better to go for the higher-priced ones. (It would be interesting to have Abernethy's opinion on whether the Darwinian stress of such a terrible room would cause tourists to opt for "reproductive restraint.")

Similarly, *Atlantic* readers can prepare for the horrors of "The Crisis of Public Order" (July 1995) by first "Treading Lightly in a Costa Rican Rain Forest" at an exquisite and expensive eco-resort where even nature is in perfect order. Or they can get ready for "the brutal realities of nation-building" (May 1995) by imagining themselves at a charming hotel in Corsica, where the rooms start at $300 a night. My favorite of these travel pieces is Geoffrey Wheatcroft's "Oh, to Be in Antigua: This Caribbean island makes an Englishman feel right at home," which immediately precedes a harrowing piece about the failure of sex education in the October 1994 issue. Wheatcroft, who lets his readers know none too discreetly that he's been to Oxford, regrets that the Caribs "were fated almost to disappear," and thinks the slave period in the island's history is "maybe best passed over," but goes on to discover "a fascinating series of echoes . . . between Antigua and England." What a pleasant surprise, after dismissing all that history, to find that the island is "a little shoot of England" which "grew on the Caribbean imperceptibly"! "We know what happened to the Antiguans as a whole," he says, "and it is rather touching. They became Englishmen." After pointing to similarities between Antigua and the West of England, he concludes: "And so if you want to see what England was like once—what is still an England of the imagination—go to Antigua."

Though he lacks the causal key that would explain the surprising "echoes" he observes—say, the history of colonialism—Wheatcroft is not entirely innocent of recent reading. He does pause to attempt a rebuttal of Edward Said's contention (in *Culture and Imperialism*) that profits from Antiguan sugar slavery are important to the plot of Jane Austen's *Mansfield Park*. But poor Wheatcroft seems not to know that a master prose stylist and polemicist, Jamaica Kincaid, has been there before him, with what is certainly the best writing about Antigua. In *A Small Place* (1988), Kincaid shows from the point of view of an angry and eloquent black Antiguan precisely why

There are good Muslims (those who support "stability" and Israel), bad Muslims (most of the rest), and African Muslims (not really Muslims, because their beliefs are tainted with "animism")

Antigua is *not* England and why Antiguans did *not* become Englishmen. Like so many travel writers and tourists, Wheatcroft believes his mobility and privilege make him omniscient: "You can walk around the town [St. John's, the capital] in no time at all, maybe pausing for a little shopping, and then rent a car. . . . Seeing it can be done quickly. You can drive round the coast in an afternoon." Perhaps "seeing" can be done quickly, but Kincaid's book shows that understanding takes longer, that some things cannot be seen at all from the point of view of the glib travel writer. (Not surprisingly, the same Wheatcroft wrote a long piece on Winston Churchill for the February 1994 issue, arguing that, in spite of his virulent racism and other faults, Churchill was "the savior of his country . . . and of European civilization too.")

Prince Valiant in Africa

If Wheatcroft's Antigua piece takes first prize for *Atlantic* travel writing, surely the most piquant combination of travelogue and cover story is the juxtaposition of "Prince Valiant's England: A Few Brief Shining Moments" with Robert Kaplan's "The Coming Anarchy" in the February 1994 issue. Although Prince Valiant's time may well have been as chaotic and brutal as anything described by Kaplan, it has today been subdued into comfortable tourist fodder and stirring comic strips. Starting from a lovely color photo of the Somerset landscape, the reader progresses toward "the elegant Georgian charm of Bath" and finishes, of course, at the Queensberry Hotel ($135–225 a night). (Jane Austen comes up again, twice.) Then, with the turn of a single page, the trembling reader lurches from Georgian charm to Gothic horror, with a photo of soldiers walking past the bleached bones of civilian victims near the airport in Monrovia, Liberia. From "brief shining moments" of European chivalry to "The Coming Anarchy: How Scarcity, Crime, Overpopulation, Tribalism, and Disease are Rapidly Destroying the Social Fabric of Our Planet."

One wonders briefly about the "we" here. Whose planet? But Kaplan quickly makes it clear that these thoughts will be relentlessly subordinated to a "strategic" and "security" perspective, identifying and dealing with new post–Cold War threats to "our security." The "we" turns out again to be the guy with the Weber grill, holding on to paradise by whatever means prove necessary.

And what a lengthy catalog of atrocities, centered in West Africa but spreading over the globe: twenty-one pages of skinhead Cossacks, juju warriors, criminal anarchy, disease, and environmental collapse. There's even the "hot zone" threat: "some experts" (unnamed) worry that viral mutations and hybridizations (caused in some unspecified way by the specter of "soaring" African birthrates) will create a new, easily transmitted version of the AIDS virus. The photos of disaster include an execution in Liberia, corpses in Yugoslavia, and a strange one of Kurdish children with spent cartridges in the foreground. As his various critics have pointed out, Kaplan focuses exclusively on the negative, and he does so only in order to wallow in a gratuitous and titillating pessimism, not to formulate recommendations for improvement. He's not interested in places like Ghana, Uganda, or Ethiopia, where conditions are improving, but only in countries that can be made to fit his dystopian vision.

Anarchy in Dakar?

When "The Coming Anarchy" first appeared, I was living in Dakar, Senegal, directing ten American students working on research projects. Each student was hosted by a Senegalese family whose hospitality and diplomacy combined

French culture with African customs and lineages stretching back to the time of Louis XIV. Each of them was working by day with Africans (teachers, researchers, agricultural technologists, consumer advocates) who struggle intelligently to overcome the continent's formidable problems. Each was becoming fluent in Wolof, a language that would give them the opportunity to know the culture in some depth. All of us were enjoying the night life of Dakar, where one is much safer from violent crime than in the United States. When we met to open our mail in the pleasant garden behind Le Glacier Modern (a hundred flavors of *gelato*, all better than you can get in most American cities), we found that no fewer than three of the students had received copies of Kaplan's article from their parents, with anxious questions about their children's safety.

They were at a loss as to how to reply—there was such an epistemological wall between Kaplan's "knowledge" of Africa and our own. No one would dispute that horrible things are going on in Africa, and I don't mean to argue that Le Glacier Modern or the homes of the Dakar bourgeoisie are "typical" African spaces, but they are real, and Kaplan ignores them, along with the efforts of those young researchers and teachers. This critical difference was pointed out by an American who wrote to the editor (May 1994) to testify that she had actually lived in one of the Ivory Coast shantytowns where Kaplan saw only social disintegration, and had seen "men and women who are living with dignity, mutual respect, and a strong network of social values." (These perceptual differences are not limited to Kaplan: *Granta*'s most recent special issue on Africa [Summer 1994] is filled with horror pornography, and even a good journalist like Christopher Hitchens fell into the trap in "African Gothic," a record of his hasty tour of the continent for the November 1994 issue of *Vanity Fair*.)

The masthead lists Kaplan as a "contributing editor," and his articles appear often enough to help establish the magazine's tone as a whole. A look at any of his pieces reveals *The Atlantic*'s scaremongering, but "The Coming Anarchy" is so rich (and rich with falsehood) that virtually every paragraph cries out for detailed refutation. Here are just a few of the main problems:

• As Alexander Cockburn points out in *The Nation* (March 28, 1994), "nowhere does he [Kaplan] admit the Western role in plagued economies." Though he laments destructive logging in Côte d'Ivoire, for example, he does not speculate on where the hardwood is going or on how IMF and World Bank policies of export-driven development force such destruction. One letter-writer in *The Atlantic* complained that the article "is almost completely ahistorical," taking no account of colonialism and continuing historical inequities in Africa, the Middle East, and elsewhere, so that "the reader is left with the impression that these societies have become inherently ungovernable" due to some internal defect. "Resource depletion," "scarcity," "crime," and other agents of Kaplan's nightmare happen all by themselves.

• Though he repeatedly mentions the "work of specialists," most of his experts turn out to be of the security studies variety, like Israeli military historian Martin van Creveld, or Olin Strategic Studies Fellow Samuel Huntington, who speculates about "the clash of civilizations" and the

Disease is rampant and everyone is dying, yet overpopulation seems to be the most serious problem

threat of Islam. Thus Kaplan makes obvious errors like his suggestion that family structures are weak in West Africa, and he has no appreciation for the cultural vibrancy of, say, West African popular music. Like Wheatcroft, he has passed by and has seen, but really has little local knowledge of the places he's talking about. They are simply grist for his generalizing mill.

- Race looms large in Kaplan's notion of anarchy. The French, he says, are valiantly struggling to maintain "stability" (one would have thought that profits were involved) in West Africa, but when they leave, only disorder can follow because Kaplan cannot imagine black people governing themselves. A disproportionate seven of the article's fifteen photos of worldwide chaos involve disorderly black people. While he sees only filth and confusion in African shanty-towns, he takes the trouble to go deeper and discover the hidden orderliness of Turkey's shantytowns, where the occupants are many shades lighter. Perhaps it also helps that the Turks, though Muslim, are staunch U.S. allies. While *The Atlantic* isn't by any means *The New Republic*, concerns about Israeli security often af-

fect the magazine's worldview. Other recent Kaplan pieces fret about the deterioration of the Egyptian state, "whose stability has been a pillar of U.S. foreign policy," and the threat of chaos in Syria (November 1994, February 1993). And *The Atlantic* loves the studied ignorance of Bernard Lewis; the same issue that carried Kaplan's worries about Syria also featured Lewis's ponderous rumination on whether "liberal democracy" is incompatible with Islam. (One wonders whether corporate capitalism and campaign contributions are incompatible with democracy, but this is not Lewis's area of "expertise.") Clearly, there are good Muslims (those who support "stability" and Israel), bad Muslims (most of the rest), and African Muslims (not really Muslims, because their beliefs are tainted with "animism," etc.).

- Kaplan is confused about the current meaning of nationalism and the nation-state. On the one hand, he acknowledges that postcolonial boundaries are often arbitrary and postcolonial states serve their citizens poorly; perhaps some states should vanish. On the other hand, every defiance or circumvention of state power frightens him, because the only kind of order he can imagine is state-imposed, from the top down. Like others before him, he prematurely declares the demise of the nation-state, which is doing well in spite of repeated death notices this century.

- He builds his portrait of these places out of clichés (children "teem," populations "surge," etc.), and it's wildly self-contradictory. Disease is rampant and everyone is dying, yet overpopulation seems to be the most serious problem! Several Kaplan critics pointed to evidence that birthrates are going down, and even sympathetic letters to the editor inquired about the contradiction between surging populations and mass death. While Kaplan argues that global soil degradation is directly caused by local population growth, many areas acquired their serious soil problems by growing precisely the export crops Kaplan seems to favor: cotton, coffee, cocoa. California's sparsely populated Central Valley, with its soil depletion, would seem to undermine Kaplan too, but "surging populations" and "soaring birthrates" are Gothic monsters, not subject to the rules of logic.

- The atrocities Kaplan cites are atrocious, all right, but they don't necessarily represent a new trend in human history. Berkeley historian Franz Schurmann (writing for *Pacific News*) points out that the conclusions Kaplan draws from current butchery in Liberia and Sierra Leone could as easily have been made on the basis of similar events in highly "civilized" parts of Europe and Asia during World War II. Kaplan cites the destruction of Dubrovnik as a new kind of war: "When cultures, rather than states, fight, then cultural and religious monuments are fair game." But when the states of England and Germany fought, didn't the Germans bomb Coventry and St. Paul's? Didn't the Allies burn Dresden? Didn't Hitler order the burning of Paris? Similarly, Kaplan cites Liberian Prince

Johnson's gruesome video of the killing of Samuel Doe to show that in the anarchic future, "technology will be used for primitive ends." But wasn't film used this way fifty years ago to document German "experiments" on prisoners? Kaplan finds "shadowy cross-border organizations" like Islamic terrorist groups to be a new phenomenon, but haven't the CIA and the other big intelligence services always operated without respect for national boundaries and sovereignties?

- "Where there is mass poverty," Kaplan maintains, "people find liberation in violence. . . . Physical aggression is a part of being human. Only when people attain a certain economic, educational and cultural standard is this trait tranquilized." Apparently the United States, with its $300 billion annual military budget, fits Kaplan's definition of tranquility, but it would probably be hard to convince the citizens of Baghdad or Grenada that only the poor are capable of violence.

Limousine Dreams

Logical refutation of Kaplan's blunders seems, however, beside the point—in a nightmare like this, the real organizing principles are more likely to be psychological or metaphorical than logical. Kaplan's *Blade Runner* scenario requires a more mobile, flexible, up-to-date image of "the West" than the protected suburban backyard or the cozy hotel room, and he has one, left over from the era of Reagan and Milken: the rich nations, he argues, are like an air-conditioned stretch limo, cruising the blasted streets of New York. Inside the limo: the post-industrial portions of North America, Europe, and the Pacific Rim. Outside: homeless beggars, skinhead warriors. As with the backyard and the hotel room, no reciprocal relationships are elaborated between the richness of those inside the limo and the poverty of those outside. It's an accident, or a fact of nature, or perhaps evidence of superior intelligence and initiative on the part of those in the limo (cf. *The Bell Curve*). All that the inhabitants of the limo seem to require from their environment is a spot of pavement, and they are mobile enough to just bugger off somewhere else if this is not provided to them. (The limo image is ironic in light of Kaplan's macho author note, which boasts that he travels "bush-taxi class.")

But notice what has just happened: this elaborate image has brought Kaplan's global argument all the way back home to the streets of America—where its emotional center of gravity was really located all along. The last of the fifteen color photos illustrating the slide into global anarchy introduces, without any special comment ("naturally," as it were), a scene from the Los Angeles "riots" into the sequence. As the limo picks its way among the potholes of Manhattan, with Kaplan firmly on the inside looking out, he begins to make more analogies between global chaos and "what obtains in American inner cities." And the reason he is so frightened by diminutions of state power in Africa, India, or Pakistan becomes apparent: "As crime continues to grow in our cities and the ability of state governments and criminal-justice systems to protect their citizens diminishes, urban crime may . . . develop into low-intensity conflict." In

spite of the walled communities and private police forces, the stretch limo may be stopped at a roadblock and its privileged occupants forced to deal at street level with the unfortunates outside.

As Kaplan's inflated global thesis collapses onto the streets of America, it begins to make a kind of nativist, know-nothing "sense." Perhaps Kaplan's worries have nothing to do with Africa or the Balkans, which function only as images for American states of mind. If the article seems wildly inaccurate as history, perhaps it is perfectly accurate as a reading of a certain kind of white American psyche. *Atlantic* readers *know* the slums of Abidjan are as horrible as Kaplan says, because they've seen Harlem or Southside Chicago or South Central L.A. on television. They're sure the planet is over-populated, because there are too damned many welfare mothers breeding at their expense. They *know* that global anarchy is coming, because they *feel* the U.S. is falling apart. The ideal reader for the piece would be someone like Saul Bellow's racist Mr. Sammler, fulminating about how the *schwartzes* have spoiled everything. And inevitably, Kaplan quotes Bellow waxing nostalgic about his schooling in the good old days of American cultural homogeneity: "It was a country, then, not a collection of 'cultures.'" (Right, Saul. And I bet you walked five miles to school and back—uphill both ways.) On the last page of the article, Kaplan's anxiety about the decline of the nation-state becomes clear: he's worried about whether the culturally diverse United States can stave off the pressures of fragmentation and protect the riders in the limousine. America's heterogeneity already threatens its stability as a nation-state, and Kaplan warns that "immigrants bring their passions with them." (Presumably nonimmigrants have no passions, Tim McVeigh notwithstanding?)

The final page of the article, then, becomes a polemic against multiculturalism, Afrocentrism, and the "violent affirmation of negritude" in the American school system. After roaming the world, Kaplan ends up wishing the United States had the cultural stability of "crimefree" Roman Catholic Quebec, with its "Francophone ethnicity" (whatever that is), and castigating black journalists at the *Los Angeles Times* for disrupting American unity. At last, Africa assumes its real importance in Kaplan's scale of values: "In an age of cultural and racial clash, when national defense is increasingly local, Africa's distress will exert a destabilizing influence on the United States."

Enter the Gangsta

If I'm right that Kaplan's fear of global anarchy begins and ends at home, one would expect his juju warriors to make an American appearance, and they do not disappoint. The cover story for the very issue that carried letters to the editor about Kaplan's piece (May 1994) is "The Code of the Streets," illustrated by a photo collage of a gangsta youth, shirtless, with a gold chain around his neck, baseball cap on backward, the waistband of his undershorts showing above lowslung jeans. His right hand makes a gesture *Atlantic* readers will be unable to interpret (peace or war?); behind his back, his left hand holds a huge pistol, pointing it—where else?—directly into the eye of the reader. Inside, this figure can be seen doing a number of other things: fighting, stealing a gold chain, driving

a convertible, shooting another man in a drive-by, smoking a spliff, smoking a cigar, and caressing his girl's naked behind. The collages have titles like "Drive-By" and "Trophies" that make them set pieces in a standard narrative of gangsta life. This man certainly poses a direct, in-your-face threat to *Atlantic* readers. He must also fascinate them, since he has such a colorful life, and does things some of them might want to do, in between more sensible visits to Hadrian's Wall or the Georgian hotels of Bath.

The accompanying article by University of Pennsylvania sociology professor Elijah Anderson describes itself as "an essay in urban anthropology" by a "social scientist," and purports to explain "how the inner-city environment fosters a need for respect and a self-image based on violence." As might be expected from the ads for Merrill Lynch and the Geo *Prism* that accompany it, the article is a guide to the streets for the extremely square—we learn such insider details as the meaning of the word *juice*. Although the article is based on "research on violence and inner-city poverty funded by the Guggenheim Foundation," it remains extremely abstract and general, without place names, proper names, or direct quotations from interviews.

Anderson depicts "*the* poor inner-city black community" (my italics), apparently the same from New York to Detroit to L.A., and peopled with two kinds of black families, the "decent" families and the "street-oriented" families. This latter category shades over into the "hardcore street-oriented," but it seems not to make much difference because "depending on the demands of the situation, many people in the community slip

back and forth between decent and street behavior." These descriptive categories are circular and tautological rather than explanatory, and the essay rarely rises above the level of thin generalization. Too many sentences begin with "some" or "many" or "increasingly"— indicators of imprecise trend-watching. There's more specific information about "the street" in a single good rap song, or in a book like John Edgar Wideman's *Brothers and Keepers*, than in this neat little fairy tale. The collaged illustrations are much more colorful and frightening than the writing, but both tend to abstract young black males from the specifics of any particular context. Perhaps the point is that *Atlantic* readers looking out through the tinted glass of the limo don't really want to know *too much* about "the street."

What they want to *do* about the street is clear from another alarming cover story, Adam Walinsky's "The Crisis of Public Order" (July 1995). Walinsky devotes page after page to showing how

crime in America is even worse than you thought: "We have fled our cities. We have permitted the spread of wastelands ruled by merciless killers. . . . And now a demographic surge is about to make everything worse." It's "One Long Descending Night," according to Walinsky, who cites an estimate that 85 percent of black men in the District of Columbia will be arrested during their lifetimes. Yet Walinsky has but one recommendation for the awesome and complex problem he describes: half a million new cops immediately, with more to follow.

"The New Intellectuals" by Robert S. Boynton (March 1995) provides an interesting twist on the question of how *The Atlantic* represents black Americans. Although Boynton passes over a lot of important distinctions by putting Stanley Crouch and Shelby Steele in the same category as Toni Morrison and Cornel West, his article is generally sympathetic. He presents the current spate of black intellectuals as the legitimate heirs of New York intellectuals like Alfred Kazin, Philip Rahv, and Irving Howe, and he praises them for portraying race as a "manifestation of a larger project." Because they conceive of "the problems of African-Americans as inseparable from the problems of Americans," he does not see them as Kaplan's disruptive outsiders. But the magazine's graphic spin on the story seems to be doing something else. The cover illustration shows a black fist clenched in a Black Power salute, but holding a fountain pen (is it one of those Watermans advertised inside?). Another full-page graphic shows three such hands —two with fists clenched and one that has awkwardly metamorphosed into Rodin's Thinker.

Like many *Atlantic* graphics, these images are extremely crude, but that's not the point. The point is that the magazine finds it hard to imagine black intellectuals without conjuring up black bodies in a posture of threatening insurgency, like those in the gangsta collages. The text on the cover reinforces this notion that there's something anomalous and surprising about black thinkers: "Sophisticated, morally aware, at times fiercely contentious—the breed known as 'public intellectuals' has seemed close to extinction. Suddenly they're back. And they're black."

The "suddenly" and the deferral of "black" until the end suggests that an *Atlantic* subscriber is not expected to think of black people as sophisticated or morally aware, and that this new development—blacks who *think*—will catch him or her on the blind side. Perhaps it's not irrelevant that although *The Atlantic* has published many distinguished American writers (Grace Paley, Robert Penn Warren, James Dickey, Ann Beattie,

Bernard Malamud, and many others) and in fact published a long excerpt from Bellow's *Mr. Sammler's Planet*, one does not think of the magazine as a launching pad for black writers. (James Alan McPherson is the only one who comes immediately to mind.) The point is that for some *Atlantic* readers, the notion of black intellectuals may be more confusing and more genuinely threatening than the dramatic but familiar terrors a writer like Kaplan has cribbed from Conrad, Kipling, and Rider Haggard.

Population Bombs

From Kaplan's "surging" African populations to the February 1993 cover story "How Many Is Too Many," *The Atlantic* pays an astonishing amount of attention to issues of population. While in certain parts of the world, *The Atlantic* finds too much reproduction going on, here in the U.S. some people aren't reproducing fast enough, according to Gina Maranto's June 1995 cover story "Tick-Tick-Tick-Tick-Tick: How Long Can Women Put Off Bearing Children?" The article attacks what it believes to be a feminist injunction that women postpone childbearing to develop careers. It does this with a barrage of bad news for potential mothers: the number of eggs you start with begins to dwindle while you're still in the womb, your eggs are getting older every minute, infertility treatments don't work, etc., etc. (There's even a subsection entitled "The 'Bad Eggs' Explanation.") Maranto's references to research are very detailed, and the article is full of ringingly authentic words like "blastomere" and "aneuploidy." Certainly, infertility is miserable for those who want kids and can't get them, and the public *has* been

misled about the efficacy of wonder treatments. And Maranto's concluding public policy recommendations (more parental leave, good public day care, job flexibility for parents) are eminently rational, though not likely to happen in the Age of the Newt.

However, having reviewed the gloomy evidence of declining fecundity after age thirty (it's even worse after thirty-six) for several pages, the story gives away its nature as a scare story pure and simple when Maranto piles up in a single column more horrors than you'd see in a week of *General Hospital*: low birth weight; stillbirth; chlamydia (silent sterilizer of those who've had too many sexual partners); pelvic inflammatory disease (ditto); smoking; alcohol; drugs; cancer (cervical, uterine, and ovarian, "ravages" of); premature ovarian failure (only anecdotal evidence so far); and early menopause (ditto). Put this catalog together with the distressed woman (white, with wedding band) on the cover listening to her biological clock tick away, and it's clear that the article is not just a friendly effort to inform women trying to balance difficult alternatives. The message is "GET PREGNANT NOW or you'll suffer heartbreak later on." The idea is to scare a hell of a lot of women, and perhaps sell some magazines. Not bad for an "opinion leader," even for a "lifestyle sheet." Again, Maranto deploys the *Atlantic* pattern of visceral fear surrounded by piles of scientific evidence to make it all seem ever-so-rational.

The Maranto article is one manifestation of an *Atlantic* trend that is now several years old—the tendency to align the magazine "moderately" but firmly with the backlash against feminism. Like blacks who think, women who earn money threaten the backyard kingdom of Mr. Barbecue and the invisible Mrs. Barbecue. Wendy Kaminer's "Feminism's Identity Crisis" (October 1993) and the virulent letters it stirred up offer evidence of how hot feminist issues can get in *The Atlantic*. But perhaps the magazine's most famous backlash piece is the "Dan Quayle Was Right" cover story by Barbara Dafoe Whitehead (April 1993). Recall that Dan Quayle thought it wrong for TV character Murphy Brown to have a child out of wedlock, despite her comfortable financial position. According to Whitehead's contributor note, Quayle got the idea from a *Washington Post* column that she had written.

Whitehead wants to put the shame back in divorce and single parenthood, and naturally she has lots of frightening "social-science evidence" to prove that bad things are going to happen to your child if she grows up in a "disrupted" rather than an "intact" family. She starts from the provincial assumption that a

Steve Pietzsch
© The Atlantic Monthly Company

1950s-style American nuclear family has been a universal norm, when in fact the isolated nuclear family as we know it is itself a recent experiment. Her argument then sets up a straw man, proving that "the case against the two-parent family is remarkably weak," when no one has made such a "case" in the first place. Whitehall's "social-science evidence" often consists of correlating two things to imply a causality that has not really been established, as when she blames divorce and single parenthood for the fact that "the proportion of children in poverty has increased dramatically, from 15 percent in 1970 to 20 percent in 1990."

Right, but perhaps this has something to do with changes in the economy? Or with cuts in federal poverty programs? Perhaps the general route in American social relations has something to do with our current phase of consumer capitalism, not just with bad behavior?

After the sensational headline, the most striking thing about the article itself is its dullness. Twenty-one double-column pages, scarcely relieved by illustrations. Almost a page to establish the stunning fact that the death of a parent is not a good thing for a child! A small sample of Whitehead's slow-mo prose: "It has taken thousands upon thousands of years to reduce the threat of parental death. Not until the middle of the twentieth century did parental death cease to be a commonplace event for children in the United States. By then advances in medicine had dramatically reduced mortality rates for men and women." Page after turgid page predicting a grim future for children of divorce, when the

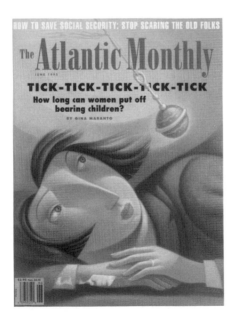

question ought to be how to make it better. I kept wishing they'd given the space to Barbara Ehrenreich, whose sentences have a more pleasing shape, and whose concrete historical analyses of American social change are often brilliant. But I suspect it's the very length and dullness of such pieces that make them convincing to some *Atlantic* readers—a sort of truth-by-the-pound principle. First a blunt proposition that one is viscerally inclined to agree with, then a pile of evidence that one doesn't necessarily have to read, but that confers an aura of reasonableness on the original proposition.

An ad for De Beers' apartheid-produced diamonds appeared in the same issue as Whitehead's argument, and I can't help but imagine that the ad and the article are linked. As we all know, "a diamond is forever," and Whitehead would like to restore the traditional patina of eternity to heterosexual congress. But look what else De Beers wants us to accept with that engagement ring. Across the profile of a white woman's face runs this copy: "Because she believes dogs have souls and angels have wings. Because she gave nine months of her life to watching someone grow. Because she named him after me. Diamonds. Just because you love her." Or should it read "Just because you love yourself"? Is this disgusting narcissist and his forcibly bubble-headed wife what Whitehead means by an "intact" family? (Note that all questions of "surging" overpopulation disappear when Dad can afford a diamond—and an idle wife.)

Having been promoted from "research associate" to "vice-president" at the Institute for American Values, Whitehead makes another appearance on the cover in October 1994. This time, it's sixteen lighthearted pages on "The Failure of Sex Education," proposing abstinence as the only solution. But just ask any high school kid—sex education hasn't been tried yet, so it's a little premature to call it a failure and to hold it responsible for rising overall rates of teen pregnancy. Whitehead's two cover stories are just part of an *Atlantic* trend toward conservative positions on sex and gender issues, culminating recently with George McKenna's "How Lincoln Might Have Dealt with Abortion." Starting from the false premise that legal abortion is "one of the most carefully cultivated institutions in American society," when it is in fact under constant threat from all quarters, McKenna modestly wraps his pro-life position in Lincoln's authority and prestige. Excavating Lincoln's position gives McKenna plenty of time to put forward the (false) analogy between abortion and slavery. (In case you're curious, it turns out that Lincoln was a pro-life "moderate" like McKenna himself.)

The Myth Myth

One more instructive *Atlantic* contribution to gender debates is the August 1994 story "The Sex-Bias Myth in Medicine." Author Andrew Kadar tries to prove that men, not women, are neglected and misunderstood by the medical care system. Judging by the letters to the editor from members of his profession, he does not succeed, but the article fits into a category frequently seen in *The Atlantic*—the pseudo-debunking article. There's "The Power-Line Cancer Myth" (November 1994): the belief that living near power lines is not good for

you "may be unfounded." There's "The Plutonium Fallacy" (April 1995): plutonium might not be quite as "dangerous as alleged." There's "The Diversity Myth" (May 1995): U.S. national stability really arises from the imposition of Anglo values by violence. And the gun control myth. And the sex education fallacy. . . . Each of these stories offers an appearance of genuinely unconventional thinking, of a rational reconsideration of commonly held beliefs. But in each case, the leads and headlines inflate the value of what's actually being demonstrated, and the articles can't live up to their own advertising.

What, Me Reactionary?

In most of these cases, *The Atlantic Monthly* takes a position very close to that of

Rush Limbaugh or Jerry Falwell, but does it much more tastefully, and for reasons that are expressed more delicately. Although it doesn't argue from a Christian platform, the magazine's actual positions on issues like sex education, divorce, immigration, and abortion overlap with those of the Christian right. Barbara Dafoe Whitehead's author note (April 1993) laments how her ideas about Murphy Brown were abused: "The Republicans, of course, went on to use 'family values' as a code for anti-feminist and anti-gay positions." But not us here at *The Atlantic Monthly*! We're moderates hoping Clinton will keep his campaign promises to take the lead on family issues. It's hard to take such micropositioning seriously when it occurs inside an issue that screams "Dan Quayle Was Right" from its front cover.

One symptom of such positioning is the way longtime *Atlantic* editor James Fallows fends off Rush Limbaugh (May 1994). Fallows got his start at the maga-zine by biting the hand of Jimmy Carter (for whom he was writing speeches) in an overhyped two-part shaggy-dog exposé called "The Passionless Presidency" (May and June 1979). Fallows opined that Carter might "look past the tired formulas of left and right" (sound familiar?) to offer the nation something new. Having got the knife in and twisted it for two months, Fallows concluded by saying he planned to vote for Carter in 1980 nonetheless! His Limbaugh essay similarly boggles the mind: Fallows distances himself from Limbaugh not because Rush is a bully and a fraud whose bad ideas do material harm to millions of living humans, but because Rush has ceased to be amusing—the article is titled "Why Rush Got Boring."

In the final analysis, this is what *The Atlantic Monthly* has been offering its readers for the past several years: the chance to be just as backward as a bible-thumper on issues like race, immigration, the environment, and "family values," while maintaining an aura of reasonableness—even genteel boredom. The articles give an appearance of careful deliberation, weighing objections and making exceptions, but the graphics and the headlines flatten nuances with a steamroller, stirring up anxiety, fear, and apocalyptic paranoia. The comfortable people inside the limousine are getting scared, just as scared as the little people who send money to Pat Robertson and company—and when they get scared, they get vicious, in spite of their suitcoats and college degrees. These days, when a stretch limo goes by, there's often a gangsta of some sort hidden behind the tinted glass.

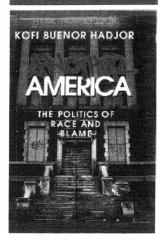

IT'S RAINING MEN

Notes on the Million Man March

Robert F. Reid-Pharr

Perhaps the most curious feature of last fall's Million Man March was the way that this massive political demonstration, at least twice the size of the historic 1963 March on Washington, actually worked to reinforce the racial commonsense of the nation. At a political moment when the enemies of black America have consolidated with frightening determination, Minister Louis Farrakhan, his supporters, and even his detractors encouraged the notion that at the root of the difficulties facing African Americans is a certain male lack—an inability, or unwillingness, to take responsibility as *men*, to stand up for community and self.

It was probably an unintended irony that the rhetoric of the march organizers echoed Daniel Patrick Moynihan's infamous 1965 report, "The Negro Family: The Case for National Action," with its diagnosis of pathologies plaguing black families and communities. This resonance, which has gone largely unremarked, is central to the way the march forced so many of us to rehearse the as-

Christopher Smith, Impact Visuals

sorted racial, sexual, and political identities by which we define ourselves, and which define us. "Who are you?" the march asked. "Black or not–black? Man or not–man?"

It should be clear to most observers that the way Farrakhan and the other march organizers answered these questions—with appeals to a revitalized patriarchy—worked to reinforce traditional gender norms. What is less obvious is the way that this black spectacle restaged the *racial* commonsense of the nation, the same commonsense that animates much of the conservative rhetoric about issues and policies most directly associated with black communities, especially affirmative action and welfare. In the face of shrinking public resources and an evangelical zeal to "reinvent" (read: dismantle) government, African Americans were once again advised that self-help is the best medicine. The black man was instructed to return home and start providing for kith and kin, to stop making excuses about the scarcity of legitimate,

well-paying jobs, and to access his inner manhood, that great and mysterious wellspring of masculinity hidden deep within his psyche, waiting to be harnessed to the project of a beautiful black tomorrow. This all-powerful masculinity was offered as the solution to, and compensation for, the stark curtailments of resources and opportunities that confront African American men (and everyone else) in this country.

If blackness hinges on heterosexuality, then either black gays are not really black or the notion of blackness is untenable

In this light, at a celebration of black masculinity predicated on the absence of black women, it is interesting to consider the question of black gay men's participation in the event. For if the real message of the march was that it is going to take a heroic black masculinity to restore order in our various communities, especially poor and working-class communities, then it follows that gay black men are irrelevant, or even dangerous, to that project. And if the march itself was intended to re-create a masculine community of agency and responsibility, through the archetypical figures of father and son, then the surreptitious presence of the *lover* threatened to undo the logic of the event itself.

. . .

In the weeks prior to the march, the gay press was full of speculation over the proper stance black gay men should take toward Farrakhan, the other march organizers, and the march itself. The Los Angeles–based Black Gay and Lesbian Leadership Forum vacillated on the question, finally encouraging gay men to attend and to make their presence known. Activists staged a premarch rally and convinced Ben Chavis, the march's executive director, to agree to have an openly gay speaker address the crowd from the podium. (Chavis reneged at the last minute.)

The debate revolved around the question of whether black gay men should support an event so closely identified with Minister Louis Farrakhan, who has made no secret of his homophobia. (In Oakland, California, in 1990 Farrakhan told a crowd, "If God made you for a woman, you can't go with a man. . . . You know what the penalty of this is in the Holy Land? Death.") More to the point, black gay men, even if they stayed home, were again confronted with a rather awkward set of questions. Faced with a celebration of a stable—that is, Afrocentric, bourgeois, and heterosexual—black masculinity, gay men who felt compelled by the march had to decide among a number of plausible responses. They could reject the event itself as "not truly black" because of the homophobia and misogyny in which it trafficked. They could think of the march as representative of a flawed blackness that might be repaired by making a significant black gay presence visible at the event (which many did) or by intervening with the march organizers (which a few attempted). And finally, they could acknowledge the basic logic of Farrakhan's rhetoric. For if the definition of blackness hinges on heterosexuality, then either blackness and homosexuality are incommensurable (and black gays are

BLACK BY BIRTH
GAY BY GOD
PROUD BY CHOI

Donna Binder,
Impact Visuals

not really black) or the notion of blackness is untenable, as witnessed by the undeniable existence of large numbers of black gay men.

This last position, of course, is most difficult to accept. It flies directly in the face of much within contemporary black gay and lesbian thought, which most often represents black gays and lesbians as integral, if beleaguered, members of the black family—witness *Brother to Brother*, *Home Girls*, *Sister Outsider*, works shepherded by Essex Hemphill, Barbara Smith, and Audre Lorde, respectively. Indeed, the gay response to the march dramatizes the fact that there are remarkably few spaces—even those inhabited by black gays and lesbians—in which one might contest the most basic assumptions that underlie American race and

gender identity. Even in the midst of raucous and intense disagreement, the idea of race emerges unscathed. Indeed, blackness has been bolstered, insofar as we all were forced, at least those of us who are black *and* otherwise, to scurry for cover under the great black mantle, to fly our colors, the good old red, black, and green, even as we attempted to resist the homophobic assumptions that structured the event.

. . .

More than a political demonstration with concrete political demands, Farrakhan's march was a sort of race spectacle. Following Guy Debord, we should look to locate its meaning not in the striking images it produced or in our individual responses, but in the social re-

Christopher Smith,
Impact Visuals

lationships constructed by and through these images. Debord doubts that transcendence can be located within the spectacle. For him, spectacles are never progressive events; rather, they represent and reaffirm the larger society. Debord writes, "For what the spectacle expresses is the total practice of one particular economic and social formation; it is, so to speak, that formation's *agenda*. It is also the historical moment by which we happen to be governed."

It is ironic that Booker T. Washington's sensibility so deeply informs the rhetoric of Louis Farrakhan

His point is well taken. Those of us interested in progressive politics need to reconsider the efficacy of the marches, protests, and demonstrations that have convulsed the American public sphere in the last century, as well as the ways in which their themes (civil rights, antiwar, gay pride) are constrained by the nature of the event. Mustering enthusiasm for these events requires a fair dose of ignorance about the contentiousness that invariably surrounds them—disagreements that most often turn on the organizers' unwillingness to push the boundaries of the event. I am reminded here of the successful struggle initiated by Anna Arnold Hedgeman to have women included among the speakers on the platform at the 1963 march, as well as the ease with which civil rights stalwart Bayard Rustin was shut out of the same event because of his homosexuality. That march has become such an important part of the American national memory

Paul Hodgdon

because it so clearly articulated the rather limited language and values of a liberal America. Indeed, King's "I Have a Dream" speech receives much of its force from the evocation of an ethos that is at once Christian and American nationalist, supporting, in the process, a liberal integrationist agenda that insists upon the expansiveness—and expansion—of the nation.

Mass public spectacles have been a regular means by which changing ideas of race have been disseminated to the American populace. As early as 1895, Booker T. Washington called for black reconciliation with the very whites who were the architects of segregation, disfranchisement, and systematic racist terror, thereby rearticulating the emerging racialist—and segregationist—common sense. Washington's particular genius, evident in his Atlanta Cotton States Exposition speech, was his ability to articulate a conservative racial politics to whites, particularly white southerners, while captivating many blacks with a message that spoke to their basic desire to be admitted as equal participants in American public life. "In all things that are purely social," he argued, "we can be as separate as the fingers, yet one as the hand in all things essential to mutual progress."

It is a compelling irony that the sensibility behind Washington's words should so deeply inform the 1995 rhetoric of Louis Farrakhan. Specifically, both men call for black self-sufficiency, if not self-determination; both swallow, more or less whole, frankly segregationist notions about the proper interaction between the races; and both, oddly enough, subscribe to the myth of America. As Farrakhan argued at the march:

There's no country like this on Earth. And certainly if I lived in another country, I might never have had the opportunity to speak as I speak today. I probably would have been shot outright, and so would my brother Jesse, and so would Maulauna Karenga, and so would Dr. Ben Chavis and Reverend Al Sharpton and all the wonderful people that are here. But because this is America, you allow me to speak even though you don't like what I may say.

Of all the curiosities uttered by Minister Farrakhan during the march, including the extended numerological analyses, the excoriation of presidents past and present, the religious rhetoric of atonement, and so forth, I was least prepared for this hackneyed bit of American exceptionalism. It was tempting to read this gesture as mere anomaly, the kind of unnecessary bombast that cushions overly long or ambitious speeches. But I suggest we take this piece of Farrakhan's rhetoric seriously—indeed, that we recognize in it the key to his success that day, as he spoke to the assembled masses on the Mall and to the nation.

Minister Farrakhan's particular talent is his ability to sensitize wildly diverse black audiences to their very real oppression while steering them, not simply away from a critique of the political and economic structure of the United States, but toward a reinvestment in the very ideological processes that work to create, and maintain, those structures. It is true that Farrakhan regularly points out the evil of the American enterprise: slavery, segregation, disfranchisement, continued and continual racial degradation. But instead of leading his followers toward radical critique, Farrakhan chooses instead to return again and again to an essentially therapeutic mode, in which he plays the role of the good father come back to set the (national) house in order.

At the Million Man March—"a glimpse of heaven," as the Nation of Islam's newspaper, *The Final Call*, had it—Louis Farrakhan put himself forward as the emblem, the ideal type, if you will, of a newly emergent black masculinity. He appeared as a shining exemplar of a renewed Black Man, striking the posture of the stern—if gentle—father, savior,

**1995
Million Man
March**

*Ron Thomas,
Reuters/Archive Photos*

patriarch, messiah. He scorned our enemies while asking us only to look inward, to find the evil within and cast it out. If we did so, he prophesied, if only we could learn to humble ourselves, we would surely see a new dawn of cleanliness and order, the Black Millennium. He stood, then, as a sort of Emersonian representative man, embodying a masculinity so pure that simply by gazing upon it one could extinguish the fires of ambiguity and uncertainty that rage in the hearts of black men across America.

The agreement on the part of the march's organizers (supported even by progressives like Cornel West) to discourage black women's participation implicitly shored up Farrakhan's myth-making. I never could quite understand *why* a demonstration about the plight of black Americans had to be gendered in the first place. (Wouldn't two Million Black People beat one Million Black Men?) With this strategy—an obvious insult to black women—the march organizers showed themselves to be concerned primarily with lending a certain ontological stability to men whose identities are increasingly complex. The injunction to keep the women at home helped channel public debates about the march into familiar territory, the ongoing "crisis of African American gender relations." In that sense, the sexist rhetoric and the many responses it provoked simply represented (black) business as usual. It was a forceful restatement, à la

Farrakhan returns again and again to an essentially therapeutic mode, in which he plays the role of the good father come back to set the (national) house in order

Moynihan, of the terms we have used to discuss (African) American cultural, political, and economic life since at least the 1960s.

Fundamental changes in American political and economic life are currently being debated, in a conversation largely dominated by the Republican right. What is disconcerting about this is the way rhetorics of blackness (such as Ronald Reagan's "welfare queen" and George Bush's "Willie Horton") have been coupled not simply with critiques of black communities, but with even more blistering attacks on affirmative action, welfare, education, government interventionism, inner-city crime, and so forth. While the march was still in progress, President Clinton made a speech at the University of Texas in which, after distancing himself from Farrakhan, he praised the black men who attended the event for taking responsibility for themselves, and *their* communities. He then went on to make a rather predictable speech on race relations in which he suggested, among other things, that it is not racism that motivates a mother to pull her child close when she passes a black man in a crime-ridden neighborhood.

What is disturbing about this line of argument is not only the crude manner in which it reaffirms the myth of the Dangerous Black Man, but the way that it reiterates the racialist logic that stands

Farrakhan and Chavis worked to yoke the energy of the event to a simplistic and segregationist racial ideology

at the root of this country's many woes. The idea that there are discrete black communities, beset by black problems, which can and should be solved exclusively by black people taking responsibility for themselves, is precisely the logic of segregation, no matter how empowered individual black people may feel in the process of its articulation. What connects Clinton and Farrakhan,

then, is that neither has yet seen his way clear of the pernicious racialism that increasingly dominates American public life.

. . .

Despite my reservations about the ideological underpinnings of the march, it would be untrue to say that I do not understand what drew hundreds of thousands of individuals to Washington on that October day. I went, full of skepticism yes, but also expectant, even hopeful. The first thing that struck me was that it was *not* a march, but more of a *happening*. I am accustomed to marches on Washington, with thousands of people—singly or in various more or less well-organized groups—streaming down Pennsylvania Avenue en route to the Mall. Usually the architects of the mass action try to divvy up the crowd into state-based bodies, collectivities of gender and race, various political and social organizations, groups of students, dignitaries, and so forth. The Million Man March, however, had none of this. The few banners and signs that dotted the crowds were largely homemade, expressing local and specific concerns. Moreover, there were surprisingly few individuals who could be clearly identified as members of the Nation of Islam, or even Muslim. The emphasis was on similarity, the incredible and moving oneness we all shared.

I should acknowledge, here, how exciting, titillating even, this oneness actually felt. The beauty of the men was startling. It hung in the air like the smoke of incense, intoxicating us all, calling into existence a fantastic vision of community—a glimpse of heaven, indeed. The

Christopher Smith,
Impact Visuals

entire event, not to mention the debates that framed it, was wholly overdetermined by a kind of black-inflected homoeroticism. It seemed that we men could enact millions of tiny instances of love and desire—a touch, a glance, murmurings of "Pardon me, brother," "Excuse me, sir"—precisely because the women were absent. What remained was a sort of naked masculinity.

A teenage boy comes up to me. I see his baggy clothes, his corn-rowed hair, the cocky lilt in his walk, before I see him. His face is flushed as if he has just witnessed something beautiful and terrible both, like he has just survived a natural disaster or awakened from some horrible fever. He takes my hand, places his other arm around my shoulder, and says, "All this unity, all this love," presses close to me for an instant, then releases me and keeps moving. I am stunned, caught up in the moment. I imagine that I really have seen this boy, that he has seen me. I am no longer afraid, but on

the contrary, rather giddy, glad to be here, to have been a part of all this.

At Union station, I buy a disposable camera and begin taking snapshots of other anomalies in the crowd: women, the elaborately dressed, the not-black. In looking back over these pictures, now as then, I think that there is something satisfying about seeing reflected, if only for a brief while and through a deeply flawed lens, an image of an equitable, just, and peaceful community. It felt like freedom, a new beginning. Indeed, for a moment, if only a moment, I felt that I had regained that which was lost, had seen beyond the horizon.

· · ·

Still, as Paul Gilroy has suggested, it is unsettling that the notion of (black) freedom seems so inevitably dependent on polarities of sex and gender, and accompanied by a certain desperate insistence on black sexual potency. It seems that the idea of freedom has been so overwritten by fantasies of race and gender that it has become nearly impossible to imagine it without reference to these same fantasies. "The Black Man," as the rhetoric of both right and left would have it, is the most *un*free of American citizens. As one-third of the black males in this country languish in prisons or under the stewardship of assorted probation and parole boards; as black men continue to be overrepresented in the drug trade, and among the legions of persons with chronic illnesses—HIV, cancer, heart disease, alcoholism; as we give our lives over to violence or to a certain silent despair, we have become the very emblem of ugliness, bestiality, and barbarism by which the rest of America, particularly white America, can view itself as liberal and free. The image in my mind now is of Rodney King's beating: the endless blows, the irrationality of the white policemen's rage as they labored to drive this black beast deeper into their collective unconscious. It is possible to chart the last several decades of American cultural and political life by lining up our black male martyrs, criminals, and celebrities: Martin Luther King, Malcolm, Medgar Evers, Louis Farrakhan, Clarence Thomas, Mike Tyson, Willie Horton, Yusef Hawkins, O. J. Simpson. The list goes on.

If freedom was truly the ultimate goal of the march, then it was of a discrete,

limited kind: freedom from the crushing burden of images—the criminal, the addict, the vengeful lover, and the invalid. Instead we were presented with an ocean of men, orderly, directed, clean-cut, and remarkably eloquent. Even in their silences. At the march, in the act of rethinking and reenacting our disparate identities, we felt an intimation of some larger notion.

Here, then, despite the regressive racial and gender politics that framed the Million Man March, there were countless improvisational moments of transcendence. The reality of all public spectacles is that the outcome is never certain; no one can confidently predict what its attendees will take away from it, what meanings its many participants will attribute to it. The sad part is that the march organizers evinced so little respect for this wondrously messy and ambiguous process. Once again we were urged to mount the tired horse of black patriarchy. Ministers Farrakhan and Chavis worked to yoke the energy of the event to a simplistic—and segregationist—racial ideology. I still yearn, then, for a vision of the good, for a public dialogue and a civic life that celebrates multiplicity, that prizes ambiguity, and thereby recognizes the play of identity and difference that makes possible community as well as change.

Position

UNMASKING MARCOS

Whatever happened to the Subcomandante?

Ilan Stavans

Tout révolutionnaire finit en oppresseur ou en hérétique.
—Albert Camus

The Subcomandante Insurgente Marcos, or *El Sup*, as he is known in Mexico. His skin is bleached, whiter than that of his compañeros. He speaks with palpable erudition. The sword *and* the pen: he is a rebel, yes, but also an intellectual, a mind perpetually alert. And like some ranting dissenter, he is always prepared to say *No*—*No* to five centuries of abuse of the indigenous people of Chiapas and the nearby Quintana Roo in the Yucatan Peninsula. *No* to tyranny and corruption, *No* to the sclerotic one-party state that has mortgaged Mexico and her people for generations, and for generations to come.

No, No, and *No.*

El Sup is also like Sisyphus, or possibly like Jesus Christ: he bears on his shoulders an impossible burden, the aspirations and demands of an embattled people. He must know, in his heart, that the rock is too heavy, the hill too steep; his efforts will change very little in the way people go about their lives south of the Tortilla Curtain. His real task, the best he can do, is to call attention to the misery of miserable men and women.

He isn't a terrorist but a freedom fighter, and a peaceable one at that. He took up arms because debate is unfruitful in his milieu. He is a *guerrillero* for the nineties who understands, better than most people, the power of word and image. He uses allegories and anecdotes, old saws and folk tales, to convey his message. Not a politician but a storyteller—an icon knowledgeable in iconography, the new art of war, a pupil of Marshall McLuhan. As he himself once wrote, "My job is to make wars by writing letters."

El Sup, a tragic hero, a Moses without a Promised Land. He stands in a long line of Latin American guerrilla heroes, at once real and mythical, an insurrectionary tradition stretching back nearly half a millennium. Figures like the leg-

Subcomandante Marcos

Jack Kurtz, Impact Visuals

endary Enriquillo, who orchestrated an uprising among aborigines in La Española around 1518, about whom Fray Bartolomé de Las Casas writes eloquently in his *Historia de las Indias*. And Enriquillo's children: Emiliano Zapata; Augusto César Sandino, the inspiration for Daniel Ortega and the Sandinistas; Simón Bolívar, the revolutionary strategist who liberated much of South America from Spanish rule and who dreamed in the 1820s of La Gran Colombia, a republic of republics that would serve as an Hispanic mirror to the United States of America; Tupac Amaru, the Peruvian Indian leader of an unsuccessful revolt again the Iberians in 1780 whose example still inspires the Maoists in Peru; Edén Pastora, *Comandante Cero*, an early Sandinista guerrillero turned dissenter;

He is knowledgeable in iconography, a pupil of Marshall McLuhan. As Marcos himself once wrote, "My job is to make wars by writing letters"

and of course, Fidel Castro and Ernesto "Ché" Guevara. A robust tradition of revolutionaries, overpopulated by runaway slaves, *indios subversivos*, muralists, and disenfranchised middle-class intellectuals.

El Sup: newspaper columnists and union organizers credit him for the wake-up call that changed Mexico forever. He had gone to Chiapas in 1983 to politicize people. "We started talking to the communities, who taught us a very important lesson," he told an interviewer. "The democratic organization or social structure of the indigenous communities is very honest, very clear." He

fought hard to be accepted, and he was, although his pale skin marked him as an outsider. (Though the preeminent spokesman of the Zapatista movement, he could never aspire to a position greater than subcomandante, as the highest leadership positions are customarily reserved for Indians.) The next ten years were spent mobilizing peasants, reeducating them and being reeducated in turn. The rest, as they say, is history.

And rightly so: after all, on the night of January 1, 1994, just as the so-called North American Free Trade Agreement, NAFTA, between Canada, the United States, and Mexico, was about to go into effect, he stormed onto the stage.

Lightning and thunder followed.

It was a night to remember. As José Juárez, a Chiapas local, described it, "it was on New Year's Eve when President Carlos Salinas de Gortari retired to his chambers thinking he would wake up a North American. Instead he woke up a Guatemalan."

No, said the Subcomandante. Mexico isn't ready for the First World. Not yet.

Everywhere people rejoiced. *Un milagro!* A miracle! A wonder of wonders! So spoke Bishop Samuel Raúl Ruíz García, the bishop of San Cristóbal, whose role in the Zapatista revolution angered conservatives but was endorsed by millions worldwide, turning him into a favorite for the Nobel Peace Prize.

With his trademark black skintight mask, El Sup was constantly on television. *Un enmascarado:* Mexicans turned him into a god. Since pre-Columbian times Mexico has been enamored with the mask. A wall between the self and the universe, it serves as a shield and a hiding place. The mask is omnipresent in

Mexico: in theaters, on the Day of the Dead, in *lucha libre*, the popular Latin American equivalent of wrestling. And among pop heroes like El Zorro, El Santo the wrestler, and Super Barrio, all defenders of *los miserables*, masked champions whose silent faces embody the faces of millions.

Suddenly, the guerrilla was back in fashion. The "news" that the Hispanic world had entered a new era of democratic transition had been proven wrong.

Once again weapons, not ballots, were the order of the day. Within the year, the lost "motorcycle diary" of Ché Guevara was published in Europe and the United States—a record of a twenty-four-year-old Ché's travels in a Norton 500 from Argentina to Chile, Peru, Colombia, and Venezuela. A free-spirited first-person account unlike any of his "mature" works, it recalled Sal Paradise's hitchhiking in Jack Kerouac's *On the Road.* El Sup had discovered new territory: the revolutionary as easy rider.

El Sup had a rifle, yes, but he hardly used it. His bullets took the form of faxes and e-mails, cluster bombs in the shape of communiqués and nonstop e-mail midrashim through the Internet. He wrote in a torrent, producing hundreds of texts, quickly disproving Hannah Arendt's claim that "under conditions of tyranny it is far easier to act than to think." In less than twelve months, during sleepless sessions on the word processor in the midst of fighting a war, El Sup generated enough text for a 300-page volume. And he sent it out without concern for copyright. His goal was to subvert our conception of intellectual ownership, to make the private public and vice versa.

He was a master at marketing. By presenting himself as a down-to-earth dissenter, a nonconformist, a hipster dressed up as soldier, he made it easy to feel close to him. To fall in love with him, even. In one communiqué, for instance, he addresses the Mexican people:

Brothers and sisters, we are the product of five hundred years of struggle: first against slavery; then in the insurgent-led war of Independence against Spain; later in the fight to avoid be-ing absorbed by North American expansion; next to proclaim our Constitution and expel the French from our soil; and finally, after the dictatorship of Porfirio Díaz refused to fairly apply the reform laws, in the rebellion where the people created their own leaders. In that rebellion Villa and Zapata emerged—poor men, like us.

In another, he writes to his fellow Zapatistas:

Our struggle is righteous and true; it is not a response to personal interests, but to the will for freedom of all the Mexican people and the indigenous people in particular. We want justice and we will carry on because hope also lives in our hearts.

And in a letter to President Clinton, El Sup ponders:

We wonder if the United States Congress and the people of the United States of North America approved this military and economic aid to fight the drug traffic or to murder indigenous people in the Mexican Southeast. Troops, planes, helicopters, radar, communications technology, weapons and military supplies are currently being used not to pursue drug traffickers and the big kingpins of the drug mafia, but rather to repress the righteous struggle of the people of Mexico and of the indigenous people of Chiapas in the Southeast of our country, and to murder innocent men, women, and children.

We don't receive any aid from foreign governments, people, or organizations. We have nothing to do with national or international drug trafficking or terrorism. We organized ourselves of our own volition, because of our enormous needs and problems. We are tired of so many years of deception and death. It is our right to fight for a dignified life. At all times we have abided by the international laws of war and respected the civil population.

Since all the other compañeros of the Zapatista National Liberation Army were more modest, El Sup stole the spotlight. He was unquestionably *la estrella*. And his enigmatic identity began to obsess people. His education, some said, is obviously extensive. He must be a product of the Distrito Federal, the Mexico City of the early eighties.

Was he overwhelmed by the outpouring of public affection? "I won't put much stock in it," he told one interviewer. "I don't gain anything from it and we're not sure the organization will, either. I guess I just don't know. About what's going on. I only get an inkling of what's going on when a journalist gets angry because I don't give him an interview. I say, 'Since when am I so famous that they give me a hard time about being selective, and the lights, and I don't know what all.' That is pure ideology, as they say up there, no? We don't have power struggles or ego problems of any kind."

Being selective: *el discriminador*. But his ego, no doubt, is monumental. He courted attention relentlessly. By 1995, stories circulated that internal struggles within the Zapatistas were growing, fought over El Sup's stardom.

Meanwhile, unmasking El Sup became a sport. Who is he? Where did he come from? I, for one, thought I knew, though not through any feat of journalistic prowess. I haven't been to the Chiapas jungle since the Zapatistas launched their rebellion. And if he is who I think he is, I haven't spoken to him since long before his communiqués began streaming from the Lacandonian rain forest.

The clue to his identity came in early 1995, after Salinas had ceded power to his successor, Ernesto Zedillo Ponce de León, in the aftermath of a series of political assassinations that had rocked the PRI, the governing party. The enemy grew restless. El Sup had become too dangerous. And too popular! He was better known than any politician. He commanded more attention than any of the soap operas on Mexican TV, the opiate of the Mexican masses. Enough was enough. It was time for him to go.

Desenmascarar. What the Mexican government performed was an ancient ritual at the heart of the nation's soul: the unmasking. Quetzalcoatl was unmasked by the Spaniards, Sor Juana by the Church, and Pancho Villa by a spy. To unmask can mean to undo, or to destroy, but it can also mean to elevate to a higher status: every six years, as the country prepares to receive its new president, the head of the PRI literally unveils his successor before everyone's eyes.

In the public eye—El Sup's own terrain—the Mexican government revealed his true self: Rafael Sebastián Guillén Vicente, a thirty-seven-year-old former college professor. A revelation, indeed, which El Sup immediately disputed . . . before vanishing into the night. Just like that, he disappeared. Off the TV screens. Out of the spotlight. He became a nonentity: *Un espíritu.* Other Zapatistas replaced him in the high command of the Zapatista army.

In Mexico, of course, the government is always wrong; that is, since it promotes itself as the sole owner of the Truth, nobody believes it. And yet, El Sup might well be Guillén. I personally have no trouble equating the two. They sounded the same, right down to their rhetoric—

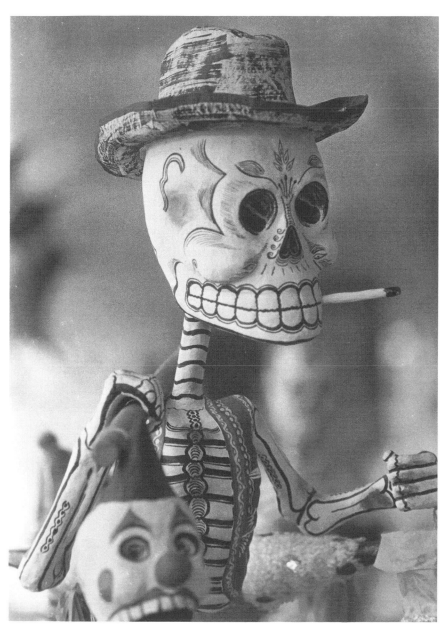

Day of the Dead
reveller

AP/Wide World

a language I learned at the Xochimilco campus of Mexico City's Universidad Autónoma Metropolitana (UAM), the decidedly radical school where Guillén taught. In discussing his communiqués with several old college friends, we were struck by the similarities between his postmodern tongue and the often hal- lucinatory verbiage at Xochimilco, full of postscripts and qualifications and ref- erences to high and low, from modernist literature and academic Marxism to pop culture. El Sup said his idols were the nationally known "new journalists" Carlos Monsiváis and Elena Ponia- towska, whom my whole intellectual generation deeply admired and whose own works trespass intellectual boundaries with glee. When asked to describe the books that influenced him, he would cite the 1970s writing of Octavio Paz, Julio Cortázar, Borges, Mario Vargas Llosa, and Gabriel García Márquez, although he would be careful to distance himself from the right-wing politics of Paz and Vargas Llosa.

El Sup mooned journalists with his writings. His speeches, like the authors we studied at UAM, seamlessly mix fiction with reality, becoming masterful self-parodies, texts about texts about texts. In a reply to a letter from the University Student Council of the Universidad Nacional Autónoma de México (UNAM), he writes that with great pleasure the Zapatistas have received the students' support. He asks them to get organized following the pattern of the Zapatistas, and concludes:

If you accept this invitation, we need you to send some delegates so that, through an intermediary, we can arrange the details. We must organize everything well so that spies from the government don't slip through. And if you make it down, don't worry about it. But keep up the fight over where you are, so that there can be justice for all Mexican people.

That's all, men and women, students of Mexico. We will be expecting a written response from you.

Respectfully,

From the mountains of the Mexican Southeast.

P.S.: El Sup's section: "The repeating postscript."

Another postscript follows, and then more and more.

P.P.S.: As long as we're in the P.S.'s, which of all the "University Student Councils" wrote to us? Because back when I was a stylish young man of 25 . . . there were at least three of them. Did they merge?

P.S. to the P.S. to the P.S.: In the event that you do (whew!) take the Zócalo, don't be selfish. . . . Save me some space where I can at least sell arts and crafts. I may have to choose between being an unemployed "violence professional" and an underemployed one, with underemployment wages (much more marketable that way, under NAFTA, you know).

P.S. to the nth power: These postscripts are really a letter disguised as a postscript (to hide it from the Attorney General's Office and all the rest of the strongmen in dark glasses), and, but of course, it requires neither an answer, nor a sender, nor an addressee (an undeniable advantage of a letter disguised as a postscript).

Nostalgic P.S.: When I was young (Hello, Attorney General's Office. Here comes more data), there used to be a lightly wooded place between the main library, the Facultad de Filosofa y Letras, the Torre de Humanidades, Insurgentes Avenue and the interior circuit of Ciudad Universitaria. We used to call that space, for reasons obvious to the initiates, the "Valley of Passions," and it was visited assiduously by diverse elements of the fauna who populated at 7 P.M. (an hour when those of good conscience drink hot chocolate and the bad ones make themselves hot enough to melt); they came from the humanities, sciences, and other areas (are there others?). At that time, a Cuban (Are you ready, Ambassador Jones? Make a note: more proof of pro-Cas-

The Bettman Archive

tro tendencies) who used to give lectures seated in front of piano keys the color of his skin, and who called himself Snowball, would repeat over and over: "You can't have a good conscience and a heart. . . ."

Final fortissimo P.S.: Have you noticed how exquisitely cultured and refined these postscripts are? Are they not worthy of the First World? Don't they call attention to the fact that we "transgressors," thanks to NAFTA, are striving to be competitive?

"Happy Ending" P.S.: Okay, okay, I'm going. . . . This trip is coming to an end, and the guard, as usual, is still asleep and someone is tired of repeating "Is anybody out

there?" and tell myself, "Our country" . . . and what is your answer?

El Sup's unconventional style was a commonplace at UAM in the early eighties. I was a student there at the time, the same time that Guillén, about five years my elder, was teaching. Some of my friends took classes with him, remarking on his sharp intellect and infectious verbosity. Crossing paths with him in hallways and cafeterias, I remember him bright and articulate.

Well-known as an incubator for Marxist, pro-Cuba, pro-Sandinista activity, UAM's Xochimilco campus had been built by the government in the early seventies. It included two other

campuses in far-flung corners of the city. It was built in an attempt to dilute the massive student population at UNAM, the oldest institution of higher learning in the country.

In her book, *La noche de Tlatelolco*, Poniatowska chronicled the protests of 1968. It was UNAM's student body, some 30,000 strong, who led the protests, which were brutally crushed in the massacre at Tlatelolco Square. El Sup, although not Guillén, was born during that massacre—a ritual birth, an origin in which his whole militant odyssey was prefigured. If the revolution couldn't be won in the nation's capital, he would join the unhappy peasants in Chiapas and Yucatan—he would become an urban exile.

When Xochimilco opened, it immediately superseded UNAM in antigovernment militancy. It became a magnet for subversive artists, would-be guerrilla fighters and sharp-tongued political thinkers. The place was known for its unorthodox educational methods, and fields of study often lost their boundaries. Professors not only sensitized us to the nation's poverty and injustice, they encouraged us to take action. Friends would take time off to travel to distant rural regions and live with the indigenous people. Most eventually returned, but many didn't—they simply vanished, adopting new identities and new lives.

Injustice, inequality, freedom of speech —we wanted changes. "Down with the one-party system!" We would take advantage of cheap fares and travel to Havana, to become eyewitnesses to the profound transformation that had taken place in a corner of the Hispanic world. The Sandinistas in Nicaragua captured

our attention and love. We admired their courage and identified with intellectuals like Julio Cortázar, Ernesto Cardenal, and Sergio Ramírez, who had put their literary careers on hold to work for the Nicaraguan government, or who had orchestrated international campaigns to support the Sandinista fight. We were excited—and we were blind. Our personal libraries were packed full with Marxist literature. Our writers were busy fashioning a style in which art and politics were inseparable. We disregarded any argument that tried to diminish our utopian expectations.

Indeed, finding bridges between political theory and activism became a sport. Those of us who studied psychology embraced the anti-psychiatry movement and were expelled from asylums for allowing patients to go free. I, for one, worked with a metropolitan priest, Padre Chinchachoma, who devoted his ministry to homeless children. He believed that to help the children he needed to live among them, in Mexico City's

The government rationale was clear: if Third World adolescents are always full of antigovernment feeling, they should be provided with a secluded place to vent their rage

garbage dumps—foraging with them for food, making and selling drugs for money, and occasionally engaging in acts of vandalism. I read Padre Chinchachoma's books with great admiration. He was my messiah, my Sup before El Sup.

Xochimilco—exciting, contradictory. Our teachers were dissatisfied middle-

class Mexican leftists, exiled Argentinean intellectuals and other Latin American émigrés. Our idols were Ché Guevara, Felix Guattari, Antonio Gramsci, and Herbert Marcuse. Wealthy professors urged us to agitate among peasants in the countryside. And, what's more, we were aware that the government perceived our radicalism, our animosity, as productive.

In fact, it wanted our hatred. Its rationale was clear: if adolescents in the Third World are always full of antigovernment feeling, they should be provided with a secluded space to vent their rage. They'll scream, they'll organize, but as long as they're kept in isolation, nothing will come of it. And so we did, investing our time and energy in countless hopeless insurrectionary projects. But it wasn't a waste of energy. Something great did come out of it: El Sup.

I left Mexico in 1985, but I often look back at my years at UAM as a turning point. Between the pen and the sword, I thought I was wise for choosing the pen. But El Sup was even wiser: he chose both.

My politics and artistic views have changed somewhat. I have become a critic and scholar, and have adopted a new language. In the process, I acquired a new mask of my own: I became part Mexican and part North American—at once both and neither.

Evidently, El Sup is also an academic, although a less reticent one. I was the coward, the egotist. He was the hero. We are both bridges—across cultures, across social classes. I chose the library as my habitat, while he made Mexico itself his personal creation.

So what if he is Guillén, and vice versa? Simply that his unmasking has served its purpose: El Sup has faded away from public attention. His once-omnipresent visage now appears infrequently, if at all, a haggard reminder of the still miserable conditions in the South.

Now there's talk of him, El Sup, becoming a leftist candidate in national politics. But history has little room for heroes shifting gears, and even less for legends who undress themselves. Besides, no career is more discredited in Mexico than that of a politician. Better to vanish: only then will his trademark become truly indelible. Or better still: to become a novelist. After all, Latin America is depressing in its politics, but vivid in its imaginings. Viva El Sup, the intangible—a giant of the imagination.

ICONOPHOBIA

How anthropology lost it at the movies

Lucien Taylor

Ethnographers consider film to be like a book, and a book on ethnology appears no different from an ordinary book.
—Jean Rouch

The least advanced of men can convey information, that is, they can write by means of pictographs.
—Alfred C. Haddon

In 1977, the acclaimed Africanist anthropologist P. T. W. Baxter reviewed a film about an East African people called the Rendille for the British *Royal Anthropological Institute Newsletter* (*RAIN*). It was a film for which he felt instinctive ambivalence, and he set out to say just why it was that he was so suspicious of ethnographic films. He decided that anthropology and film are fundamentally incompatible, distinct in "aims" and methods. Each, said Baxter, "seeks quite different aspects of truth and utilises different means of stitching scraps of culture together creatively." Whereas anthropology is open-minded and detached, film is anything but. Substituting a single glass lens for our two human eyes, it is imperious and monocular; its beauty is distorting; it tries to simplify and disarm, as well as to impose. By implication, text, and anthropological text in particular, is none of these things—neither imperious or monocular, nor simplifying, disarming, or imposing. Thus, anthropologists search for complex connections between disparate particularities, while filmmakers, rather like development planners—the preeminent put-down in Africanist anthropology of the period—suppose that life is simple, and the issues clear. Baxter "resent[s]" films; he is "reluctant to submit" to them.

A decade later (1988), in terms a little less bellicose but equally ardent, the eminent Marxist anthropologist and distinguished theorist of ritual Maurice Bloch echoed this distrust. In *RAIN*'s successor, *Anthropology Today*, he tells us that not only is he "not very interested" in ethnographic films, he can "hardly bear to watch them" at all. Contemporary ethnographic filmmakers, he says, imag-

From The Nuer (1970), dir. Robert Gardner, Hilary Harris, and George Breidenbach. © Film Study Center, Harvard University

Filmmaker
and theorist
Trinh T. Minh-ha

ine they can learn something about people simply by "star[ing]" at them and listening to their words out of "context." Moreover, whereas writing anthropologists are beginning to consider how ethnographies are "constructed," ethnographic filmmakers are becoming ever more naive about the nature of representation. If, he says, ethnographic films must be made at all, they should be made with a "thesis," but without any anthropological collaboration. "I think there is great scope for anthropology on television," says Bloch, "but for a discussive intellectual form of anthropology; I want less staring at Mursi spitting at each

other." Watching Mursi spit at each other provides him with precious little context for their "words," or, presumably, for the rest of their actions. For Bloch, then, "context" is not something outside a text, something that puts a text in its place. Textuality itself, and textuality alone (a "thesis"), is the condition of possibility of a legitimate ("discussive, intellectual") visual anthropology. Visuality itself becomes merely ancillary, illustrative rather than constitutive of anthropological knowledge.

Lest these two cases seem isolated, anecdotal, and outdated, a similar fear of the filmic, indeed a suspicion of the visual *tout court*, is evident in the leading article of a 1992 collection of essays entitled, oddly enough, *Film As Ethnography*. In the keynote paper, "Anthropological visions," Kirsten Hastrup—Scandinavian anthropologist and leading authority on (in a word) "experience"—sets out to combat what she perceives as "a burst of interest in visual anthropology" that recapitulates an obsolete anthropological discourse. Hastrup rehearses Baxter's and Bloch's apprehensions, adding to them a whole series of oppositions between films and texts, as ideal types. Film, she says, is capable of producing no more than a thin description of a "happening." Text, on the other hand, can articulate a thick description of an "event," a happening invested with cultural significance. The idea would seem to be that a happening is an objective occurrence, represented indifferently, while an event is an incident witnessed firsthand, invested with first-person subjectivity. A happening is something viewed from afar, dispassionately, more or less from nowhere, while an event is narrated perspectivally—that is, from the point of view of a human participant, evoking that participant's personal experience. Film, Hastrup goes on to say, consists of no more than concrete images of what-once-was, while text transcends the particular and conveys a more comprehensive truth, the truth of the "ethnographic present." Although a picture of a happening can, at a later date, invoke the memory of its "space" for a firsthand participant, only writing can evoke the existential texture of the "place" to someone who wasn't there. Borrowing from the French thinker Michel de Certeau, Hastrup argues that ethnographic films represent reality by way of "maps" that "totalise" observations, whereas ethnographic texts offer guided tours through a "discursive series of oppositions." Filmmakers thus commit the "sin" of separating words from things, a sin for which postmodern textual anthropologists (presumably including Hastrup herself) atone by returning their readers to the hearth and home of lived experience. Texts can move freely between the past, present, and future, implying "meanwhileness" and "conjunction," but the "knowledge" contained in ethnographic films is irreducibly iconographic. Ethnographic writing alone can be reflexive, and thereby transform knowledge into consciousness. In the same vein, only anthropologists (not filmmakers) have admitted that the person of the ethnographer is part of the plot. In sum, there is no conflict between ethnographic films and anthropological texts. Not because they are complementary, but because films are, quite simply, logically inferior.

· · ·

How you respond to such generalized iconophobia depends, surely, on where you come from, and on whether you are a writer or a filmmaker. To me the most striking quality of these examples is the extraordinary *anxiety* the academic authors evince toward images, especially film images. The filmic detachment of words and things (if indeed that is what films do) is characterized in a quasi-religious idiom as *sinful*. The fear that films will somehow destroy or discredit their anthropological makers and viewers—as Bloch puts it, "when anthropologists begin to dedicate a large part of their time to ethnographic films it is usually because they have lost confidence in their own ideas"—is surely part and parcel of an abhorrence of imagery in general, a sentiment that, together with an array of attendant anti-iconic prohibitions, has existed from time immemorial. The fear of icons and graven imagery, profound in the monotheisms of Judaism and Islam, is neither novel nor restricted to anthropologists. But what about this apprehension is peculiarly anthropological?

Even in 1970s Paris, film-going was hardly the antisocial experience apparatus theorists imagined

One of the more interesting attributes of this anthropological aversion is its recapitulation, apparently unawares, of a large body of critical work—most of it French and published in the late sixties and early seventies, in magazines like *Cahiers du Ciném*, *Cinéthique*, and *Tel Quel*—that sought to elaborate, and then supersede, a semiology of cinema. Much of this work coalesced under the rubric of "apparatus" theory. To oversimplify, film critics like Jean-Louis Comolli, Jean Narboni, Jean-André Fieschi, Jean-Louis Baudry, Christian Metz, Jean-Pierre Oudart, and Marcelin Pleynet argued that film is an ideological instrument that is as coded as any other symbol system, that it has inherited the scientific perspective of the Quattrocento, and that its vision is monocular, ideal, and transcendent—and by implication, omnipresent, omniscient, and omnipotent. As Christian Metz would later describe it, this is a seeing "which has no features or position, as vicarious as the narrator-God or the spectator-God." Through

the process of editing, film disincarnates this transcendent subject's glass eye and lets it roam pretty much wherever it will. Far from the ensuing shots, with their different angles and focal lengths, producing a multitude of conflicting and embodied perspectives, these potentially diverse subjectivities are collapsed into an artificially harmonious and singular subject through a process of ideological suture. By means of editorial conventions that simulate space-time continuity, the spectators are obliged to identify with the superhuman gazes of the apparently unified subjects on the screen.

Under the influence of Lacanian psychoanalysis, apparatus theorists likened spectators to young children. Films, the argument went, force spectators to "misrecognize" their specular identity in much the same way that children do during the "mirror" stage. The experience of children and filmgoers alike is, as Metz memorably suggested, one of "under-motricity" and "over-perception." Both are characterized by a hypertrophy of the visual. Stuck in their seats, in a dark and antisocial cinema, spectators cannot help but renounce all voluntary control, regress into an infantile, dreamlike state, and give themselves up to the spectacle unfolding before their eyes on the two-dimensional screen—a condition in which they identify primarily with the Archimedean camera eye, but also, if to a lesser degree, with the characters up on the screen. The severance of the subject of desire (the viewing self) from the object of that desire (the screen or screen subject) transforms the filmgoer, no less than the infant, from a participant into a voyeur.

The iconophobia of Baxter, Bloch,

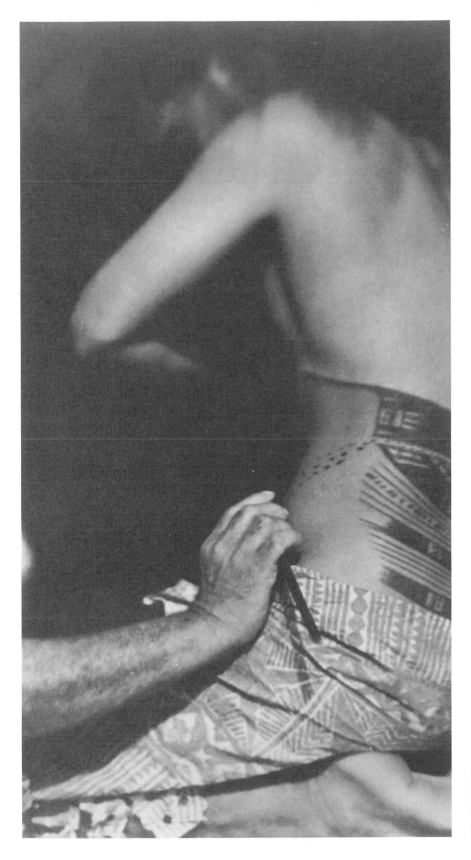

*From Moana,
dir. Robert Flaherty.
Courtesy of the
Museum of Modern
Art/Film Stills
Division*

From Forest of Bliss
*(1985), dir. Robert
Gardner.
Photo: Ned Johnston.
© Film Study Center,
Harvard University*

and Hastrup has many affinities with apparatus theory, at least in its broader strokes. For Baxter, film has none of the virtues of text. It is not tentative, detached, open-minded, or uncertain; on the contrary, it is bossy, one-eyed, distortingly beautiful, simplifying, and disarming. Film imposes itself "through the temporary suspension of disbelief," which would seem to be what Metz means by spectatorial "disavowal": filmgoers are of course (at least since the first screening of *L'arrivé d'un train en gare* in Paris in 1895) fully aware that they are watching a representation of reality on the screen, rather than reality itself, and yet they are obliged to *pretend* that it is reality if it is to have the desired effect. In a realistic film, there is a complicity of disavowal between the filmgoer and the filmmaker, a refusal of reciprocity between viewer and viewed. Metz has expressed this in an intentionalist idiom, "The film is not exhibitionist. I watch it, but it doesn't watch me watching it. Nevertheless, it knows that I am watching it. But it doesn't want to know. This fundamental disavowal is what has guided the whole of classical cinema into the paths of 'story' relentlessly erasing its discursive basis, and making it (at best) a beautiful close object." Baxter is as reluctant as Metz to "submit" to such a filmic regime. Whereas a filmgoer is imprisoned in the temporal order of the film, a book-reader has the freedom to pause or stop, as well as to flip back and forth through the pages. Freethinking and freewheeling adult that he is, Baxter resents "not being able to pause, to turn back, to recheck and to compare statements and pieces of data." Bloch and Hastrup also underline film's disavowal

of its discursive basis. As Bloch implies, filmmakers seem not to recognize that their works are "constructed." Ethnographic filmmakers, says Hastrup, deny —or worse, don't even realize—that they are part of the plot.

• • •

Baxter, Bloch, and Hastrup are an apparatus theorist's dream come true. However, as one detractor has since gibed, film does not mystify all of its spectators with a "delirium of clinical perfection." For spectators are by no means—or, rather, with all due respect for the anthropologists, not always—the wretched little creatures that apparatus theorists imagined, alienated from their true selves, "chained, captured or captivated" before an almighty screen. Even in classical narrative cinema, and certainly in ethnographic and documentary film, the discursive underpinning, or authorial voice, is not uniformly disavowed. Above all, cinematic production and reception is not some transhistorical, transcultural given. Spectatorship is a "total social fact" if anything is, embedded in a cultural context and historical moment, and thus susceptible to sociological as well as psychological interpretation. Even in 1970s Paris, filmgoing was hardly the antisocial experience apparatus theorists imagined. It's not only in Jamaica that spectators sometimes shoot at the characters on the screen. After all, film is not a purely visual medium. It has always—but especially since the advent of talkies in the 1920s and 1930s—involved a complex interplay of picture and sound. Sounds, images, and words gush around (and into) each other continually. Indeed, many ethnographic films accord a particularly

© *Napoleon Chagnon*
From Yanamamo:
The Last Days of
Eden *series.*

elevated place to dialogue. The picture as a whole is transformed by the simultaneous sound track, which is in turn modified by the adjacent picture. Film is a sensory medium, nearly as much as the human subject is a sensory being, and it is more often than not made up of both images and words. As W. J. T. Mitchell has so eloquently argued, language and imagery continually contaminate one another.

As spectators, Baxter, Bloch, and Hastrup all seem equally insensible to the properties of the medium, especially to the relationship of documentaries to the real (or, as film critics like to say, "pro-filmic") world of which they try to provide a record. (Realist fiction films, of course, absolutely elide the pro-filmic in telling their stories.) They seem also, more generally, to be unaware of how films are fabricated. One could, in fact, just as plausibly make a case for the very opposite of *all* their main propositions. Let's, for a moment, do that. In semiotician C. S. Peirce's terms, anthropological prose, like any other, is a succession of pure symbols. It is arbitrary and artificial, completely conventional. Film, by contrast, consists not only of symbols and of *icons* (since it resembles what it refers to in some way or another), but also of a series of *indices*. For it has a "motivated" or materially causative relationship with what it refers to; as semioticians would say, there is a natural bond between the signifier and the signified. Film is photochemically permeated by the world, and analog video electrically infused with it.

The indexicality of ethnographic film makes it open-ended, and thus susceptible to differing interpretations in a way anthropological writing is not. In view of this indexical "excess"—one that is latent within shots as much as it is generated by their juxtaposition—one could argue that film is not more, but *less* bossy, one-eyed, distorting, simplifying, disarming, imposing, and so on, than text. Indeed, one could make the further argument that since an observational aesthetic has for some time now enjoyed pride of place among ethnographic filmmakers—an aesthetic that favors long takes, synchronous speech, and a tempo

Film can no more be transposed wholesale into text than poetry can be transposed into prose

faithful to the rhythms of real life, and that discourages cutting, directing, reenacting, interviewing—their films are unusually open to multiple interpretations. In particular, the aesthetic of long takes is more realistic than the "psychological montage" of continuity cutting, which fragments events in such a way as to simulate the shifts in our attention if we were present, because (so the neorealist argument goes) it does not suppose that events have a singular meaning and dictate the attention of viewers accordingly. On the contrary, this "technical realism," as André Bazin put it, restores to the viewers some of the autonomy they have in interpreting reality when they are confronted with it as witnesses in real life. It allows action to develop within a single shot, over an extended period, and on several spatial planes; it constructs relationships within frames as much as between them; and it honors the homogeneity of space by preserving the relationships between objects rather

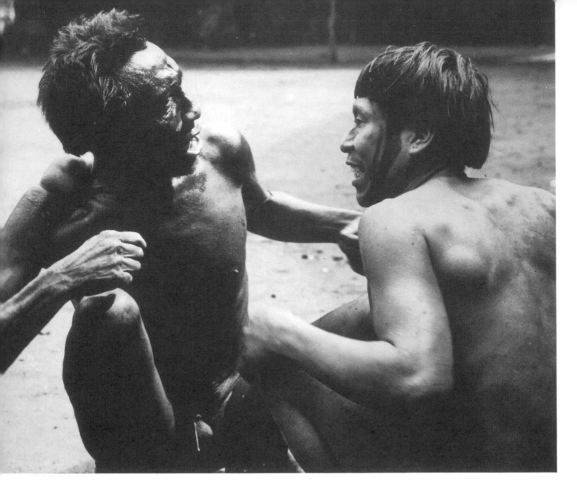

than substituting the abstract time and synthetic space of montage. Long takes, by exhibiting a deficiency of authorial intelligence (for which they have been taken to task by nearly everyone since Sergei Eisenstein), reflect an ambiguity of meaning that is at the heart of human experience itself.

An observational aesthetic, then, does not relinquish authorial control entirely, but it does so differently from other documentary forms. Observational films are still authored, but less authoritatively. They are still reductive, but watching observational films is a more digressive experience than watching other documentaries. In these regards they empower the film's subjects and the spectators alike: the subjects are less mutilated by the montage, and the spectators may garner meanings or simply come away with sensations and impressions that are at

odds with the maker's. It is not exactly that observational films permit "aberrant" or "alternative" readings, for there may be no correct, dominant or intended *writing* to which they may be counterposed: the metaphor of reading/writing, with its connotations of scientific rhetoric and decipherment, is inappropriate. But certainly observational films are open in the sense and to the extent that they permit multiple *viewings*.

Baxter is assuredly right that film will not let him pause or go back, as he might with a text. In certain respects it *is* a very domineering medium indeed. Unlike still images and text, the temporal order of projected film precludes what Peter Wollen has called a "free rewriting time." (Video, as well as film on an editing table, are different matters.) However, as a spectator, Baxter is at liberty to take from the images meanings that were never attached to them, perhaps never even imagined by the filmmaker, to a far greater degree than he is with the lines of an ethnographic monograph. Thus Baxter's problem with film may not in fact be that it is too bossy, but that it isn't nearly bossy enough. It doesn't give him the answer; it demands too much work from the viewer. (Reality doesn't give up the answer either, and it also can be obtuse and intransigent.) This is exactly what Bloch resents about the medium too; it doesn't hand him his thesis on a plate. If he wants more "discursive, intellectual" films and less staring at spitting Mursi, it may be that he doesn't want a film at all, or rather that he simply doesn't want to go to the bother of looking.

At the very least he doesn't want films that require him to be engaged in actively generating meaning out of the scenes that pass before his eyes and ears —a form of engagement closer to the experience of an onlooker at the event than to a reader of an ethnographic monograph. Discursive, intellectual films, in Bloch's book, are those that are pretextualized, that elaborate a thesis, that have already done his work for him— films, in short, that mimic anthropological prose. No wonder they always fall short! "The idea that ethnographic film speaks for itself is wrong," he writes. Most anthropological writers would agree. Peter Loizos, a scholar of Greek gender relations, is one of the few to appreciate the divergent capacities of films and texts. But even he, in the final analysis, wants to insist that "as anthropologists we most fruitfully admit films in evidence when we can relate them . . . to sources outside the film itself." The hint

of juridical discourse here intimates that film is on trial. But why? Why does it pose such a threat?

Hastrup's inattention to the experiential realism of movies is all the more unusual in that her writings argue that the vocation of contemporary anthropology is to restore us to the sensuous flow of what phenomenologists like to call the flesh-of-the-world—a calling that seems almost inherently cinematic. Although she claims film is bound to present only "real-time" sequences, one of the medium's signal features is, in fact, its ability to manipulate time and space. Observational and vérité films, in particular, offer embodied "itineraries" through space, and tell perspectival stories, in a way that academic monographs rarely do. Storytelling has been at the heart of cinema since its inception, of course, but it is only recently that ethnographic monographs have tried to move beyond abstract, synchronic, and synthetic classification—beyond, in Hastrup's terms, maps. She claims the "more comprehensive truth of the ethnographic pres-

Filmic ethnography, whether about Mursi spitting at each other, an Icelandic ram exhibition, or anything else, requires as much "local knowledge" as written ethnography

ent" is the exclusive preserve of writing, on Hastrup's account. Yet the ethnographic present has never been in greater disrepute, as a comprehensive and mystifying totalization that removes one's subjects from the entanglements of history—indeed, as Johannes Fabian would say, takes them out of time altogether.

Little wonder, then, that Hastrup suggests that texts alone can convey the "timelessness" that is part of human experience when most of us would have thought that experience was distinguished precisely by its *timeliness*—its concrete and contingent coordinates in time and space. Cinema, of all the media of human expression, has long been praised for its ability to simulate a world of living flux, what André Bazin famously called "objectivity in time." The cumulation of successive film frames evokes the sensation of movement over time quite literally *through* movement over time, and captures the experience of animate presence in a way that neither photographs nor text can. As Metz put it, "Film gives back to the dead a semblance of life." By contrast, one could argue as credibly as Hastrup's claim to the contrary that the prosaic text of the anthropologists, and not least the denial of "coevality" between observer and observed, has clear affinities, not only with timelessness, but also with lifelessness.

Hastrup reserves another property for texts: the capacity to transcend "the instance of fieldwork." But the moment an editor makes (or imagines) the first splice, a film has already embarked on the slippery road to abstraction, synthesis, and transcendence. If finished films still bear scars of the encounters that produced them—indexical "stigmata" of their histories—might that be a virtue, and not the vice she takes it to be? Hastrup believes that texts, and texts alone, can capture the existential space of cultural experience, and yet it is the motivated, existential, "real relation," as Peirce put it, between the cinematic signifier and signified, the filmic and the pro-filmic,

that makes it so expressive of lived-body experience. In addition, documentary films that foreground the active engagement between filmmaker and filmed in the production of cinematic meaning predate by half a century the current vogue for reflexivity among ethnographic writers. Moreover, quite apart from any self-conscious baring of the device on the part of the filmmaker, the indexicality of the medium, and particularly its use of experience, make it inherently reflexive—that is, at once subject and object to itself—in a way that has no precise parallel in other media or arts.

Hence Hastrup's presumption that films alone separate words and things, and that only postmodern ethnographic texts may recover the originary vitality of prereflective existence—that only *writers* may disclose something of what it is feels like, in any particular local setting, to be-in-the-world—is eccentric in the extreme. As it happens, only since the introduction of magnetic sound stock in the late 1950s have documentary editors been able to *afford* to separate sounds from pictures, and so words from their speakers (Hastrup's "things"). But with texts, as with noniconic symbols in general, taking words away from their utterers is absolutely free, a penstroke or touch of the keyboard away. It is as old as (written) history itself! What is the distinguishing hallmark of literacy if it is not its radical disjunction of the utterance (the *énoncé*) from the moment of utterance (the *énonciation*)? A sin, if you like, but hardly one that postmodern ethnographic texts can manage to atone for.

But this is all academic. For film is *es-*

sentially a sensory medium, fusing "words and things," in a way that writing, or at least expository academic writing, is not. As film theorist Vivian Sobchack has recently reminded us in *The Address of the Eye*, "More than any other medium of human communication, the moving picture makes itself sensuously and sensibly manifest as the expression of experience by experience." Film, unlike any other art form, thus depends upon experience twice over: as form and content, discourse and representation, subject and object—in short, as signifier and signified. Acts of moving, hearing, and seeing are at once presented and represented as the originary structures of embodied existence and the mediating structures of discourse. It is the double duty, as Sobchack calls it, that experience performs in the cinema that would seem to make the medium so fit for exploring existence in all its ambiguity, fit for expressing the undifferentiated significance of the human condition; fit, that is, for simultaneously embodying and evoking the intuitive lived experience of what Husserl and later Heidegger would call the *Lebenswelt*, the lifeworld.

· · ·

If anthropological writers, naturally enough, have only their own best interests at heart in their depreciation of film, what do ethnographic filmmakers and specifically *visual* anthropologists have to say on the subject?

Surprisingly, many ethnographic filmmakers seem to accept the aspersions cast on their trade. They concede without protest that ethnographic films are marginal to the evolution of anthropological knowledge. Films are pretty pic-

tures, excellent at arousing empathetic identification with an exotic people or an alien way of life—useful for popularizing anthropological knowledge with the help of some well-chosen voice-over, but little more. "Ethnographic film," writes Asen Balikci, "is characteristically descriptive to the point of largely excluding analysis. . . . film is not an appropriate medium for sophisticated analysis." Timothy Asch, the filmmaker of the canonical Yanomamo series, hoped against hope that one day anthropologists would stop conceiving of ethnographic film as "entertainment" and start thinking of it as (guess what?) "data." And ethnographic "hypermedia" expert Peter Biella has argued that the "observational style . . . cannot present theory." (This, despite the fact that the etymology of "theory" is "to look" or "to gaze," and that if there's one thing that observational filmmakers do, it's that.) Comments like these are a dime a dozen in almost every issue of the various international journals devoted to ethnographic filmmaking.

There are others, though, who see continuities between ethnographic films and anthropological monographs, who feel that ethnographic films should not so much illustrate as actually embody anthropological knowledge. This position is often traced to Sol Worth, collaborator with John Adair on the celebrated "Navajo Project." (Wondering whether the Navajo might have a "film grammar" of their own, one related to their language and worldview, they handed out 16 mm triple-turret Bell and Howells to neophyte Navajo filmmakers to see what they would do with them. Not a lot, they found out, unless the filming could be shown to be beneficial to their

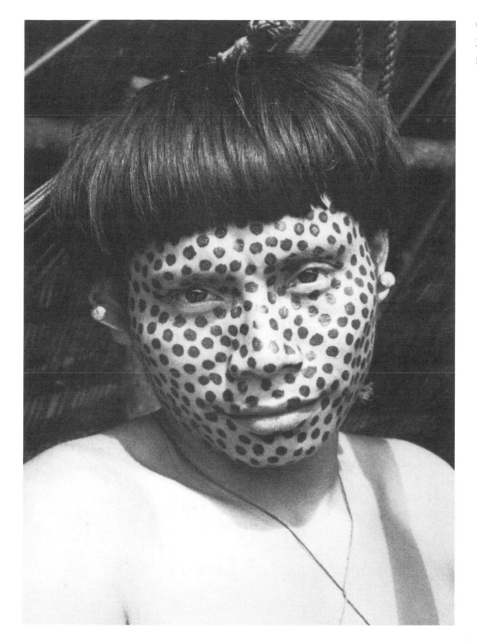

sheep.) In 1976, Worth proposed an "anthropology of visual communication," urging scholars to explore how anthropological knowledge can be inscribed in film and other iconic symbol-systems. Implicitly arguing against naive realist theories of visual representation, Worth insisted that ethnographic film offers not a "copy" or a "magic mirror" of the world "out there" but "*someone's statement about the world.*" Worth wanted to take us beyond "our deeply held and largely unexamined notion that . . . motion pictures are a mirror of the people, objects, and events that these media record photochemically," just as he wished to question "the jump we make when we say that the resultant photographic image could be, should be, and most often is something called 'real,' 'reality,' or 'truth.'" In the hands of well-trained anthropologists, film may be not only a record *of* culture (which it invariably is) but also an analytic record *about* culture. Once one allows the possibility that film could make a scientific statement about the world, we can step outside the seductive myth system that would have us believe that it is only a crass copy of it. This frees us, says Worth, from "the impossible position of asking whether [they] are true." And some of us, he says, "are arguing that it is as silly to ask whether a film is true or false as it is to ask whether a grammar is true or false. Or whether a performance of a Bach sonata or a Beatles song is true or false."

A year earlier, in 1975, fellow anthropologist of visual communication Jay Ruby enumerated a series of specifications for ethnographic films—that they "describe" a "whole culture" or a "defineable" unit thereof, that they be in-formed by an explicit or implicit "theory" of culture, that they be articulated within an "anthropological argot," that they contain explicit reflexive "statements" revealing the author's "methodology," and that they thus furnish a "scientific" "justification" for every selection made, including the framing and length of every shot, the film stock, the lens, the "type" of sound, and all editing decisions. But for all his insistence on hardcore ethnography and an authentic "anthropological argot," Ruby never pauses to provide a definition of either. Ethnography is invoked, almost fetishistically, as a magical elixir of anthropological truth.

Of course, even for written texts, many of Ruby's prescriptions would be a tall order. Anthropological monographs no more provide a "scientific justification" for the "multitude of decisions" involved in their production than do ethnographic films—be it shot length or word choice, sequence or sentence, film form or literary style, "type of field sound" or choice of informants. Rather than introducing a critical distance by foregrounding a text's constructedness, Ruby's "reflexivity" is supposed to produce an absolute transparency, a state of complete self-consciousness—a state that is logically impossible in the human sciences just as it is in the arts. While it is, of course, possible for me to dream up a reflexive hall of mirrors in which I could represent (my representing) myself representing my original representation, there is no Archimedean Prime Representer at the end (or beginning) of the line. What the Welsh writer and documentary editor Dai Vaughan says about film is true of representation in general: "Events *must* be contrived for the camera; and to make the audience aware of the contrivance is to fall into the absurdity of an endless regression. . . . Once we have accepted that there is no purely technical criterion for realism—no gimmick of presentation which can guarantee authenticity—then we are forced to recognize that we must rely upon the integrity of the artist for its creation and upon the judgement of the viewer for its proof." Is it any different for written ethnography? As Vaughan suggests elsewhere, "Wilfully or by oversight, some materials may be wrongly labelled. Some things may have been less rehearsed or more rehearsed, less spontaneous, less calculated, less uninfluenced by the camera's presence than we-as-viewers suppose them to have been. But there is no sharp demarcation between the misunderstandings of documentary and the misunderstandings of life."

Ruby's hope that films and texts might one day be virtually identical can only be maintained by downplaying what distinguishes them. Although he sees himself as making a case for a truly *filmic* ethnography, his terminology (descriptions, definitions, methodologies, statements, and justifications) reveals that in his conception, visuality is entirely absorbed by the "logos" of anthropology—by, that is, Margaret Mead's "discipline of words."

Ruby's domestication of the visual and Worth's proposed shift from a visual anthropology to an anthropology of visual communication go hand in hand. The degree to which Worth sought, despite himself, to *linguify* film is quite remarkable. He claimed that conceiving of film as a statement about rather than a copy of or "magic mirror" to the world would somehow liberate us from asking whether it's true or false, when precisely the opposite is the case. It is not the world itself, or even our experience in it, that has a truth-value, but rather our representation of it. If film were nothing but a magical mirror held up to the world, we would not have to ask if it were true at all. It is because it aspires to be, or cannot resist being, discourse that we are still obliged to ask such questions of it. It is no coincidence that films are criticized as biased or subjective far more frequently than photographs.

Worth compared textuality with his proposed mode of anthropology, which he called pictorial-visual. But rather than expanding anthropology to include the distinct properties of this "pictorial-visual," he smothered it with metaphors of prosaic textuality. In his attempt to relativize the role of language, he in fact enshrined language as paradigmatic for meaning by reducing anthropological films to "statements about" and "records of." But film can no more be transposed wholesale into text than poetry can be transposed into prose. His problem, in short, is the problem at the core of semiotics, for the paradigm of semiotics has always been linguistics.

Worth was half right to distinguish between a record "about" and a record "of" culture, even if the distinction could be articulated more accurately as one between *discourse about* and *record of*. But Worth failed to recognize that every film is by definition both of these things at once: it is not that film is not linguistic at all, nor even that it is a language unlike any other, but that it is, incongruously and oxymoronically, at once both

a language and not a language. If film does not provide a mimetic copy of the world, it does very definitely throw up a "magical mirror" to it. It is anything but reducible to someone's statement about it. As Roland Barthes put it in *Camera Lucida* (1981), quite possibly with Worth in mind:

It is the fashion, nowadays, among Photography's commentators (sociologists and semiologists), to seize upon a semantic relativity: no 'reality' (great scorn for the 'realists' who do not see that the photograph is always coded). . . . the photograph, they say, is not an analogan of the world; what it represents is fabricated. . . . [However] the realists do not take the photograph for a 'copy' of reality, but for an emanation of past reality: a magic, not an art.

. . .

Worth described Nelson Goodman's seminal *Languages of Art* as a catalyst for his own work; a curious claim, for Goodman's writing is notable for its treatment of what sets images and texts apart. He suggests that nonlinguistic systems "differ from languages . . . primarily through lack of differentiation—indeed through density (and consequent total absence of articulation)—of the symbol system." While Baxter, Bloch, and Hastrup associate this undifferentiated, unarticulated quality with deficiency—with (anthropological) absence—Goodman proposes on the contrary that a symbol system's degree of differentiation is inversely proportional to its density. A symbol system is dense, its symbols "replete," to the extent that the various properties of its symbols are important to its overall meaning. A dense image is also "continuous"; the various features that make up the whole defy reduction into isolated, unique characters, each with its own singular referent. In this regard, pictures are dense in a way that texts are not. Film, of course, as an ongoing fission-fusion of words, sounds, and moving pictures, all flowing into and through one another, is both dense and differentiated, continuous and discontinuous, all at the same time.

Goodman's notion of density, in itself, does not directly address the indexicality of film, which is what sets it apart from the larger class of icons, nor indeed the mobility that distinguishes it from still photos. But at least it does not assume that language is paradigmatic for meaning, and so does not criticize film for lacking qualities that are essentially linguistic. As the heydey of structuralism and semiotics has passed, both Lacan's claim that the unconscious is structured like a language and Lévi-Strauss's conviction that kinship systems display grammars as intricate as those of languages have been discredited. Few people nowadays believe that language offers an apposite analogy for culture or society. But so long as anthropologists continue to hold that language is paradigmatic for anthropology, then a "pictorial-visual" mode of anthropology can only come into being by divesting itself of its distinguishing features. And if that is the case, then why bother?

. . .

Because we humans express ourselves through images as well as through language, and because anthropology constitutes an exploration of the human con-

From Ika Hands (1981), dir. Robert Gardner. © Film Study Center, Harvard University.

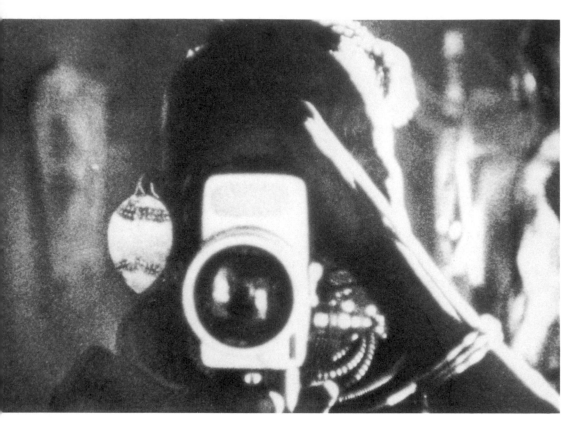

dition, it seems needlessly delimiting to conceive of the form of anthropology itself as exclusively linguistic. If anthropology is to create a space for the visual—in this case, film—it must seek neither to disavow discontinuities between the two media nor to transform one into another. For a start, this would entail a shift from the attempt to convey "anthropological knowledge" on film—the attempt to *linguify* film—to the idea that ethnography can itself be conducted filmically. Filmic ethnography, whether about Mursi spitting at each other, an Icelandic ram exhibition, or anything else, requires as much "local knowledge" as written ethnography. Bloch declared, "The idea that ethnographic film speaks for itself is wrong." But what if film doesn't speak at all? What if film not only

constitutes *discourse about* the world but also (re)presents *experience of* it? What if film does not *say* but *show*? What if film does not just *describe*, but *depict*? What, then, if it offers not only "thin descriptions" but also "thick depictions"?

If film critics and visual anthropologists have had an equally hard time compiling an inventory of the rules and regulations of film, it may be because these rules are not half as hard and fast as those of plain prose, and because they're partly improvised as filmmakers go along. If, as Barthes claimed, one of the connotations of film, or photography, is that it has a capacity to offer a "message without a code," then, try as analysts might, this record or trace of the world will never wholly submit to semiotic decoding. In other words, if the rules of film resist for-mulation, this may not be because film-makers are even more unconscious about the form they manipulate than everyday language speakers are about their syntax. It may be that the relative syntactic poverty of the medium is precisely its semantic strength, that which allows it to respond to the diversity and density of human experience as flexibly as it does. In Jean Mitry's words:

[Cinematic] forms . . . are . . . as varied as life itself and, just as one doesn't have the knowledge to regulate life, so too one hasn't the knowledge to regulate an art of which life is at once the subject and the object.

Whereas the classical arts sought to signify movement with the immobile, life with the inanimate, the cinema must express life with life itself. It takes up there where the others leave off. It thus escapes all their rules as it does all their principles.

Of course, at a certain point this becomes mumbo jumbo. If films were indeed to forgo *all* rules, they would soon be incomprehensible, all noise and no signal. And film is usually verbal as well as visual, and as such ethnographic filmmakers have to confront thorny problems of verbal and visual representation, both. Semiotics is not all wrong: films are constructed sequentially, they narrate stories, and so have syntagmatic features; in these and other respects they are indeed imbued with at least paralinguistic qualities. Films can be studied for their records of and about the world, and in anthropological film reviews that it exactly what is done. But the foundational metaphor of semiotics remains language, and semiotics continues to derive its force from looking at nonlinguistic sys-

tems of signification *as if* they were languages. At a certain point the analogies break down, and semiotics (and semiotics-derived communication theory) loses its purchase. What makes film so captivating is that it is something other, or more, than just language. Indeed, given the apparent affinity of film with life itself, moving images evoking moving life, hearing evoking hearing, and seeing seeing; given the centrality of the lifeworld to anthropology; given the exemplary open-endedness of ethnography, whose wealth of detail is always supposed to transcend the theoretical services to which it may be put; and given the attention anthropologists have devoted lately to representations of the body and to the embodiment of experience, the backlash against film no less than the ongoing desire to linguify it seem all the more unlikely.

Or do they? Jean-François Lyotard, for one, has argued that the ambiguity and opacity of the perceptual medium will always upset orders of prosaic textual representation, with their yearning for clarity and lucidity. This may be true. It is a curious irony that of the anthropologists who are so fearful of film, one (Bloch) is an expert on "ritual" and the other (Hastrup) a specialist in "experience." Bloch has long made a convincing case for the non-propositional, performative, "illocutionary" quality of ritual, but with the constraint of individual freedom at its core. Perhaps what irks him most about film is, paradoxically, the qualities it shares with ritual— its illocutionary aspects and its temporal coercion: it permits no free rewriting time. (What could be more liminal than sitting silently in a dark cinema, eyes transfixed on an illusionistic screen seemingly teetering between two- and three-dimensionality?) And maybe what so galls Hastrup is precisely film's simulation of lived experience. As ethnographic filmmaker David MacDougall has remarked, "the truth is that anthropologists were made anxious by this cinema which eluded them, which was neither science nor mere exoticism, but which trespassed upon their dreams and memories of fieldwork."

However, contrary to Lyotard and a lot of postmodernist hype, this doesn't mean that the discursive is inherently inferior to the figural, or the textual to the visual. (How dispiriting it would be to have to resort to writing to make that case.) For if there is an intrinsic impoverishment to the image in knowledge, as surely there is, then there is equally evidently an impoverishment to knowledge in the image. Density is diminished by being articulated, as is differentiation if all the pieces are put back together again. Moreover, the phenomenologists' and neorealists' hopes that film would reunite viewer and viewed in the sensuous intersubjective flesh-of-the-world have clearly been dashed. The answer is not, *pace* Bloch and Hastrup, to wax lyrical about the Good object of the written word and to hoot and holler about the Bad object of film (any more than it is to make a Bad object out of the written word and a Good object of film), but to recognize that the textual and the filmic are both multiple rather than monolithic, and culturally and historically variable in their imbrications rather than God-given in their differences. Through dialogue and narration, subtitles and intertitles, end credits and opening credits, film is shot through with language, just as imagery ineluctably infuses language.

Anthropological writers seem to have turned their backs on film because they begrudge documentary its unique affinity with the human experience they too take as their (missing) object. Films have a way of exceeding theoretical bounds, and of showing anthropologists' purchase on the lived experience of their subjects to be rather more precarious than they would like to believe. In its plenty, film captures something of the lyricism of lived experience that probably attracts many anthropologists in the first place. Dai Vaughan has argued that film's plenitude "defies its reduction . . . into a simple linear statement approximating the condition of prose." Might it be that anthropologists resent documentary's resemblance—insofar as it may be said to resemble literary forms at all—not to their own plain prose, but to poetry?

The Good Parsi

The Fate of a Colonial Elite in a Postcolonial Society

T. M. LUHRMANN

During the Raj, one group stands out as having prospered because of British rule: the Parsis. The Zoroastrian people adopted the manners, dress, and aspirations of their British colonizers, and were rewarded with high-level financial, mercantile, and bureaucratic posts. Indian independence, however, ushered in their decline. Tanya Luhrmann's analysis brings startling insights to a wide range of communal and individual identity crises and what could be called "identity politics" of this century. In a candid last chapter the author confronts another elite in crisis: an anthropology in flux, uncertain of its own authority and its relation to the colonizers.

$49.95 cloth $22.95 paper

Still the Promised City?

African-Americans and New Immigrants in Postindustrial New York

ROGER WALDINGER

Still the Promised City? addresses the question of why African-Americans have fared so poorly in securing unskilled jobs in the postwar era and why new immigrants have done so well, using New York as a prism to examine the changing relationships between race, immigration, and economics. Roger Waldinger points out that immigrants from Asia, Latin America and the Caribbean have flourished in self-created ethnic employment niches, while African-American networks no longer provide connections to the lower-level jobs.

$35.00 cloth

The Anatomy of Prejudices

ELISABETH YOUNG-BRUEHL

"Clearly written and accessible…this is a major work in personality and culture that asserts the plurality rather than the unity of prejudice. The author…integrates psychoanalytic concepts with sociological and historical readings… Impressively erudite, [she] knows 'how culture shapes the study of itself.' Young-Bruehl confronts a great and enduring scourge of humanity while enriching many fields. Along with new and challenging ideas, this book provides an indispensable survey of past scholarship."
—LIBRARY JOURNAL

$35.00 cloth

Chicanos in a Changing Society

From Mexican Pueblos to American Barrios in Santa Barbara and Southern California, 1848–1930

ALBERT CAMARILLO

WITH A NEW PREFACE BY THE AUTHOR

"Camarillo is without a doubt the top Chicano historian in the United States… *Chicanos in a Changing Society* is the best treatment of race and ethnic relations in the historical development of the United States Southwest. It tells a rich and complex story of how California's mexicano population was deprived of its land, politically disempowered, and socially segregated into ethnic enclaves or barrios."
—Ramón Gutiérrez,
University of California, San Diego
26 halftones, 25 tables • $16.95 paper

EXTREME PREJUDICE

Dinesh D'Souza and the coarsening of American conservatism

Michael Bérubé

Discussed in this essay

The End of Racism,
*Dinesh D'Souza,
New York:
The Free Press*

Strolling through the Detroit International Airport on my way to my parents' home in Virginia Beach, I came upon a newsstand-bookstore that was devoting eight or ten shelves of space—roughly one-quarter, I believe, of its "new best-sellers" wall—to Dinesh D'Souza's *The End of Racism*. I had heard a great deal about the book before it was published, and had just recently been asked (twice, actually) by the *Chicago Tribune* to review the thing. I declined, partly on the grounds that I've already read more D'Souza than any human should, having perused both *Illiberal Education* (1991) and his rarely mentioned first (and best) effort, *Falwell: Before the Millennium* (1984). That's the book where D'Souza writes, "listening to Falwell speak, one gets a sense that something is right about America, after all." So why would I want to read the new seven-hundred-page D'Souza, the magnum opus, the D'Souza *Ulysses*? Do I really have any obligation to keep plowing through the book-shelves of the Right, demonstrating

again and again that there's no there there?

Within hours I was in my parents' living room, asking my father whether he thought a *Tribune* review from me would make any dent in the media campaign bringing bulk shipments of *The End of Racism* to airport bookstores, or whether I wouldn't just be giving the book greater visibility and credibility simply by agreeing to treat it as a serious object of some kind. "Well, Michael," my father replied, "you may not have to worry. From what I hear, the book isn't doing very well, in reviews or in sales." When I asked where my father had heard such a thing, he turned to me and asked, with a straight face, if I hadn't seen the new "desperation" ads the Free Press was running for the book. "Two for one deal," he said. "Buy *The End of Racism* at the already low, low bargain price, and receive *The Mark Fuhrman Tapes* for free."

Of course, it's manifestly unfair to compare D'Souza and Fuhrman. To my knowledge, D'Souza has never personally beaten or framed a black person, nor has he suggested creating a large bonfire of black bodies. In *The End of Racism*, he merely proposes a theory of "rational discrimination" based on the recognition that there are vast "civilizational differences" between black and white Americans. At the close of his first chapter, D'Souza offers a brief catechism on the subject: the main problem for blacks is not racism, but "liberal antiracism"; the civil rights movement failed because "equal rights for blacks could not and did not produce equality of results"; and, consequently, the cause of "rational discrimination" is "black cultural pathology." D'Souza's middle chapter ("Is America a Racist Society?") expands on the premises of rational discrimination, which may be unfair to individuals but valid about groups-as-wholes:

Only because group traits have an empirical basis in shared experience can we invoke them without fear of contradiction. Think of how people would react if someone said that "Koreans are lazy" or that "Hispanics are constantly trying to find ways to make money." Despite the prevalence of anti-Semitism, Jews are rarely accused of stupidity. Blacks are never accused of being tight with a dollar, or of conspiring to take over the world. By reversing stereotypes we can see how their persistence relies, not simply on the assumptions of the viewer, but also on the characteristics of the group being described.

This, perhaps, is right-wing sociology's finest moment: *reversal of stereotypes!* Why didn't *we* think of that? OK, now let's get this straight. Koreans are *not* lazy, Hispanics do *not* try to make money, Blacks are spendthrifts, and . . . hey! wait a minute! those clever Jews really *are* trying to take over the world! Get me Pat Robertson!

Many of my black friends were understandably alarmed to hear that D'Souza's book endorses the practice of "rational discrimination." One told me that she'd read only so much of the book—up to the point at which, on page 169, D'Souza notes that the civil rights movement failed because it did not consider its political consequences, namely, that "racism might be fortified if blacks were unable to exercise their rights effectively and responsibly." After that, she decided the book might as well be called *The Negro A Beast*, after Charles Carroll's best-seller of 1900. Such a title, I replied, would almost surely keep the book out of major airport bookstores, and so was probably rejected by the Free Press's marketing department. But then again, I added, there's no reason to think of D'Souza as antiblack; on the contrary, the theory of "rational discrimination" may prove even more dangerous to white Americans than to any other group. It doesn't take a Malcolm or an Ishmael Reed to figure this one out: White people blow up federal buildings. White people pillage savings and loans. White people built Love Canal. White people commit horrid, unthinkable murders of helpless children and pregnant women, and then they blame them on black men. All the great serial killers of the West are white people. Now, don't get me wrong. I'm not saying that all white people are crazy or greedy or dishonest. Some of my closest friends are white. But would you want your daughter to marry one?

• • •

Dinesh D'Souza

Len Be Pas

fers from Herrnstein's and Murray's in that it also includes extended hallucinations masquerading as "historical overview." More on this below.) The authors of these books then appear, calm and composed, on national media, saying they know their work is bound to cause controversy but should at least be granted an honest hearing. (See also, under this heading, David Brock's *The Real Anita Hill*.) Phase two of their mission accomplished, they then head back to base camp at *Commentary* magazine to write assessments of their reception, showing that despite their honesty and all-around reasonableness, they were savaged and brutalized by the knee-jerk liberal press. All of which demonstrates *a fortiori* the liberal stranglehold on political discourse in the United States; for as the ever-reliable Eugene Genovese memorably put it in a recent issue of the *National Review*, surveying the public response to *The Bell Curve*, "once again academia and the mass media are straining every muscle to suppress debate."

So much for the new genre and its characteristic media-saturation strategy. Now for some of the highlights of *The End of Racism*.

I presume that many of my readers are familiar with some of D'Souza's more extraordinary arguments in *The End of Racism*. Still, it may be worth pausing briefly over some of the highlights. For I believe this book, together with *The Bell Curve*, is an instance of a wholly new genre of encyclopedic pseudoscience, and it is fundamental to the workings of this genre that the books in question be too bloated and overstuffed for the ordinary reader to fathom. In this new genre, measured commentary, reportage, and scholarship are blended with ultraconservative and even fascist policy recommendations, regardless of the logical relation between the scholarship and the recommendations. (D'Souza's book dif-

• "The popular conception seems to be that American slavery as an institution involved white slaveowners and black slaves. Consequently, it is easy to view slavery as a racist institution. But this image is complicated when we discover that most whites did not own slaves, even in the South; that not all blacks were slaves; that several thousand free blacks and American Indians owned black slaves. An examination of these frequently obscured aspects of American slavery calls into question the facile equation of racism and slavery."

- "The American slave was treated like property, which is to say, pretty well."
- "Most African American scholars simply refuse to acknowledge the pathology of violence in the black underclass, apparently convinced that black criminals as well as their targets are both victims: the real culprit is societal racism. Activists recommend federal jobs programs and recruitment into the private sector. Yet it seems unrealistic, bordering on the surreal, to imagine underclass blacks with their gold chains, limping walk, obscene language, and arsenal of weapons doing nine-to-five jobs at Procter and Gamble or the State Department."
- "Increasingly it appears that it is liberal antiracism that is based on ignorance and fear: ignorance of the true nature of racism, and fear that the racist point of view better explains the world than its liberal counterpart."

Almost as striking are D'Souza's incisive rhetorical questions:

- "If America as a nation owes blacks as a group reparations for slavery, what do blacks as a group owe America for the abolition of slavery?"
- "How did [Martin Luther] King succeed, almost single-handedly, in winning support for his agenda? Why was his Southern opposition virtually silent in making counterarguments?"
- "Historically whites have used racism to serve powerful entrenched interests, but what interests does racism serve now? Most whites have no economic stake in the ghetto."

Yet these are merely the book's most noticeable features—the passages that make a reviewer suppose that the easiest way to slander D'Souza is to quote him directly. *The End of Racism* is not, however, the sum of its pull quotes. More important are its characteristic tics and tropes, which are harder to convey but crucial for an understanding of how his text operates. There is, for instance, the repeated insistence that behind every civil rights initiative looms the specter of cultural relativism, and that the father of cultural relativism is Franz Boas. The last time I encountered this argument—and I am not making this up—I was reading neo-Nazi pamphlets on the cultural inferiority of the darker peoples. D'Souza is unique, however, in finding the evil Boas everywhere he looks, from the founding of the NAACP to the unanimous majority in *Brown v. Board of Education.*

Indeed, the only figure who comes in for as much abuse as Boas is W. E. B. Du Bois, apparently because Du Bois was so simplistic as to blame white people for lynchings, Jim Crow, and the race riots of 1906 (Atlanta) and 1908 (Springfield).

Once you've been tarred by D'Souza as a cultural relativist, there is no hope for you. Everything you say testifies only to your moral turpitude

(Actually, to be fair to D'Souza, his book nowhere mentions those riots.) As D'Souza explains at some length, Du Bois was a cultural relativist. And once you've been tarred by D'Souza as a cultural relativist, there is no hope for you.

Charles Murray

assumptions." Johnnetta Cole writes that the "problem" with single-parent households "is that they are deprived of decent food, shelter, medical care, and education," and D'Souza writes that "Johnnetta Cole finds nothing wrong with single-parent families"—and that, more broadly, "leading African American intellectuals abstain from criticizing and go so far as to revel in what they describe as another alternative lifestyle." Houston Baker writes a book claiming that 2 Live Crew was rightly banned in Broward County for obscenity, and sure enough, D'Souza cites him (and his book) as one of the Crew's leading defenders. How can this be? You guessed it—cultural relativism. "Instead of seeking to counter the cultural influence of rap, leading African American figures unabashedly condone and celebrate rap music as the embodiment of black authenticity."

In *The End of Racism*, we find that successful black people are especially whiny (unless they're conservatives); accordingly, they draw from D'Souza a scorn that is indistinguishable from hatred. In 1993, Senator Carol Moseley-Braun argued that the Senate should not recognize the Confederate flag as the official symbol of the United Daughters of the Confederacy; D'Souza calls her protest "histrionic"—and, because he knows who pays his bills, fails to mention that Jesse Helms made a project of taunting Moseley-Braun thereafter. In his penultimate chapter he takes up the narratives of middle-class blacks who deal with countless racist slurs and slights every day, and reacts with disbelief to their professions of resentment:

Everything you say testifies only to your moral turpitude. Henry Louis Gates, Jr. suggests that it's racist to say to him, "Skip, sing me one of those old Negro spirituals" or "You people sure can dance," and D'Souza replies, "Why are [these statements] viewed as racist? Because contemporary liberalism is constructed on the scaffolding of cultural relativism, which posits that all groups are inherently equal." A century earlier, Du Bois had called for "anti-lynching legislation" and "enfranchisement of the Negro in the South"; D'Souza remarks that "this represented a program strongly influenced by Franz Boas and Boasian

These are the observations of relatively well-placed men and women: an executive, a government worker, and a college professor. Since no reasons are given that would justify such reactions [i.e., D'Souza did not cite them], one might conclude that we are dealing with cases of people who live in a world of make-believe, in mental prisons of their own construction. For them, antiracist militancy is carried to the point of virtual mental instability. It is hard to imagine whites feeling secure working with such persons.

D'Souza's ability to empathize with beleaguered white persons is admirable, and no doubt if he continues to succor the hurt feelings of his powerful white colleagues who don't see why Skip gets so huffy when he's asked to sing "Roll, Jordan, Roll," his career as a prominent right-wing intellectual—and his fellowship from the American Enterprise Institute—is pretty much guaranteed. It was not long after the book was published, in fact, that the *Wall Street Journal* devoted half a page of op-ed space to an excerpt from D'Souza's concluding chapter—the part where he finally gets around to delivering his payload, his brief for the repeal of the 1964 Civil Rights Act.

D'Souza's rationale for repeal is clear: ever since the passage of the Fourteenth Amendment, he claims, the federal government has been "the primary threat to black prospects." In a truly free market, by contrast, racial discrimination would not exist, since "discrimination is only catastrophic when virtually everyone colludes to enforce it." D'Souza's case in point is major league baseball, about which he poses a truly novel thought-experiment: "Consider what would happen," he writes, "if every baseball team in America refused to hire blacks." Lest we are unable to imagine such a thing, D'Souza guides us step by step:

Blacks would suffer most, because they would be denied the opportunity to play professional baseball. And fans would suffer, because the quality of games would be diminished. But what if only a few teams—say the New York Yankees and the Los Angeles Dodgers—refused to hire blacks? African Americans as a group would suffer hardly at all, because the best black players would offer their services to other teams. The Yankees and the Dodgers would suffer a great deal, because they would be deprived of the chance to hire talented black players. Eventually competitive pressure would force the Yankees and Dodgers either to hire blacks, or to suffer losses in games and revenue.

There's something disingenuous about D'Souza's plans for integration, since D'Souza had argued earlier, citing Joel Williamson, that Jim Crow laws were "designed to preserve and encourage" black self-esteem. But let's assume, for the nonce, that D'Souza is serious here, and let's assume also that franchises like the Celtics or the Red Sox of the 1980s could not win games without a sizable contingent of black ballplayers. How precisely is this argument supposed to work in American society at large? Are we supposed to believe that bankers and realtors don't discriminate against black clients for fear that their rivals down the street will snap up all those hard-hitting, base-stealing young Negroes? Or is it that when black motorists are tired of being pulled over in California, they will simply take their business to the more hospitable clime of Arizona?

. . .

Few commentators have noted that Dinesh D'Souza is himself the most visible contradiction of the right's major premise in the culture wars—namely, that campus conservatives are persecuted by liberal faculty and intimidated into silence. For here, after all, is perhaps the most vocal Young Conservative of them all, a founder and editor-in-chief of the *Dartmouth Review* who's since gone on to Princeton University, the Reagan administration, and lucrative fellowships from the Olin Foundation and the American Enterprise Institute. He is, in short, a phenomenon. No matter how diligently his critics pore through his work, demonstrating time and again that the stuff doesn't meet a single known standard for intellectual probity, *he is taken seriously*. Liberal heavyweight champ Richard Rorty is tapped to take his book apart in the *New York Times Book Review*; Harvard's Stephan Thernstrom weighs in with a trenchant critique in the *Times Literary Supplement*. On the other side of the aisle, both Genoveses stand up to testify to the book's importance, calling it "impressive" and "courageous." D'Souza is denounced and celebrated, defended and reviled. He appears in *Forbes*, the *Atlantic*, the *American Scholar*. Meanwhile, over on page A4 of the hometown paper there's a story about how the Philadelphia police have terrorized the city's black citizens for years; on page B10, an NFL star's brother, a young black businessman, has been stopped by highway police and beaten to death. No probable cause, no previous record. No one notices.

Not long ago Michael Lind wrote about what he called "the intellectual death of conservatism," recounting how he watched in amazement as Heritage Foundation founder Paul Weyrich suggested lacing illegal drugs with rat poison—and no one in the room demurred. The publication of *The End of Racism* seems to me a larger version of the same phenomenon: not only a deliberate and at times terrifying attempt to move the center of political gravity as far right as possible, but also so egregious an affront to human decency as to set a new and sorry standard for "intellectual" debate. It is remarkable, I think, that this latest and most virulent brand of postwar American conservatism has so far produced only one prominent defector, only one conscientious objector—the aforementioned Michael Lind. And it is similarly remarkable that D'Souza's book has provoked only one resignation from the AEI—that of prominent black conservative Glenn Loury.

Still, however much one might lament the resolute ideological conformity on the right, it strikes me as a gesture of political impotence for commentators on the left to criticize *The End of Racism* for failing to meet any reasonable standard for sound scholarship, informational accuracy, or logical coherence. It's rather like complaining, after your arms have been removed from their sockets, that your opponent has failed to abide by *Robert's Rules of Order*. Does anyone seriously expect that Lynne Cheney, say, will tender her resignation to the American Enterprise Institute as well, on the grounds that D'Souza has flouted the intellectual standards of which she claims to be the defender? And what of Adam Bellow, son of Saul, who, according to D'Souza, "worked closely with me throughout the preparation of the manuscript"? Wasn't there anything he could have done to make *The End of Racism* a saner, a more respectable book? Or was he too busy searching the world over for the Tolstoy of the Zulus?

I think it is important that the American right is now so supremely self-confident, so assured of its control over the direction of public policy and political debate, that no one at the Free Press or the AEI worried whether *The End of Racism* might damage the credibility of conservatism. Such self-confidence is altogether impressive, even sublime. What does it betoken? The *Wall Street Journal* excerpt of the book should probably be our guide. It's significant that the *Journal* trumpeted only D'Souza's call to repeal the Civil Rights Act of 1964; apparently, the time is not yet right for the *Journal* to reprint neo-Nazi pamphlet material on the omnipresent cultural influence of Franz Boas. But outright repeal of the Civil Rights Act is still unthinkable in American politics; the most the American right can do, for the moment, is to shoot holes in the Voting Rights Act of 1965, and torpedo those liberal intellectuals, like Lani Guinier, who actually take the legislation seriously. The "race issue" of 1996 wasn't supposed to be civil rights in toto; it was supposed to be the abolition of affirmative action, spearheaded by the so-called Civil Rights Initiative in California. Isn't D'Souza jumping the gun? Isn't the Civil Rights Act too ambitious a target?

But perhaps the jumping of the gun is precisely the point. D'Souza's not writing for 1996, or even for 2000; he's writing for generations yet to come. Like Bob Dornan's presidential candidacy, *The End of Racism* may be a short-term disaster but a long-term success in pushing the rightward edge of the envelope for what can be plausibly considered as a substantive contribution to public debate. It is a disgraceful book by any measure, but it may yet be a landmark— even though, like the *Lyrical Ballads*, Fauve painting, and, say, *Mein Kampf*, it be maligned and ill-understood upon its first appearance. And who knows? May-

The *End of Racism* may yet be a landmark, even though, like the *Lyrical Ballads*, Fauve Painting, and *Mein Kampf*, it be maligned and ill-understood upon its first appearance

be the times they are a-changing, and soon it will be as common as rain to hear Dornanesque presidential candidates call their opponents "pot-smoking, triple-draft-dodging adulterers" and to see policy analysts guffawing about how ridiculous it would be to create jobs programs for gold-chained, limping black men. Once upon a time Barry Goldwater was considered an extremist—so much so that the presidential race of 1964 was the only election since 1852 in which a Democratic nominee other than FDR won more than 50 percent of the popular vote. Now, with his defense of gay military personnel and his dismissal of personal attacks on Clinton, Goldwater has almost become the custodian of the party's "liberal" wing. What if *The End of*

Racism, like Goldwater's nomination, is merely a shot across a bow? What if, by the year 2016, the American right has carried out Rush Limbaugh's jocular suggestion that a maximum of two liberals be kept alive on each college campus—and those few thousand of us who remain amidst the rubble are sighing nostalgically for the days when there

The *Wall Street Journal*'s editors are willing to flirt with anything, even crypto-fascism, so long as it promises to unwrite federal commitments to social justice

were still liberal Republicans like Dan Quayle who were at least ambivalent about the prospects of sterilizing populations with measurable "civilizational differences" from whites?

Allow me my phantasmic scenarios. I now live in a nation where a mainstream, nationally syndicated columnist like George Will can defend Bob Dornan's candidacy on the grounds that it's exciting and will shake things up. I live in a nation where it is not considered "extreme" to eliminate capital gains taxes or to turn social programs over to the states so that Republican governors can undo the deleterious effects of the Fourteenth Amendment. I live in a nation where Dinesh D'Souza is considered a "courageous, insightful, and eloquent critic of the American social scene" (Linda Chavez) and a book like *The End of Racism* appears on airport-bookstore shelves festooned with no fewer than eight testimonial blurbs—including those of Chavez, Eugene Genovese, Charles Krauthammer, and a few token liberals like Andrew Hacker and Gerald

Early, who really ought to have known better.

What, finally, does the publication of *The End of Racism* say about the relations between the "responsible" right and the "extreme" right? In the wake of the Oklahoma City bombing, American conservatives were outraged that anyone could have drawn a connection between Rush Limbaugh's or Gordon Liddy's mirthful, hypothetical incitements to murder, and the deadly explosives used by right-wing fanatics. Many on the American right, to their credit, denounced the bombing—usually a few hours after denouncing those few pinkos and bleeding hearts who had had the gall to suggest that the bombers might not have been Islamic fundamentalists. Not a single white conservative, however, has voiced any reservations or regrets about the publication of *The End of Racism*. Adam Bellow has not stepped forward to admit that mistakes were made; Bob Dole has not charged that the book will erode our moral fiber; Gertrude Himmelfarb and Lynne Cheney have not confided to *Commentary* their worries that the book may not meet the ideal of scholarly objectivity. Perhaps it will not be considered outrageous, then, for liberals like me to draw the obvious conclusions—that there are no rightward boundaries for what conservatives will consider acceptable public discourse on race, and that the *Wall Street Journal*'s editors are willing to flirt with anything, even crypto-fascism, so long as it promises to unwrite Federal commitments to social justice. As I contemplate *The End of Racism*, I await the requisite soul-searching on the right. But in all honesty, I'm not holding my breath.

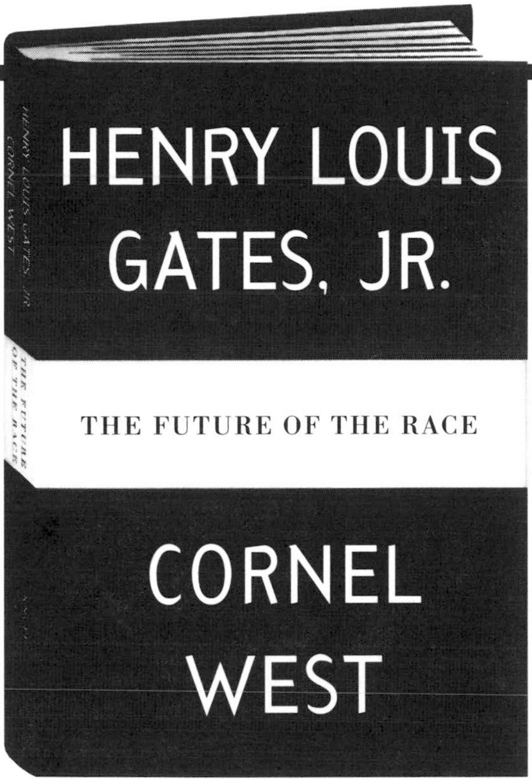

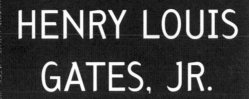

HENRY LOUIS
GATES, JR.

THE FUTURE OF THE RACE

CORNEL
WEST

A PUBLISHING EVENT

THE FUTURE OF THE RACE

THE GROUND-BREAKING BOOK in which two of our foremost African-American intellectuals—taking W.E.B. Du Bois as their model—talk in their very different ways about the dreams, fears, aspirations and responsibilities of the black community—especially the black elite—on the eve of the 21st century.

At all bookstores 🐎 Knopf

WITHER MARXISM?

Russell Jacoby

In the modern battle of the books Marxists and leftists have won, at least if quantity is the criterion. The number of titles on Marxism, socialism, and communism; the array of studies on leftist groups and individual activists and theorists, obscure and not-so-obscure; the numerous monographs on every dimension of Marx's works; the history and sociology and literary criticism that tackle every facet of life and culture in a Marxian mode: all these tower over the corresponding literature inspired by conservatism.

Things are slowing down a bit. I recently received updated sales figures for my own 1981 contribution, *Dialectic of Defeat: Contours of Western Marxism*. Every six weeks last year some soul was moved to buy this book, giving me a total of eight copies sold for the year. For a comparison, consider that according to *The New York Times,* thirteen people purchase a "Star Trek" book each minute. If *Dialectic of Defeat* sold at that rate, 1994 sales would finish up after thirty-seven

seconds; complete sales over fifteen years would not reach two hours.

Of course, neither numbers of titles nor sales define the battle of the books. The fact that there are many more books on the Marxist Antonio Gramsci than on Robert Michels, a critic of Marxism, does not mean that Marxism is in good shape. (A check of the UCLA library finds two hundred and forty books either by Gramsci or with Gramsci in the title, compared to thirty-three on or by Michels.) On the contrary. News of the resounding, perhaps lethal, setbacks to Marxism is everywhere. If success leads to celebration, defeat calls for reflection and study: what remains of Marxism?

Introductory sociology and history courses have long presented arguments "refuting" Marxism: the working class has not developed as anticipated by Marxists; revolutions have occurred in the preindustrial, not industrialized, nations; and the Marxist economic system, not capitalism, fundamentally violates

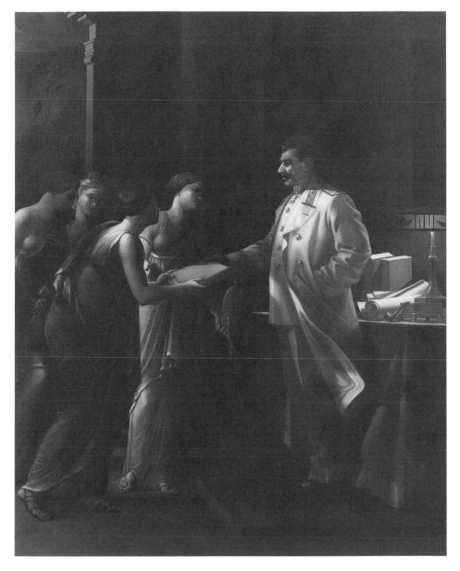

Komar & Melamid
(Russian), Stalin and
the Muses (from
Nostalgic Socialist
Realism series). Oil on
canvas. 1981-82.
Courtesy Ronald
Feldman Fine Arts,
New York.
Photo: D. James Dee

human nature. (Three strikes and you're out.) The collapse of the Soviet system and China's disengagement from communism compound the doubts. Marxism seems finished as a historical force, and perhaps as a theory. Conservatives joke that Marxism survives in two places on the planet—Cuba and American college campuses. Are they right?

In 1993 a humanities center at the University of California, Riverside, set itself the task of bucking conventional wisdom. "Some of us," explain the conveners of the conference, grew tired of the "orgy of self-congratulation" for the free market and of the "many hasty postmortems of Marxism." They invited various "distinguished thinkers," including Jacques Derrida, to consider and reconsider Marxism. The editors boasted

Komar & Melamid (Russian), View of the Kremlin in a Romantic Landscape *(from Nostalgic Socialist Realism series). Oil on canvas. 1981-82. Courtesy Ronald Feldman Fine Arts, New York. Photo: D. James Dee*

that their conference would not be "another autopsy [of Marxism] administered by Anglophone economists and policy analysts who typically were and are very far from the sites of struggle and transformation."

Any effort to rethink Marxism free of platitudes deserves support. Yet this sentence already contains questionable suppositions or clichés. "Anglophone," adopted from the Canadian situation, seems inappropriate here. What does it mean? That Francophones or non-English speakers will revitalize Marxism? The phrase suggests a Third Worldism that can no longer be sustained.

Moreover, the idea that those who are close to "the sites of struggle" are automatically closer to truth belongs to the legacy of orthodox Marxism that needs

reexamining, not repeating. And who are these combatants from distant struggles? Of the thirteen contributors included in the collection *Whither Marxism?* eleven teach at American universities. Is, for instance, Gayatri Spivak, identified as the Avalon Professor of Humanities, Department of English and Comparative Literature, Columbia University, a messenger from a remote struggle?

At this conference Derrida gave a lecture that is published, to use his own words, in "augmented" and "clarified" form as *Specters of Marx.* No one will challenge the "augmented," but "clarified" is not a term that Derrida's work in general, or this work in particular, brings to mind. Little is clear, and less is clarified. For better or worse, Derrida does not cater to his audience. After fifty pages, when most readers or listeners would be panting for a lucid sentence, Derrida announces his lecture is about to begin. "If I take the floor at the opening of such an impressive, ambitious, necessary or risky, others might say historic colloquium."

Down-in-the-mouth Marxists have rallied to Derrida's *Specters* because—surprise—the master of obscurity announces his loyalty to Marxism or, to be more precise, to a *spirit of Marxism*. He informs us that deconstructionism has never been anything else but a "radicalization" of a "certain spirit of Marxism." He does not invoke Marx as a great philosopher to be ritualistically honored. No, Derrida wants to prevent "the neutralizing anesthesia of a new theoreticism."

If there is a spirit of Marxism which I will never be ready to renounce, it is not only the critical idea or the questioning stance. . . . It is even more a certain emancipatory and messianic affirmation . . . . And a promise must promise to be kept, that is, not to remain 'spiritual' or 'abstract,' but to produce events, new effective forms of action, practice, organization, and so forth. To break with the 'party form' or with some form of the State or the International does not mean to give up every form of practical or effective organization.

Derrida knows this may startle well-trained deconstructionists who have learned that nothing exists outside the text. Marxist practice? Organization? Effective action? "Already," he writes, "I hear people saying: 'You picked a good time to salute Marx!' Or else: 'It's about time!' 'Why so late?'"

To affirm a commitment to Marxism in the 1990s with a call for effective action: Derrida can be honored for swimming against the current. To keep the promise is something else. What do these ringing affirmations and appeals for action mean? A short answer: very little. It is impossible to revitalize Marxism without frontally addressing its history, specif-

To affirm a commitment to Marxism in the 1990s with a call for effective action: Derrida can be honored for swimming against the current.

ically its history of failure and defeat and the reasons for them. This Derrida barely does, and consequently the book lacks ballast. It almost seems to float.

Nor is the ethereal quality mitigated by Derrida's engagement with the Marxist tradition. His own intellectual breadth and depth are hardly in doubt, but his knowledge of Marxism seems skewed, restricted to Marx's own texts, which he examines intensively, and recent French writings on Marxism, especially Balibar's. For Derrida little exists between these points, with the exception of several brief pieces by Maurice Blanchot. Hence his pronouncements about Marxism might have textual validity but lack historical resonance.

Francis Fukuyama's sanguine vision of the future, set forth in his *The End of History and the Last Man*, rightly irritates Derrida; in opposition he calls for a "'New International'. . . a link of affinity, suffering, and hope, a still discreet, almost secret link, as it was around 1848, but more and more visible . . . an alliance . . . among those who . . . continue to be inspired by at least one of the spirits of Marx or of Marxism . . . a kind of counter-conjuration." This may warm the hearts of Marxist deconstructionists, but is less Marxism than mysticism.

Derrida may suspect that his Marxism seems disemboweled, almost a "new theoreticism"; this may explain the paranoid leftism that surfaces in his text. Seeking to conjure away the ghost of scholasticism he conjures up, he offers a dark vision of absolute control. Today there is a "*dominant* discourse" positing the death of Marxism that is orchestrated and synchronized:

The politico-economic hegemony, like the intellectual or discursive domination, passes by the way of techno-mediatic power. . . . This power . . . cannot be analyzed or potentially combated . . . without taking into account so many spectral effects, the new speed of apparition (we understand this word in its ghostly sense) of the simulacrum, the synthetic or prosthetic image and the virtual event, cyberspace and surveillance, the control, appropriation, and speculations that today deploy unheard-of powers.

In his critique of Fukuyama, Derrida occasionally descends to earth, and at times he sounds like a solid Marxist. In fact, he uncharacteristically offers a "ten-word telegram" detailing the "plagues" of the "new world order" that Fukuyama and other cheerleaders of capitalism ignore. (Characteristically, Derrida's ten-word "telegram" runs to some fifteen hundred words.) These plagues include unemployment, homelessness, foreign debt, arms industry, interethnic wars. Derrida is not wrong, but he has little illuminating to say about these subjects. The "plagues" are invoked to demonstrate the continuing evils of the free market, but the disasters of capitalism do not necessarily confirm Marxism.

At best, *Specters* might be considered an extended study of the textual import of "specters," "ghosts," and "spirits" in select texts of Marx, mainly *The Eighteenth Brumaire* and *The German Ideology*. Derrida likes to bounce off, around, and inside texts: this is his forte. Some of these "readings" are ingenious and amusing; others illuminating. Unfortunately, too much of this book reads like Derrida satirizing Derrida. The book begins portentously: "Someone, you or me, comes forward and says *I would like to learn to live finally*. Finally but why? *To learn to live*: a strange watchword. Who would learn? From whom? To teach to live, but to whom?" These are remainders that Derrida picks up at a philosophical discount house.

As someone who loves language, translations, and puns, Derrida has a very difficult time writing a clear sentence. His effort to illuminate Marx's obsession with ghosts and spirits is not helped by his own obsession: he cannot quote Marx without giving us Marx's German. Is this always necessary? Since Marx in his critique of Stirner is frequently quoting and punning himself, the going gets rough. A passage of Marx with Derrida's retranslations and German additions reads:

If one has achieved this level [where talk passes through millions of spirits, aus den Menschen Millionen Geister reden], if one can explain with Stirner: "Yes, ghosts are teeming in the world [Ja, es spukt in der Ganzen Welt]," then "it is not difficult to advance to the point" where one makes the further exclamation: "Only in it? No, the world itself is an apparition [Nur in ihr? Nein, sie selber spukt]."

*Komar & Melamid
(Russian),* Laika
Cigarette Box. *Oil on
canvas. 1972. Courtesy
Ronald Feldman Fine
Arts, New York.
Photo: D. James Dee*

What remains astonishing in Derrida is the extent to which he relinquishes the very tradition of Marx, Freud, and Nietzsche he honors; these masters of subversion broke with the scholasticism and pedantry that Derrida revels in.

In style and method Derrida's *Specters* sharply differs from that of Anthony Giddens in *Beyond Left and Right* and Ronald Aronson in *After Marxism*. In fact, for those who like to dabble in national traditions, these three books might be taken as emblematic of recent French, English, and American political theorizing. In accord with Foucault's sentiment that he leaves it to the police to figure out what he is saying, or whether he is consistent, Derrida's text is often incomprehensible and maddening—and just occasionally brilliant. In accord with a no-nonsense English approach, Giddens's is straightforward and unadorned—as well as weightless. What is he saying—and why? Aronson employs the basic American approach: throw everything in and perhaps something will come out. His has a cast of thousands, running from his grandfather

Komar & Melamid (Russian), What Is to Be Done? (from Nostalgic Socialist Realism series). Oil on canvas. 1982-83. Courtesy Ronald Feldman Fine Arts, New York. Photo: D. James Dee

and his daughter to a zillion academic Marxists.

Anyone still waiting for the promised third volume of Giddens's "contemporary critique of historical materialism" should wait no longer. Giddens has given up and offers this volume as a replacement. He is less interested in the fate of Marxism than in defining a future radical politics. He tells us that all certainties are over; we live in an age of "manufactured uncertainty." This situation is a by-product of three sets of developments that inform a radical politics: globalization or what Giddens prefers to call "action at distance"; the emergence of a "posttraditional social order"; and the "expansion of social reflexivity." He explains this last: "In a detraditionalizing society individuals must become used to filtering all sorts of information relevant to their life situations.... The growth of social reflexivity is a major factor introducing a dislocation between knowledge and control—a prime source of manufactured uncertainty."

These categories and concepts bring us only to page seven. A few pages later we learn that actually "the ecological crisis is at the core of this book." Then

Giddens offers a six-point framework for a "reconstituted radical politics," which doesn't mention ecology. The first three points include the need to "repair damaged solidarities" and reconcile "autonomy and interdependence"; the need to "recognize the increasingly centrality of what I call *life politics*. . . . Life politics is a politics, not of *life chances*, but of *life style*." And thirdly: "In conjunction with the generalizing of social reflexivity, active trust implies a conception of *generative politics*. Generative politics exists in the space that links the state to reflexive mobilization in the society at large."

All this is very interesting—for sociology graduate students and other depressed peoples. For others the book seems composed of conceptual Lego blocks. Giddens puts a concept here and adds one there, but the whole construction seems wonderfully arbitrary. He could just as well reverse the concepts or stack them differently; it makes no difference. Is it "dialogic democracies" or "democratic dialogues" that are essential? Should a new conceptual deck go here or would it look better above chapter 5?

The real object is just to keep on building; and so he does. Within a few pages, he gives us a list of six circumstances of "generative politics," four main contexts of high-consequence risks, four connected areas of dialogic democracy, three problems of regenerating civil society, and so on, with lists and diagrams. Giddens has some sensible things to say about the welfare state, but many of his ideas are inane: for instance, a suggestion of a "lifestyle pact" between the rich and poor. The main problem is that even his reasonable observations are overwhelmed

by his unstoppable and vapid theorizing. If this is a major book by a major sociologist, sociology is in trouble. If this is an example of radical theorizing, radicalism and theorizing are in trouble.

Unlike Derrida or Giddens, Aronson is forthright about the fate of Marxism: it is over. He does not mess around with Marxism as a spirit or critique. Marxism is finished as a project of social transformation; it may, and perhaps should, persist as a theory of this and that—as fragments—but it has no future as a general movement of revolution. Aronson has not abandoned a radical politics, but insists radicalism is no longer unified; now it is heterogeneous and diverse. Even the radical imperative cannot be assumed, but must justify itself.

Aronson wants to explain how he reluctantly concluded that his thirty-year commitment to Marxism was over. To this end, he offers a mini-autobiography, sketching out chapters of his life. This is less novel than it may appear. Aronson has always been obsessed by himself and his personal distance from Marxism. Twenty-five years ago he gave an address directed to his teacher Herbert Marcuse. In "Dear Herbert" (published in the 1971 volume *The Revival of American Socialism: Selected Papers of the Socialist Scholars Conference*), he complained that he felt that Marcuse's approach was too abstract, remote, and impersonal, and that he felt inferior to the refugee's lofty Marxism.

The relentless banality of Aronson's account of his less-than-fascinating life does not help his argument; it is difficult to muster much sympathy for his "all-absorbing struggle" for tenure. He describes other key events as follows: "One turning point [in his abandonment of

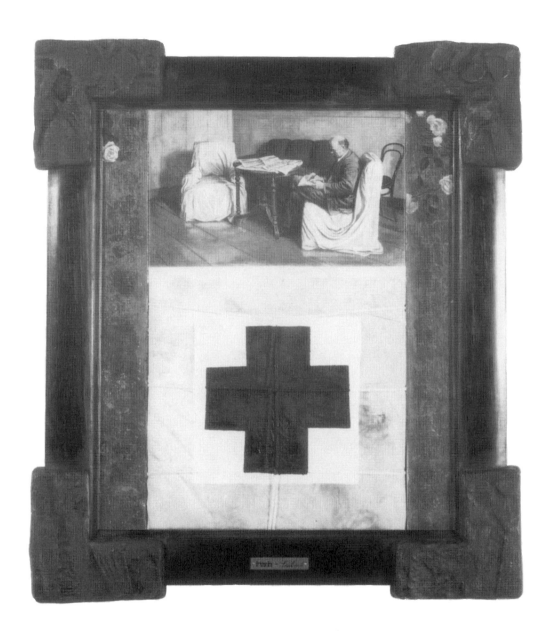

Marxism] came when reading my daughter Pamela Aronson's senior essay for James Madison College, Michigan State University, in December 1989. It was 'A Feminist Critique of Marxism.'" A second turning point was a "lecture I gave in South Africa, in August 1990, which is the first statement of the idea of this book." "The last straw" came when he heard an address on the future of Marxism at the Central Meeting of the American Philosophical Association.

Beyond outlining his intellectual trajectory, Aronson surveys at length classic and recent critiques of Marxism. He tries to be fair, weighing pro and con, and concludes that the early critics were on target: Marxism has been wrong about too much. The more recent theorists like the analytical Marxists have given up the moral and emancipatory vision. For Aronson, Marxism has proved unable to respond to the imperatives of advanced industrialization; it is a theory trapped by its origins in early capitalism.

We have entered a new period, Aronson tell us, where we are "on our own," with no revolutionary subject or total theory. A radical politics is possible, but must use multiple models and paradigms. "The problem . . . is that there is no basis for assuming in advance that blacks, women, Greens, socialists, gays and lesbians, peaceniks, native peoples and other and future activists will be struggling against the same structures or on behalf of the same goals." He closes by reflecting on the importance of morality and hope in any future radical politics.

After Derrida and Giddens, Aronson's doggedness is at least refreshing; in sticking to Marxism as a theory and praxis of emancipation, he is able to measure not only how much the dogmatic but also the nondogmatic and revisionist Marxists have surrendered. His insistence on the obsolescence of Marxism is a token of his commitment to its original vision. For this reason it is instructive to compare Aronson to those who continue to uphold Marxism—for instance, the authors collected in *Whither Marxism?*, the conference papers delivered in conjunction with Derrida's *Specters*.

The opening essay, Douglas Kellner's "The Obsolescence of Marxism?" comes on strong; according to Kellner, Marxism is in great shape. The collapse of the Soviet Union and the Stalinist regimes leaves Marxism untouched—in fact validates it for true Marxists who have long

If *Beyond Left and Right* is a major book by a major sociologist, sociology is in trouble. If this is an example of radical theorizing, radicalism and theorizing are in trouble.

criticized the Stalinist deformations. The very upheavals in the Soviet Union and Eastern Europe confirm the truth of Marxism. Calmly contradicting virtually every commentator and observer, Kellner states that "the events of 1989 show the continued viability of Marxian theories of mass politics, insurrection and revolution." For Kellner, "only the most ideological enemy of Marxism, or uninformed pseudointellectual, could seriously maintain that the Marxian theory is obsolete." This would apparently include some well-informed intellectuals included in the same volume.

IRWIN (Slovenian). The Enigma of Revolution. Mixed media. 1988. Courtesy of the artists, Neue Slowenische Kunst, and AMOK Press, Los Angeles.

After the bluster, however, even Kellner must admit that while there "has been a tremendous development of theory, there has been a steady decline in Marxist politics . . . and practice in contemporary political movements." He begins almost to sound like Aronson. Marxism as a "master theory and narrative" is over; but it remains important as "a method of social research and set of theoretical perspectives." We need a "reconstructed Marxism" that will be "more open, tolerant, skeptical and modest than previous versions."

Capitalism is vicious, but this does not make Marxism true.

As a whole, *Whither Marxism?* does live up to its promise of not celebrating the demise of Marxism. To be sure, "not celebrating the demise" does not mean saving and revitalizing Marxism. For like any collection of conference papers, it lacks coherence. The volume includes an incisive discussion of Latin American debt and impoverishment by Carlos Vilas. Inasmuch as it never had much impact in the Southern Hemisphere, the collapse of the Soviet Union, he notes, hardly affects Latin Americans. Yet Marxism is not healthy; "social movements to reduce the impact of economic restructuring and increasing poverty look feeble, to say the least." Su Shaozhi argues that the Chinese Revolution replaced Marx with Mao; and the more recent economic reforms do not refute but can be explained by Marxism. Andrei Marga offers thoughtful reflections on the fate of Marxism in Eastern Europe.

On the other hand, Stephen Resnick and Richard Wolff dream they are break-

ing new ground while they fearlessly tread old paths. They imagine they are the first to discuss whether the Soviet Union was a state capitalist society by examining surplus labor. Even a limited contact with a vast Trotskyist literature, for instance, Tony Cliff's 1955 *State Capitalism in Russia*, would disabuse them of that notion. They also imagine that the question of surplus labor is the pressing revolutionary question of the moment. "We share and seek to develop further Marx's commitment to contributing a systematic analysis of surplus labor so that future revolutionary upsurges against capitalism will be more likely to succeed." How or why an analysis of surplus labor abets revolutionary upsurges is not spelled out—in fact, not even mentioned. A good tonic to this dreary stuff is Zhang Longxi's "Marxism: From Scientific to Utopian," a bracing and eloquent call for the continuing relevance of the young Marx.

Where does this bring us? Any global summary of the state of Marxism is surely impossible. We have entered a period of objective uncertainty. The victory of capitalism has come at a terrible and incalculable cost, which is not to say that the Soviet regimes were preferable. They were not. Yet by most measures of violence, suffering, or poverty, the world is not in great shape, and the future looks worse. Can we abandon Marxism if we have not passed beyond an inhumane capitalism that gave rise to it? Perhaps not, but this logic easily degenerates into an unconvincing justification for Marxism. "If capitalism is vicious, then Marxism is valid," goes the reasoning. Unfortunately it is not so. Capitalism is vicious, but this does not make Marxism true.

IRWIN (Slovenian). Freedom Comes From the East. Mixed media. 1989. Courtesy of the artists, Neue Slowenische Kunst, and AMOK Press, Los Angeles.

It seems late, and obvious, to recall that Marxism was a materialist theory that underscored economic life—how people lived and labored. Of course, it was more than this. For decades critics pounded away at the mechanical and vulgar materialism of Marxism; much of this criticism has been to the point. The "Western Marxists"—Karl Korsch, Georg Lukács, the Frankfurt School—sought to revitalize the cultural, ideological, and psychological dimensions of Marxism; they rightly recalled that Marx distinguished his own theory from a simple materialism.

Yet valid criticism of a reductionist Marxism has too often passed into a complete surrendering of its materialist core. The many criticisms of the "productionist" bias of Marxism leave us with a Marxism that exclusively trades in spirits, texts, images, and echoes. Deconstructionism with its tendency to flatten out differences between text and context abetted this idealism. If nineteenth-century Marxism was materialistic and determinist, late-twentieth-century Marxism has become idealist and incoherent.

It would be instructive to trace the vagaries of Gramsci's concept of "hegemony" to illustrate this shift. In Gramsci "hegemony" smacked of classes contending for state power in a "war of positions"; now it means any passing idea. Literary critics who love to refer to Gramsci regularly refer to "hegemonic" literary theories—meaning that in select English departments more literary critics subscribe to one theory rather than another. This is not Gramsci.

Marxism will not be rescued by recalling its materialist roots, but it cannot be revived by forgetting them. The Marxist remembrance of the inhuman conditions of human life is its strongest card; its allegiance to economic and social circumstances constitutes its blood and muscle. Obviously, this is not news. Yet for all the gestures toward economic and social life by contemporary Marxists and post-Marxists, precious little materialism remains.

Oddly, amid the discussion of what is or remains of Marxism, none of these authors bothered to reexamine at a classic text, Georg Lukács's "What is Orthodox Marxism?" the opening essay of his *History and Class Consciousness*. Lukács's 1919 essay is hardly the answer, but he extracted an essential of Marxism that is now neglected. For Lukács it is the dialectical *method* that defines Marxism:

Let us assume for the sake of argument that recent research had disproved once and for all every one of Marx's individual theses. Even if this were to be proved, every serious "orthodox" Marxist would still be able to accept all such modern findings without reservation and hence dismiss all of Marx's theses in toto. . . . Orthodox Marxism . . . does not imply the uncritical acceptance of the results of Marx's investigations. It is not the "belief" in this or that thesis, nor exegesis of a "sacred" book. On the contrary, orthodoxy refers exclusively to method.

Along with method, Lukács brought to the fore the category of totality. Traditional social science and revisionist Marxism preferred examining units and parts, the facts as they surface here and there. "In the teeth of all these isolated and isolating facts and partial systems, dialectics insists on the concrete unity of the whole." Lukács cited Marx: "The re-

IRWIN (Slovenian). The Ljubljana Trial. Mixed media. 1988. Courtesy of the artists, Neue Slowenische Kunst, and AMOK Press, Los Angeles.

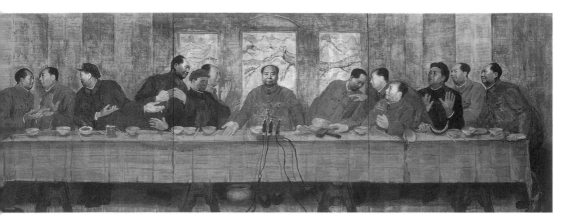

Zhang Hongtu (Chinese, 1943-). Last Banquet. Laser prints, The Little Red Book, and acrylic on canvas 1989. Courtesy of the artist and the Bronx Museum, New York City.

lations of production of every society form a whole." For Lukács, Marxism rests on the category of the whole; knowledge of the whole breaks the spell of reification. In his 1967 Preface to its republication, Lukács stated that "it is undoubtedly one of the great achievements of *History and Class Consciousness* to have reinstated the category of totality in the central position it had occupied throughout Marx's works."

Nothing seems more out of touch with contemporary Marxism and radical social theory. For if Marxists like Kellner and post-Marxists like Aronson agree on anything, it is that a Marxism that seeks the whole picture is finished; and that the future belongs to partial visions—piecemeal struggles of separate groups. In the contemporary academic jargon, Marxism as a "master narrative" is over. This has become the socialist mantra. If once upon a time leftists appealed to workers and peasants, now their speeches and writings call upon numerous communities, each of which has distinct interests and programs: African Americans, Latinos, Asian Americans, Native Americans, women, gays, the disabled, children, single mothers, seniors, teachers, unionists—and the lists get longer and longer.

Undoubtedly, the conventional wisdom expresses something of reality; these groups do exist with independent programs and identities. Yet are these immutable facts or expressions of fragmenting social forces? One indication of the conformism of a new, revised and open Marxism is its acceptance, even celebration, of the fundamental differences among groups, as if they all exist in parallel universes. It does not take vast effort to discover that the separate groups, at least within the United States, are structured by a single society. Whoever speaks of the situation of African Americans or youth or women must address the economic and political realities of American society as a whole. Even on a world scale—or exactly on a world scale—the total view is more, not less, imperative. Capital becomes global and mobile, while Marxist and post-Marxist theory becomes local and sedentary.

To be sure, the gap between theory and practice is complete. More than ever, each group, community, or ethnicity is convinced its situation is unique. Talk of the whole falls on deaf ears. Nevertheless, truth does not depend on popular ratification. In a regressive age Marxism retreats to its most abstract principles. Today even the most learned Marxists are puzzled. Eric Hobsbawm closes his new book, *The Age of Extremes*, admitting the century is winding down with "a global disorder" whose nature and resolution are "unclear." This is surely right. Only this can be stated: a Marxism that celebrates incoherence or renounces materialism and the effort to grasp the whole has renounced itself. The formulations of Hegel and Adorno still speak to the present. "The whole is the true" and "The whole is false."

Zhang Hongtu (Chinese, 1943-). Chairman Mao. Laser prints, collage, and acrylic on paper. 1989. Courtesy of the artist.

AS YOU LIKE IT

Stephen Burt

You've probably heard the joke: to make a fortune cookie true, append the words "in bed." Thus, a new friend will uncover great wisdom (in bed); don't let your boss get you down (in bed). The joke plays on our assumption that how we fare in life depends on what we do (or what we'd like to do) sexually, and with whom—on the axiom, at least a century old, that sexual proclivities are a basic component of identity. At least since Foucault's *History of Sexuality*, the best writers about sex have been aware enough of this assumption to invoke it: Is sexuality always an identity? Why do we assume that it is, if we do? Are the categories with which we think about sex mostly invariant over time (the essentialist argument), or have they changed as drastically as the names we use to talk about them (social constructionism)?

One place these questions come together is at site of what Foucault would have called "nonjuridical" power: occasions and places—the playground, the Thanksgiving dinner, the hockey rink,

the St. Patrick's Day parade—where norms are assembled and affirmed, and forms of deviance suggested or ruled out, usually without being made explicit or literal. Since the tacit transmission of symbols is the ordinary domain of literary criticism, it should not be surprising that literary critics have often turned out to be more skilled than their rivals in history, psychology, and anthropology at disentangling desire from the norms that encircle it. Where new books by Jonathan Ned Katz and Leo Bersani try (and fail) to explain, respectively, straight and gay desire in general, Marjorie Garber's unwieldy compendium of "bisexual" contexts succeeds by taking into account how complex and personal the processes are by which our separate desires evolve.

• • •

The jacket copy calls Jonathan Ned Katz's *The Invention of Heterosexuality* a "startling history of the heterosexual concept," which shows how "heterosex-

Discussed in this essay

The Invention of Heterosexuality, *Jonathan Ned Katz, New York: E. P. Dutton*

Homos, *Leo Bersani, Cambridge, MA: Harvard University Press*

Vice Versa: Bisexuality and the Eroticism of Everyday Life, *Marjorie Garber, New York: Simon and Schuster*

Ivan Velez, Jr.
From Tales of the
Closet *#8,*
© Hetrick-Martin
Institute, 2 Astor Place,
New York, NY 10003

Ivan Velez, Jr.
From Tales of the
Closet #8,
© *Hetrick-Martin*
Institute, 2 Astor Place,
New York, NY 10003

uality became this society's dominant norm." No writer is responsible for his or her blurbs, but this one accurately reproduces Katz's tone, and dodges the same questions as the book itself: what does Katz mean by arguing not only that something called "heterosexuality" isn't natural or immutable but that it was "invented" by bourgeois adults, doctors, and pamphleteers in the late nineteenth century? The book analyzes 1890s sexologists, attacks Freud, chronicles twentieth-century attitudes toward heterosexuality, and summarizes critiques of the hetero order, from de Beauvoir to Adrienne Rich and Foucault, to whom Katz acknowledges a methodological debt. But it also fails to establish in what sense, or senses, Katz is using the word.

"Heterosexual" first appeared in English in 1892, in a medical journal, where it meant "having a desire for both sexes." By the 1920s the word had spread into ordinary vocabulary, where it meant what it usually means now. But what does it mean to Katz? Again and again we are told that just because the men and women of the past did what today's straight (or bi) couples do, we should not infer that they were "heterosexual":

Looking back on past eras before the use of the term heterosexual, we can, of course, find well-documented examples of different-sex erotic acts and emotions. Yet, from the standpoint of those who lived, loved and lusted in the past, those same acts and emotions may not have referred in any essential way to the same combination of sex and gender differences that we call heterosexuality.

Or then again they may have. One would have to look at the records and see. If it would be simplistic, as well as homophobic, to keep believing that all our ways of thinking about sex are inevitable, we should not rush to conclude that because Ancient Greeks and American Puritans did not see sex the way we do, nobody else ever has. But Katz uses these two examples to demonstrate not only that "heterosexuality" isn't "natural," but that it must have been invented when he says it was.

For Katz, heterosexuality arrived in the 1890s, replacing a regime in which *fertility* was the purpose of erotic desire—an outlook Edward O. Laumann and the other authors of *The Social Organization of Sexuality* (1994) call "procreational" (sex is for making babies) as opposed to "relational" (sex is for loving couples) or "recreational" (sex is for fun). As Katz writes, "in this period, doctors of the mind, some still flying fertility's flag, some pushing tentatively beyond it, first publicly formulated the idea of *heterosexual* and *homosexual*." But the early-nineteenth-century American bourgeoisie doesn't count as heterosexual, according to Katz, precisely because its view of sexual desire *was* relational: "No middle-class sexual ethic then validated different-sex lust apart from men's and women's *love* and reproduction" (italics mine). "Our modern, historically specific idea of the heterosexual began to be constructed" in the late nineteenth century when "a proper, middle-class, different-sex lust began to be named and documented." Heterosexuality here implies sex for fun: it seems to mean erotic attraction to and only to the opposite sex, conceived of as a basic and invariant component of identity, where the explicit end of sex is not babies or love but pleasure. In this sense "heterosexuality" may well have been invented among doctors in the 1890s, and among nonspecialist Americans later; but in this sense most Americans may not *be* "heterosexual." Most of Laumann's respondents thought of sex as "procreational" (31 percent) or "relational" (44 percent); only 25 percent wanted sex to be "recreational."

I question any use of "heterosexual" that would deny that status to most of the people who vote in Republican primaries. If early-nineteenth-century courting couples were not heterosexual because they did not want to have sex without love, then neither are many or most older Americans now. In order to argue that "heterosexuality" didn't exist

in 1800, Katz is going to have to do violence to the usual meaning of the word, or play shell games with it. If you define heterosexuality as that sexual ideology that Freud and his colleagues introduced, then of course it doesn't predate them. It might be accurate to say, pace Freud, that once sex could be explicitly discussed apart from love, a norm of different-sex eros became more central to middle-class self-descriptions than it had been before. But this book doesn't say that.

Of the psychologists and sex theorists who first studied "the homosexual" in the 1880s and 1990s, most (not all) were attracted to women; for Katz, their "focus on a few powerless perverts is best explained by their . . . special interest in defining and defending their normal sexuality—heterosexuality." This seems exactly right, because it concedes that Krafft-Ebing, Freud, and the rest had

I question any use of "heterosexual" that would deny that status to most of the people who vote in Republican primaries

feelings before they had given them scientific names; the act of naming a feeling isn't without consequence for the feeling, but neither is it creation ex nihilo. Doctors coined *heterosexual* as a medical term in order to describe, reify, conflate, and enforce a preexisting constellation of behaviors and feelings. For Freud and his contemporaries "heterosexuality is mature and good, homosexuality is immature and bad." The same is arguably true in Shakespeare's *As You Like It*, though the Elizabethans would not have used those terms. Katz has confused the ramparts with the buildings and the street plan.

The practices and ideologies of heterosexuality, in anything like its ordinary meaning—the meaning that includes Laumann's "relationals" and his "procreationals"—are far older than American industrial society. The heterosexual order Katz thinks is only one hundred years old "enshrines not procreation but sex difference and eroticism"; so did John Milton, who in the 1640s earned the vilification of what Laumann would call a "procreational" establishment when he called for the legalization of divorce in cases of "incompatibility." (Milton was defending a companionate view of marriage—what Laumann would call "relational.") Thomas Jefferson's letters reveal something like "heterosexuality" emerging in the mid–eighteenth century:

Write me very circumstantially every thing which happened at the wedding. Was she there? [B]ecause if she was I ought to have been at the devil for not being there too. . . . Remember me affectionately to all the young ladies of my acquaintance, particularly the Miss Burwells and Miss Potters; and tell them that though that heavy earthly part of me, my body, be absent, the better half of me, my soul, is ever with them, and that my best wishes should ever attend them. Tell Miss Alice Corbin, that I verily believe the rats knew I was to win a pair of garters from her, or they never would have been so cruel as to carry mine away. This very consideration makes me so sure of the bet, that I shall ask everybody I see from that part of the world, what pretty gentleman is making his addresses to her. I would fain ask the favor of Miss Becca Burwell to give me another watch paper of her own cutting, which I should esteem much

more, though it were a plain round one, than the nicest in the world cut by other hands.

"She" is—according to *The Domestic Life of Thomas Jefferson* (1871)—"his lady-love, Rebecca Burwell." But what about Miss Alice Corbin? Courtship, gallantry, ribaldry, garters, a devotion to one girl coexisting with a flaunted and erotic interest in other girls (but not boys): what, exactly, does Katz believe was "invented" a hundred years after this letter was posted? Lust? The Oxford English Dictionary dates the word *masturbation* to 1857; I hope no one is going to argue that *that* practice is only as old as our word for it.

The strangest aspect of Katz's book is its implicit pining for a world before "heterosexuality" was invented: "The new strict boundaries made the gendered erotic world less polymorphous." Less polymorphous than what? This comparison without a second term is less a statement about the past than an unusually naked expression of the weird nostalgia of anglophone Foucauldians for a time when restraints on behavior were more explicit, when power was exercised more through physical correction and less through the insidious discipline of subtexts and self-images. But it's hard to believe that the views earlier Americans seem to have had of straight sex were any less oppressive for those with unusual desires. Anyone who thinks that pre–Civil War America didn't make same-sex-oriented men ashamed of their desire should look up Walt Whitman's "Hours Continuing Long" (1860):

Sullen and suffering hours! (I am ashamed—but it is useless—I am what I am;)

Scott McCloud.
From Zot! #33,
© Scott McCloud.

Will Allison.
From Pervert Club
#2, © *Will Allison.*
Write to A. M. Works,
Box 49542, Austin,
TX 78765.

Hours of my torment—I wonder if other men ever have the like, out of the like feelings?

Is there even one other like me—distracted—his friend, his lover, lost to him?

Is he too as I am now? Does he still rise in the morning, defected, thinking who is lost to him? and at night, awaking, think who is lost?

Rather than predating the closet, Whitman's pansexual utopianism coexisted with it.

Katz has stylistic problems, too: "Freud's subjects . . . all seek satisfaction of erotic desires. When their pleasure pursuit clashes with society's rules, the pressure to conform causes sparks to fly." Sometimes the jackboot gets thrown into the melting pot: "The archetypal family sex play presented by Freud is high melodrama, a hotbed of blazing loves and hates. . . . The successful working through of baby's early passionate loves and murderous hates evidently cancels any residual fallout left after junior's active participation in the nuclear family war." But *The Invention of Heterosexuality* isn't worthless. Katz documents the heterosexist advice proffered by the scarily well-meaning psychologists of the 1950s and 1960s in books like *Growing Up Straight: What Every Thoughtful Parent Should Know about Homosexuality*. It's depressing, though, that Katz spends his time on these older texts when the prevention-of-queers brigade—as Eve Sedgwick brilliantly documents in her essay "How to Bring Your Kids Up Gay"—is still at work among liberal parents in a subtler way, one that requires other countermoves.

Katz calls for the presumably not-yet-undertaken study of the sexually "normal"; in fact, the study of "the normal," of heterosexuality as a norm, has been under way for some time, in lengthy books about the evolution of companionate marriage in England and France (all of them missing from Katz's long but U.S.-centered bibliography). And the lesbian-feminist authors Katz often cites put their critiques in exactly the terms he himself recommends. "One might argue, and others have, that heterosexuality is *learned*, socially-conditioned behavior," wrote Julia Penelope and Susan Wolfe in their introduction to the first edition of *The Coming-Out Stories*, in 1977. Katz is at best doing detail work for a general argument elaborated a generation ago. As for Katz's specific thesis—that what Americans know as heterosexuality was invented by the bourgeoisie and the sex doctors on the cusp of the twentieth century—depending on which of several definitions of the word one picks out from Katz's book, his argument is either circular, at variance with the way most Americans would ever use the word, or just plain wrong.

• • •

Katz implies that his view can make a practical difference: "A historically specific understanding of heterosexuality provides a possible alternative." Leo Bersani knows better: "The power of these systems is only minimally contested by demonstrations of their 'merely' historical character. They don't need to be natural in order to rule; to demystify them doesn't render them inoperable." Bersani's *Homos* therefore attempts, not to "denaturalize" existing tropes of gayness, but to energize and build on them. Bersani is in part arguing for the practical retention of "homosexual" as a category, with its ordinary meaning, as against those who would banish such categories from enlightened discourse. Bersani makes his principal targets Monique Wittig's rather abstract redefinition of "lesbian" and Judith Butler's notion of gender identity as performance. The book's four chapters are almost separate essays, and read as if they started out as such: an overview of the new visibility of American gay men, a critique of Wittig and Butler, a reading of Freud, and a longer reading of Gide, Proust, and Genet.

Bersani argues that we have learned to think of lack (a "want" in the self for something outside it) as constitutive of personal identity, and of desire as predicated on lack. Our means of differentiating between self and others, and thus our notions of personhood, are therefore founded on desire-as-lack. We want what we don't have, or what we aren't, and we know ourselves through our wants. But "homo" desire—desire for what one already has, or is; desire for "more of the same"—isn't founded on difference or lack. Gay desire is, therefore, an explosive device by means of which the whole idea of interiority, identity, and social relations among distinct selves simply vanishes, replaced by a flux of flesh and surfaces. This turns out to be a way of "theorizing" gay identity that for Bersani is related (as other theories apparently are not) to what gay people actually do in bed. It also suggests a model of gay community that is neither theoretical nor liberal: "An anticommunal mode of connectedness we might all share."

The disdain for liberal pragmatism, for any politics that might not presuppose new theories, is decidedly Bersani's rather than my own. Bersani has the occupational disease of theorists: he can't imagine a practical politics unlinked to an abstract account of identity. Where Judith Butler praises the drag "houses" of the film *Paris is Burning* as "a community that . . . cares and teaches[,] . . . shelters and enables . . . in the face of dislocation, poverty, homelessness," Bersani retorts: "But the structures that sustain those ills are in no way threatened or subverted; here resignification is little more than a consolatory community of victims." Of course it is. What does Bersani want the Harlem queens to do, storm city hall? According to Bersani, antiessentialist queer theorists like Butler "mount a resistance to homophobia in which the agent of resistance has been erased: there is no longer any homosexual subject to oppose the homophobic subject." That would be terrible if it were true, but it isn't. The "subjects" of *Gender Trouble* don't *have* to be uniquely and essentially "homosexual subjects" to oppose homophobia, because Butler implies other ways of doing so—with costume, at the level of image; and by describing one's desires, at the level of individual relations—that is, by *coming out*, as dykes or leather queens or lesbian boys or whatever we think we are. To which we might add, at the level of mainstream politics, such dull, unerotic projects as voting, demonstrating, and lobbying, none of which requires any model of an essentially homosexual subject.

What Bersani really is trying to do is prove that there is such a thing as the "gay subject":

Diane DiMassa.
From Hothead Paisan,
Homicidal Lesbian
Terrorist #17,
© Diane DiMassa and
Giant Ass Publishing.
Write to Giant Ass,
Box 214, New Haven,
CT 06502.

My argument is not that homosexuals are better than heterosexuals. Instead, it is to suggest that same-sex desire, while it excludes the other sex as its object, presupposes a desiring subject for whom the antagonism between the different and the same no longer exists.

Homosexuality, then, places its affiliates uniquely outside affectional ties, responsibility, and maybe even personhood: "homo-ness is an anti-identitarian identity." This notion is best observed in Bersani's readings of Gide's *The Immoralist* and Genet's *Funeral Rites* and *The Maids.* For Bersani, the North African idyll of Gide's protagonist Michel, for whom "I" and "you" are replaced by "flesh" or "skin," "eliminates from sexuality the necessity of any relation whatever." Michel does banish history, ethics, and speech—almost no one in *The Immoralist* has a conversation except Marceline, who is virtually an out gay man. This congruence of sexual openness and loquacity suggests that Michel's tendencies toward self-erasure are at least as much the product of a kind of closet as of a type of lust. An inarticulate relation to oneself, or to one's body, is still a relation; even a desire to reduce (or elevate) oneself to undifferentiated "being" is a kind of relation to oneself, as the careers of the Buddha, Simone Weil, or Kurt Cobain might show.

Bersani is strongest on *Funeral Rites,* Genet's prose-poem-cum-erotic fantasia-cum-elegy for his wartime lover. Gay sex in that book really can equal oblivion; betrayal and homosexuality, which in Genet are inseparable, "erase . . . cultural relationality itself." Gay desire undermines personhood. Anal intercourse and rimming "for Genet . . . mythically embody the sterility of a relation from which the woman's body is excluded and . . . the anti-relationality inherent in all homo-ness." Genet's "abhorrent glorification of Nazism and his . . . failure to take that glorification seriously express his fundamental project of *declining to participate in any sociality at all.*" This is right, and I can't think of a straight author who fetishizes betrayal in the same way. It's also virtually explicit, not to mention climactic, in Genet:

If the two standing males had looked at each other the quality of the pleasure would not have been the same. . . . Erik and Riton were not loving one in the other, they were escaping from themselves over the world, in full view of the world, in a gesture of victory.

As if this weren't antirelational enough, Riton (a young French collaborator) shoots Erik (a Nazi) on the very next page, just after they've finished fucking. "Genet's homosexuality . . . allowed him to imagine a curative collapsing of social difference into a radical homo-ness, where the subject might begin again, differentiating itself from itself and thereby reconstituting sociality." Reconstituting it *how*? Sorry; book over. Genet's demolition job on "interpersonal" "relations" is so powerful that it's not clear, to Bersani or to me, how any social or political identity could be reconstructed from whatever—the body? the penis?—it leaves behind.

Proust, a gay writer fascinated by questions of identity and interiority, gets a sort of cursory reading by way of contrast: "It would be immeasurably sad to lose the richness of our Proustian perceptions, to settle . . . for an intersubjec-

...BUT, FRANKLY, MY DEAR, YOU LOOK NO BETTER, IF NOT **WORSE**, IN THE MORNING THAN MY **EX-WIFE** DID.

DOMESTICITY ISN'T PRETTY.

tivity cleansed of all fantasmatic curiosity." Yet Proust's jokes against the (for him, inevitable) failure of "inverts" to become a community, and the antiethical indifference exhibited by his queerest characters, allow Bersani to align *Remembrance of Things Past* with his own program of gay anti-interiority, "point-[ing] us in the direction of a community in which relations would no longer be held hostage to demands for intimate knowledge of the other." But Proust hypothesizes the *impossibility* of such a community. There are in Proust no erotic relations that are not being held captive to a revelation that can never arrive. "Indeed," writes Bersani, "the person disappears in his or her desire, a desire that seeks more of the same, partially dissolving subjects by extending them into a communal homo-ness." If you read Proust's tangled essay on inverts in *Sodom and Gomorrah* in virtual isolation you can make it say anything, even that. But for this reader, Proust's inverts are the very opposite of people erasing themselves in search of "the same": they are people who embody radical difference

within themselves, which is why they are never satisfied, never wholly known.

How did we come to entertain the notion that desire for someone of the same sex was necessarily desire for someone radically "the same"? It can be, as the mustaches and checked shirts of the late 1970s proved; but what about gay/lesbian/bi/queer people whose preferred sexual partners are usually much older, or younger, or of another race or ethnicity? Under Bersani's post-Lacanian model, wouldn't a "hetero-age" or "hetero-race" homosexual person be compensating for a personal lack, thus instituting an identity-making difference between the self and the object of desire, just as a heterosexual person compensates? (Is sex always more basic to identity than "race," or "age"?) Bersani risks conflating the Homo with the Clone. Moreover, none of Bersani's key texts is lesbian. Edmund White's great gay reportage from the seventies routinely apologized for excluding lesbians, on the grounds that White was simply more competent to describe his own, largely single-sex milieu. But he wasn't arguing

*Tim Barela.
From* Gay Comix
Special #1: *Leonard
and Larry,
© Tim Barela and
Gay Comix.
Write to 395 9th
Street, San Francisco,
CA 94103-3831.*

M.C. Betz. From
"The Buck and a Half
Club," in Real Girl
#6, © M.C. Betz.

for the special epistemological status of all those and only those desires that are "for the same." Bersani is, and if he wants readers to believe that his analysis is more than just a fascinating reading of a few texts, he ought to show that it can be applied to women.

But the generalization problem doesn't stop there. The source and meaning of desire is radically different for different individuals. What if, say, A's sex life is best understood in terms drawn from Proust, B's is most clear through the lens of Genet, and C understands why she wants who she wants only after she's heard the Buzzcocks? In other words, what if there's no "best" reading of the structure of desire, no radical incommensurability between kinds of desire, such that nobody can talk to anybody else about eros, but instead a large set of available psychological structures for both "gay" and "straight," love and sex? This would, as Stanley Fish asks theorists to do, explain both agreements and disagreements; why we haven't finished arguing about the structure and nature of "queer," and why we bother to keep arguing. It would also reduce Ber-

sani's thesis (about the anti-identitarian nature of same-sex eros) from a proposed explanation for all homosexual desire to a very skillful construal of a few books, out of which comes another model (among many) we should be glad to have at hand.

• • •

Neither Katz nor Bersani spends much time on bisexuality. Katz remarks (apropos of Adrienne Rich's "Compulsory Heterosexuality and Lesbian Existence"): "It seems to me that whenever 'heterosexual' and 'homosexual' operate as a dominant social distinction they force people into one or the other of those two sexed eroticisms—or a 'bisexual' combination." Katz, and Bersani, and the Rich of "Compulsory Heterosexuality," describe bisexuality as comparatively rare and uninteresting, at least at present.

It's Garber's job to prove them wrong. Her *Vice Versa* is a giant scrapbook: queer student groups at Harvard, vampires, H.D., *L.A. Law*, Maynard Keynes, Frida Kahlo, the "bulldagger" blues singer Gladys Bentley, Claude McKay, Tony Kushner, *Basic Instinct*, and dozens of other bi-related phenomena all get their fifteen paragraphs of fame in the first of four sections. A lot of this will seem obvious, but not everything will be to any one reader: those who know all about the "lavender marriage" of Robert Taylor and Barbara Stanwyck will not be the same ones who know about Havelock Ellis, and even the frequent plot summaries of canonical novels (like James's *The Bostonians*) are there for a reason—better-read readers can skip them. *Vice Versa* is more than an inspirational catalog; the sheer variety of Garber's sources, each with its own suggestion of what bi can be, rebukes previous books (like Bersani's) that try to extract the universal properties of real-life gay or straight desire from a handful of primary texts. But to say that Garber "makes everything bisexual"—a complaint I've heard about this book—would be less accurate than to say she reads everything for its "bisexual" component, for the angle that will demonstrate the inadequacy of our received categories:

Jealousy; the marriage model, the erotic triangle . . . the erotic appeal of transgression, the role of cross-dressing as part of bisexual play, the changing roles of men and women over time, generational difference, the persistence of the fantasy of "falling in love" which is always at odds with steady-state relationships—all of these topics come up whenever bisexuality is addressed. And all of them speak to the question of eroticism—not to one small segment of the population but to most of it.

Where previous writers have theorized that "everybody's bi," Garber turns that assertion around. By looking at people and situations in which people have felt and acted on erotic attractions to both sexes, we can see the instability and contingency of all the other categories—starting with "gay" and "straight"—by which we define ourselves. "Bisexuality means that your sexual identity may not be fixed in the womb, or at age two, or five. Bisexuality means you may not know all about yourself at any given time"—a position that neatly cuts the Gordian tug-of-war between essentialists and constructionists. How can you know exactly how you got that way if you can't be sure who you'll be next year?

If bisexuality is in fact, as I suspect it to be, not just another sexual orientation but rather a sexuality that undoes sexual orientation as a category, a sexuality that threatens and challenges the easy binarities of straight and gay, queer and "het," and even, through its biological and physiological meanings, the gender categories of male and female, then the search for the meaning of the word "bisexual" offers a different kind of lesson. Rather than naming an invisible, undernoticed minority now finding its place in the sun, "bisexual" turns out to be, like bisexuals themselves, everywhere and nowhere.

If this is a claim that self-identified super-bis can overleap all categories in a single bound, it is, to say the least, questionable. If it is a claim that sustained scrutiny of behaviors and people who might and might not count as bi forces us to examine the diversity of individual experiences of desire, gender, and embodiedness, then it is an exciting claim that the book itself proves true. Bi is an identity that no single act ever can express, with the possible exception of declaring yourself bi, and even that act of self-labeling is not always the same: a thirty-year-old woman calling herself bi as opposed to gay in Provincetown is saying something else about the shape of her desires than the boy who calls himself bi as opposed to gay in tenth grade, in a Pittsburgh suburb.

Garber flirts with, without endorsing, Gore Vidal's argument that there are no homosexual or heterosexual people, only acts: "Why, instead of hetero-, homo-, auto-, pan- and bisexuality, do we not simply say 'sexuality'?" In 1994, the New York bi zine *Cupsize* printed a letter taking Vidal's position: "'Sexuality' should suffice. I say there is NO true hetero, no true homo, only humankind, not bi but quasi, not one or both but all." The editors responded:

Clearly these labels that we've created are only rough approximations of different ways of experiencing sexual desire. I hated having to choose a label, if I wasn't living in NY I probably would have resisted it altogether. But here, in a heterosexist world that will ignore my existence unless I find ways to broadcast myself loud and clear, I need to use language to my advantage. That means concise, one word, power action. It doesn't sum up who I am by any stretch of the imagination, but it's a tool that I have to wield if I'm going to be counted and make change happen.

This is a record of a personal decision; it is all the defense that the continued use of some labels—"bi" among them—requires.

Garber suggests that transgression—the thrill of the forbidden, or the new—may always be part of sexuality. This is at least more plausible than Bersani's contention that same-sex sex is intrinsically antirelational, and Garber backs up her argument with many more instances, from John Cheever's diaries to Calvin Klein's visual gimmicks, that can be sexy in part because they're seen where they don't "belong"—homoerotic photos in magazines "aimed" at straights, flies and wide waistbands on Klein's "men's underwear for women." Garber's chatty examples, as often, support Butler's slightly abstruse theory:

The spectres of discontinuity and incoherence, themselves thinkable only in relation to existing norms of continuity and coherence, are constantly prohibited and produced by the very laws that seek to establish causal or expressive lines of connection among biological sex, culturally constituted genders, and the "expression" or "effect" or both in the manifestation of sexual desire through sexual practice.

Selfhood, and desire, can be built around the devotion to an unfinishable task, a kind of permanent rebellion—like the ability of transvestites and transgendered people to experience pleasure as localized in body parts they don't actually have—which can only be produced by the prior existence of a rule, law, norm, or fact, to be eluded or challenged.

In her less guarded moments Garber makes bi into a "third term," a root-of-all-transgressions, exactly as she did with transvestism in her last book, *Vested Interests* (1994): "Bisexuality is related to narrative as transvestism or hermaphroditism is to image." I would love to see myself as a "third term" "at the level of image," and it's flattering that Garber is willing to do it for me, but I doubt that

I have a crucial role in the production of meaning from all, or any, images. "What [Paul] Monette's narrative teaches us is what [Stephen] Spender's [autobiography] also teaches us: Bisexuality marks the spot where all our questions about eroticism, repression, and social arrangements come to crisis." *The* spot? *All* our questions? Garber defends her bevy of puns by implying that wordplay itself is bisexual: "The 'bi'-play of bisexual journalists, essayists, and activists can be allowed to go by as just 'play.'" But the pun as a rhetorical form is just as biracial, binational and bicoastal as it is bisexual—and a good deal more bilingual. Sometimes the puns become a tic—Eldridge Cleaver "despite his name, does not mince words"; "If 'vice' is not nice, then 'perverse' may be nicer. This change of label, which we might call vice-per-versa." Don't call me, I'll call you.

Garber can no more stop asking rhetorical questions than she can restrain the flood of puns: "Do we need to keep forgetting bisexuality in order to remember and rediscover it?" "Does the X

chromosome . . . mark the spot?" "Is the sexual object 'a kind of reflection of the subject's own bisexual nature' (Freud)? What is the relationship of subject to object?" But the querulous habit can lead to valid discoveries: "To compare Pat (of *Saturday Night Live*) to Dil (from *The Crying Game*) is to compare . . . what? Apples and oranges? Chalk and cheese?" Sexlessness and sexiness? Yes, and a good hypothesis comes out of that particular split hair: "Androgyny is sexy when it is the vehicle (the physical form or performance we see) and not sexy when it is the tenor (the ideal or idealization)." The questions come into their own where they skewer misplaced certainties, like those of bad science: "If the hypothalamus of gay men is smaller than that of straight men, what size hypothalamus should bisexuals have? . . . Is there such a thing as a 'bi brain'?"

Anatomy can't tell us dick about bisexuality, because bisexuality in all its variations can't possibly be a steady state of the body, or result from one consistent biological deviance from one gay or

Ivan Velez, Jr.
From Tales of the Closet #8,
© Hetrick-Martin Institute, 2 Astor Place, New York, NY 10003

*Anne D. Bernstein.
From "Confused
Things" in
Real Girl #6,
© Anne Bernstein.*

Ivan Velez, Jr.
From Tales of the
Closet #4,
© *Hetrick-Martin
Institute, 2 Astor Place,
New York, NY 10003*

straight norm. It shows how desire in general doesn't fit well into grids or scales. As Ruth Hubbard (one of Garber's few scientist heroes) puts it: "The use of the phrase 'sexual orientation' to describe only a person's having sex with members of their [sic] own gender or the other sex obscures the fact that many of us have other strong and consistent sexual orientations—toward certain hair colors, body shapes, racial types. It would be as logical to look for genes associated with these orientations as for 'homosexual genes.'" Eve Sedgwick has made a similar point: the terms we use to describe gender and especially sexual orientation are based on unstated *and falsifiable* premises of alignment among

your biological (e.g. chromosomal) sex, male or female; your self-perceived gender assignment, male or female (supposed to be the same as your biological sex); the preponderance of your traits of personality and appearance, mas-culine or feminine (supposed to correspond to your sex and gender); the biological sex of your preferred partner; the gender assignment of your preferred partner (supposed to be the same as his/her biological sex) . . . your self-perception as gay or straight (supposed to correspond to whether your preferred partner is your sex or the opposite); your preferred partner's self-perception as gay or straight (supposed to be the same as yours).

Once Sedgwick's reader realizes how many sexual "types" there must be, he or she is less likely to feel so alone. In her longer essays, Sedgwick has been less interested in instances of obvious disarray among these categories than she is in the creative and oppressive effects the command to make them line up has had on certain writers of fiction. The playful compendia of sexual dissonance whose possibility Sedgwick's list implies, and which Butler implicitly calls for, are exactly what Garber does best.

If there *is* a sense in which we are all bi, for Garber it is the inevitability of erotic "triangles." If hetero desire works by means of the love triangle, and thence by means of suppressed or rechanneled "gay" desire, then "it is bisexual triangularity that provokes, explains, and encompasses both heterosexuality and homosexuality." Furthermore, "our greatest love stories are . . . narratives of triangularity." This seems a bit glib; if the "third" point of the triangle has to be *one person* throughout the love story then it's demonstrably wrong (*Romeo and Juliet? Persuasion?*). And if the "third" point can be an institution or a set of persons against which the lovers struggle, then to say that great love stories depend on triangles is not much more than to say that a plot requires conflict.

When Garber leaves this level of implausible universality, she resumes her usual acuteness. Why do some people consistently wind up in potential love triangles? Because they "like the position of the third . . . of the child, the one who watches, who listens, who claims the right to intervene"; or because "they like to change positions." These are appeals to experience; I'm buying. "They like to change positions" turns out to help account for sequential bi desires, for psyches that thrive on eventful fluidity, and maybe for how people come to write fiction—the sexual kick of a story. That "they like the position of the third," of the watcher rather than that of the primary actor, might help explain the simultaneous desire for both men and women—and, maybe, why some people become literary critics. It also helps explain what the Anaïs Nin character does in the film *Henry and June*:

She falls in love with a couple. I think this must be very common, especially for adolescents and others relatively inexperienced in love. The couple has such glamour: they have, after all, succeeded in winning that most desirable of objects, each other. Their life affords a glimpse of intimacy and sexiness, just inaccessible enough to make them seem irresistible. . . . Not a few erotic triangles begin this way—and not a few divorces. But the initial emotion here is bisexual. It is the couple that attracts.

That identity can be a story one tells (Garber) or a continuing performance (Butler's model) is something else the authors of *The Coming-Out Stories* may have already known: "The writing itself has caused many to realize that they have 'always been coming out,' that coming out is not a single isolated act but an ongoing process of self-definition and self-clarification." We are never conscious of our first such self-clarification, because it occurs in early childhood, and every subsequent act of becoming (including the rest of childhood) may be said to have the grammatical form of "No, but what I meant to be was . . ." And if sexual self-identification is a continuing performance, a "story," then adults who come out—as bi or gay or whatever—are in a sense beginning *in medias res*. The real beginning is adolescence or earlier, not in some kind of Freudian originary moment, but in an imperfectly remembered beginning to learn how to be who you discover you are.

Vice Versa itself thus begins *in medias res*, with current political movements, and places students, schools, and adolescence at its center. Education—especially boarding school education—is in-

trinsically "bi," in the slightly recherché sense that institutions and conventions of learning and teaching produce sexual roles that don't map onto the declared sexual orientations of the students or teachers involved. One can have a crush on a teacher (or student) in his or her capacity as teacher, whether or not the teacher (or student) is the "right" sex. "We need to take seriously the legitimacy of the crush as real love," Garber declares. This includes the same-sex crushes of people who later have "normal" straight relationships, and the hard-to-talk-about crushes of students on teachers, and of teachers on students, which a wise teacher might notice and decide not to acknowledge.

Garber writes (of boarding-school crushes): "It would be as possible to call all eroticisms pseudo as to deny that any of them are. What are the hallmarks of the real when it comes to human feelings?" Science is suspect when it comes to love and desire in a way that individual narratives are not, because narratives don't claim to be more than what they are: accounts of what it felt like to be in a certain desiring situation. But many of the autobiographers Garber examines turn out to have papered over parts of their own desiring histories; the most believable and engaging school stories turn out to be the novels (especially Dorothy Strachey Bussy's *Olivia*). Personal experience is, simply, hard to explain unless you happen to be a talented and diligent writer. The autobiographers who do not cast off old loves or previous identifications are the ones Garber celebrates. Hence her lengthy, sympathetic, and entirely just defense of the late Stephen Spender's account of his

own life, bi—and unarrogantly frank about it—*avant la lettre*.

. . .

"One of the key purposes of studying bisexuality," Garber writes, "is not to get people to 'admit' they 'are' bisexual, but rather to restore to them and the people they have loved the full, complex and often contradictory stories of their lives." Restoring to some, and giving others, the ability to describe their own desires, is the real primary project of Garber's book, the one that explains both her thesis and her profusion of exempla. Its corollary is an attack on "the normal," not only the straight norm but the competing gay norms—if this book has one bogeyman, it is

the idea that it is "normal" to reach a settled sexual identity, and that that "identity" is either heterosexual or homosexual. The claim that bisexuality is "immature" is closely related to this assumption that maturity means choosing between those ostensibly polar alternatives.

If that is what maturity means, we need to value maturity less, and listen more to people who are, or have been, "neither one thing nor the other"—even if they sound as pleasantly gimmicky as *Geraldo* guest Francis Vavra, a female-to-male cross-dresser who appears, mustachioed, hatted, and earringed, in *Vice Versa*'s inner sheaf of photos. Garber's "phenomenological" approach, which starts by listening to the people being studied, is the only one Foucault explicitly ruled out as a basis for his own inquiries into sex. But a depersonalized, Foucauldian approach runs the risk of producing false or un-

recognizable accounts of what the people being described think their loves and desires are, against which dangers a dose of *Geraldo* is arguably a small price to pay.

It may even be a necessary price. There are never many stunningly insightful novelists, playwrights, or filmmakers around, and the merely autobiographical accounts will always come from people who are more than usually inclined to exhibit their private lives. The telling of these stories will be worthwhile, even in a format more like *Geraldo* than like Proust, because it will multiply available, plausible models. But if we search only for "life stories," we are likely to miss important models and metaphors of sexual identity that are not couched in narrative form, but embedded in other sorts of art. *Vice Versa's* chapter on Shakespeare's sonnets is really about their reception history, and it's dodgy even there—if some of today's professors still regard a Shakespeare who desired both sexes as unthinkable, more probably regard "a bi reading of the sonnets" as too obvious to be worth undertaking. Garber's dealings with music are likewise almost always confined to the private and public lives of pop stars, or, as with the Living Colour song "Bi," examine only the printed lyrics. I especially wish theorists would stop discussing David Bowie's shifting public image and listen to him: the double-tracked vocals on Bowie's "Life on Mars" (1970), the stretched-out, exasperated vowels in his description of a girl who goes to the movies and still feels lonely and invisible, say more to me about role playing, secret loves, and the ambiguities of the ubiquitous closet than any Bowie press release from twenty years later ever could.

Many people don't or can't have sex, aren't in love, and have to define themselves in other ways. A lot of others have just started defining themselves. If some of those people look for themselves in books like Garber's and Sedgwick's— and especially if they find themselves there—they will also be acting out the unquestioned imperative that sexuality

Many people don't or can't have sex, aren't in love, and have to define themselves in other ways

is, or should be, the truth about ourselves. It must be depressing to be told that "you must become what you are," and that what you are is the kind of sex you have, if you haven't had enough sex to really know. Even the sexually active and literate have had this problem: Lucy McKenzie wrote in the Glasgow zine *Violet* that

I've been reading Men in Love and it's made me think a lot about sex. I am completely and utterly confused by sex, it's just this huge big blob and I can't figure it out at all. . . . _____ is so good at masturbating that she managed to get a band 1A for History higher because she wanked while she studied! To be a foot fetishist or transvestite or into getting pissed on by 10 year old boys must mean you have a clear idea of what you are into—I don't know at all and it worries me a bit. . . . I feel so uncool cuz I fall for all these cheesy things. I don't feel any different from when I started to have sex either.

I suspect that for every person who asks him- or herself such questions and then finds an answer, there are three who find,

TO BE CONTINUED...

on turning twenty or twenty-four or thirty, that they have neither the answers nor the time to keep looking. One of the points of writing accessible queer-theory books is to enable such readers to find their own answers.

But what would an "answer" be in this context? What do we—we readers of "queer theory"—want? Self-conceptions that aren't self-hating, and aren't so simple as to be inaccurate; theoretical vocabularies, then; accurate readings of texts we enjoy; but really, mostly, love. The people of the past who had the last-named desideratum could be stunningly sanguine about lacking the rest; and a text, or a terminology, is no substitute for the right boy or girl. The critique Bersani and others have applied to Butler's celebration of drag applies with equal force to any attempt to give a general political or epistemological meaning to sexual feelings or behavior: if few people select their wardrobe with political change as their primary goal, neither do most people have sex or fall in love in order to change the way Americans think about gender. And changing the theories I hold about gender is not going to change what turns me on—but it may well change what I choose to do about it, or how I see myself, and those changes may make me more, or less, likely to find love.

What does it mean to fall in love anyway? To what extent, if at all, is "falling in love" the same set of emotions in, say, 1590s England as in 1990s Montevideo, Lagos, Winnipeg, or Siberia? What are the historical and economic precondi-tions for the activity we know as "falling in love," and to what extent does the experience of romantic love underpin what we have learned to think of as the modern construction of "identity" based on "sexual orientation"? Only if these questions can be adequately answered—by psychologists, historians, literary critics, and anthropologists, not to mention makers of art, from epic poets to site-specific sculptors—will we have permanently done with the "debate" between extreme social-constructionist and more historically and geographically invariant notions of sex and sexual orientation. (The idea that "a gay man" or "a lesbian" is always a single biological type of person has, I hope, largely been laid to rest.)

Our most important prejudices tend to be simple and widely shared; otherwise they would not be able to enforce the social norms they helped create. They also tend, like the car in *The Phantom Tollbooth*, to "go without saying," which means that simply to talk about them can lessen their momentum, though it can't make them vanish. Our most im-

Most people don't have sex or fall in love in order to change the way Americans think about gender

portant desires, on the other hand, are often difficult to articulate, secret, perverse-seeming, and "hard to get"—both hard to satisfy and hard to fully understand. This is why Sedgwick's discussions in *Epistemology of the Closet* of what all modern homophobia has in common are more convincing than Katz's about the one origin of one mode of desire called "heterosexuality" or than Bersani's claims about what gay desire "is." It is also why we need all the information we can get about how diversely desire has operated. The more models we have

Is "falling in love" the same set of emotions in, say, 1590s England as in 1990s Montevideo, Lagos, Winnipeg, or Siberia?

through which we can figure out what we want and need and why, the easier, at the margin, it becomes for readers of "queer theory," or queer autobiography, to find happiness in the world (in bed).

If we need to think hard before "seeing ourselves" in the explicit social categories of another era, we should worry less over, and celebrate more, our ability to see ourselves in older individual expressions of lust and love. We may not be able to know when our particular self-conceptions first occurred to somebody, or exactly how we got to be who we are now: the queer Adam (or the lesbian Lilith, or the first transgender boy) is not going to be discovered tomorrow. But we can know that there are many kinds of desire; that "sex of partner" is one among many of desire's parameters; and that when desire has been represented in certain forms, the representations have

moved and assisted readers and listeners across continents, or social strata, or centuries, or sexual orientations. Thus the cult of "Greek love" among men with good enough Greek to know their loves were hardly exact analogues of Plato's; thus the cult of Whitman in England and Germany, among men who made their desires for men part of their self-definitions, though the term *homosexual* had not yet been invented; thus Donne's "The Canonization," a poem he probably wrote to his wife (with whom he eloped), but which looks now like a poem about the strength of any persecuted love (and especially one that confounds genders). "For God's sake hold your tongue and let me love," it begins, and:

Call us what you will, we are made such by love;
Call her one, me another fly,
We are tapers too, and at our own cost die,
And we in us find the eagle and the dove,
The phoenix riddle hath more wit
By us; we two, being one, are it.
So to one neutral thing both sexes fit
We die and rise the same, and prove
Mysterious by this love.

It may be a while before modern queer theorists have written as well or as wisely about desire as that.

AFRICAN ART IN A SUITCASE

How value travels

Sidney L. Kasfir

"Which do you prefer, natural or primitive?" The Indian trader around the corner from the New Stanley Hotel in Nairobi is heavily patronized by tourists on safari. He is referring to the neatly stacked illusionistic paintings of elephants and leopards crashing through forest clearings, made by expatriates, as well as to more expressive works of "self-taught" local artists, portrayals of urban and village life from overcrowded *matatus* (the minibus, an omnipresent subject in urban East Africa) to life on the family *shamba*, or farm. Just across the street in this high-rent district is Gallery Watatu, Nairobi's premier gallery. Here the work of the local artists is the main focus of owner Ruth Schaffner's presentation of contemporary art. A few blocks away, in the crowded stalls of the Blue Market, the work of other self-taught artists is sold straightforwardly as merchandise, by African traders operating with low overheads and correspondingly lower prices.

Christopher Steiner's *African Art in Transit* addresses the pivotal role of these untranslated middlemen, the trader-dealers. These figures appear throughout the continent: while Steiner's book is set in West rather than East Africa, Abidjan rather than Nairobi, with a cast of Muslim traders rather than the mainly Hindu traders I encountered in my own research in Kenya, the roles they play in the economy of art and taste, and the problems they pose, are fundamentally the same. Approaching African art objects as commodities, Steiner focuses on the entrepreneurial skills of the West African traders: Steiner envisions the commodification of West African sculpture as a form of cultural brokerage by traders and dealers, in which value is established over the course of bargaining in both buying and selling. The book's other major concern is the meaning of authenticity for African art, considered in the context of the art market, African and international. Steiner develops each of these themes in separate but overlapping arguments. Both have a significance

that extends well beyond their physical and temporal setting in Côte d'Ivoire in the late 1980s.

In its investigation of the meaning of value in ethnographic settings, *African Art in Transit* is indebted to the landmark anthology *The Social Life of Things*. First published in 1986 (the year Steiner began his field research in Abidjan) and reprinted three times since, this dazzling collection of essays on "things" as commodities—especially highly valued things, such as art objects, oriental carpets, and saints' relics—changed the terms of the debate on the commodification of art. Editor Arjun Appadurai's "Commodities and the Politics of Value" describes commodification as but one phase in the life of an object, rather than an immutable characteristic of certain objects. He developed a post-

The African trader in Côte d'Ivoire is at the same time an insider and an outsider—African, yes, but not of the same culture that produces the artwork by which he makes his living

Marxian cultural anthropology of commodities from Georg Simmel's observation that exchange is the source of value, and not the other way round. Appadurai paid special attention to what he calls "enclaved commodities," which have very limited circulations and are customarily considered *sacred*, hence not commodifiable. Igor Kopytoff's seminal essay in the same collection, "The Cultural Biography of Things" specifically examined the commodity status of African sculpture.

. . .

One of the social markers of the African trader in Côte d'Ivoire (and in much of West Africa) is his ambiguous status as one who is at the same time an insider and an outsider—African, yes, but not of the same culture that produces the artwork by which he makes his living. Almost always a Muslim, usually Hausa or Wolof, he emphatically distances himself from the masks and figures that are considered sacred by the Baule, Senufo, and other cultures who use them. To him (and it is always a "him"), they are "pieces of wood" that can be sold for money. Physically near yet culturally far, like Simmel's stranger, the trader is free to turn spirit-imbued objects into highly marketable commodities.

At the same time, he is no stranger to other traders. Steiner describes their strong sense of ethnic loyalty, which undergirds the series of transactions running from rural villages to big city markets and excludes outsiders from participating in the exchanges except as consumers. In one transaction replete with denials, reversals, and intrigues, the author describes the purchase of two Senufo *kpélié* masks in Korhogo he witnessed while traveling upcountry with an Abidjan-based Hausa trader in 1988. (I'll call him AHT.) These were the type of masks known by the traders as "copies" (made for sale) rather than *ancien* ("old," purportedly used in ceremonies).

In the first stage of the transaction, the masks are sold by their rural Senufo carver to another Senufo, a trader who is traveling from village to village acquir-

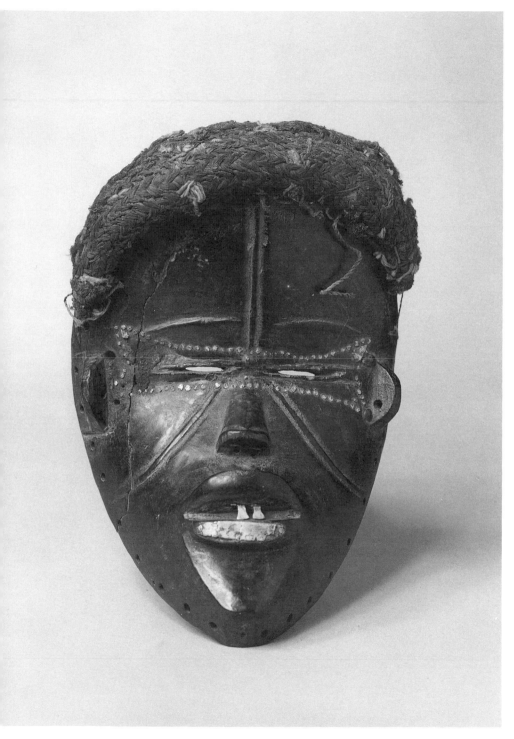

*Ge mask
(Guinea Coast,
Liberia/Côte d'Ivoire).
Artist unknown.
Wood, metal, fiber, cloth.
Early 20th century.
Reproduced with
permission by the
Baltimore Museum
of Art: gift of
Robert and
Mary Cumming,
Baltimore.
BMA 1984.83.*

**Youths at Abidjan
marketplace
shining Senufo
masks with shoe
polish**

© *Christopher B.
Steiner*

ing a store of such masks and figures. The trader then shows them (stage two) to an elderly Hausa trader (let's call him EHT)—a small-time businessman who also travels through northern villages on foot or motorbike gathering pieces to bring back to Korhogo, a well-known center for Senufo carving and the head-quarters of at least a half-dozen wealthy Hausa merchants, who conduct the art trade with dealers in Abidjan. In stage three, EHT then brings AHT and the author to the Senufo trader, who after three hours of hard bargaining over the age, and hence market value, of the ob-jects, agrees to sell them to AHT at one-fifth of his original asking price.

It isn't over yet. Stage four: back in Korhogo, Alhadji Usuman, one of the most powerful Hausa middlemen, is out-raged to discover that EHT and AHT have cut him out of the deal, in violation of accepted procedure. While all the Hausa traders in the neighborhood are noisily berating poor AHT, the Senufo trader suddenly arrives with his older brother, who, proffering the money with a flourish, demands the carvings back—stage five. They refuse; a deal is a deal. He threatens to bring in the police. Instantly,

**Storeroom, Kisii
soapstone carving
cooperative,
Kenya**

© *Sidney L. Kasfir*

three things happen: the quarrel among the Hausa traders is forgotten, EHT announces that it is actually the American who is the real "owner" (thrusting the masks into Steiner's hands to prove the point), and the Senufo brothers, seeing that it might be impolitic to involve the police in the American's business, beg off, calling the whole thing an unfortunate misunderstanding. Off they go on their motorbikes.

One striking thing about this transaction is the elaborate logic that underlies it. But another is the highly contingent nature of the bargaining, the elaborate gamesmanship and the instantaneous reversals. It is a system at once highly structured and constantly open to play. Steiner likens it to "fission and fusion" in African kinship systems. But lest one imagine the trader network as a form of straightforward economic tribalism, he asserts that while ethnic loyalty plays heavily in the rural areas, it is actually much more complicated in the big

city of Abidjan, where ties of friendship may outweigh those of ethnicity.

In reading this wonderfully complex account, I couldn't help wondering what might have gone differently if the objects had not been "copies" made for sale but "authentic" masks, sold illicitly or stolen from their owners? As Patrick Geary remarked in *The Social Life of Things*, the theft of saintly relics only increased their value as commodities: "A corpse once stolen (or said to have been stolen) was valuable because it had been worth stealing." The value of any sacred object is augmented in this process, so long as it retains its aura of authenticity in its new setting.

The most famous example of this in recent years was the case of the Cameroonian Afo-a-Kom (literally, the "Kom thing"), which also reveals the complicated issues involved in uncovering alleged theft when reputations are at stake. In 1973, while browsing an exhibition of African art at Dartmouth College, two

Idoma elephant mask.
Otobi village,
Benue State, Nigeria.
© Sidney L. Kasfir

the moral high ground), the U.S. State Department got into the act, eventually succeeding in returning the Afo-a-Kom to Laikom amid much ceremony and fanfare.

Only later was it discovered—with considerable embarrassment, and without being reported in the press—that the person most likely to have sold the piece, illicitly, in the first place was a member of the Kom royal family. (The usual route out of Cameroon would have been through Foumban, where Hausa traders similar to those in Korhogo supply objects from Cameroon and eastern Nigeria to dealers in Paris.) Paradoxically, then, the Afo-a-Kom's sojourn in the West—one might say its "commodity phase"—only increased its value, both on the art market and to the people of Kom. The publicity certainly increased its appraisal value: its name-recognition shot up after the *New York Times* investigation. And while to the Kom people themselves the Afo-a-Kom was considered an inalienable possession—something that could not be bought—it could only be more highly valued by virtue of having been taken from them and later recovered. If anything, its surreptitious removal and triumphant return were further proof of its power to resist human intervention in superhuman affairs.

• • •

It is not only unscrupulous locals who cooperate with traders and dealers. Researchers in art history and anthropology are also, however unwittingly, part of the problem. Igor Kopytoff writes knowingly of this in *The Social Life of Things* when he describes the rules by which academ-

former Peace Corps volunteers recognized the Afo-a-Kom—a beaded male throne figure that they had last seen in Cameroon at the palace at Laikom—among the show's sculpture. The item was on loan from a prominent New York dealer. The *New York Times*, which had already that year given dramatic and detailed coverage to several instances of international art theft, pounced on the story. The investigative reporter was relentless (he would later write a book on the subject). Not wanting to miss a photo opportunity (or a chance to take

ics a generation ago exempted themselves from concern for the commodification of African sculpture, even while collecting it during fieldwork. Because they didn't sell it for profit, they believed themselves uninvolved in the process.

Four years ago I had the bizarre experience of walking into a famous collector's home in Switzerland to find myself confronted by a large and elaborate Idoma mask that I immediately recognized as coming from the same village in central Nigeria where I had done extensive mask research years before (see illustration). The collector had recently purchased it from a reputable dealer in Paris. My dilemma, one shared by everybody who does this kind of research, is that it is the documentation and subsequent publication of pictures of these objects that allows dealers (in Paris or Foumban, it hardly matters) to send out "runners" to look for them—and, where possible, buy them. Had I helped create this situation, simply by writing about it? It's a variation on a familiar question: how much is the storyteller responsible for the story's interpretation?

I still don't know whether the Idoma mask was actually stolen by an agent of one of the dealers, or whether the heavy toll of IMF Structural Adjustment Policies on the Nigerian economy (and the consequent impoverishment of the Idoma, along with other rural people) had made an offer of cash impossible to refuse. As the story of the Afo-a-Kom suggests, the issues have become more complicated. The need for cash is a more common reason than actual theft these days. The seller is typically someone young and disaffected enough to place the object's exchange value above its rit-

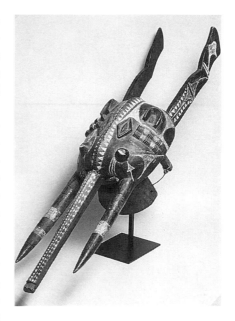

Idoma elephant mask (Nigeria). Courtesy of the Barbier-Mueller Museum, Geneva, Switzerland.

ual value, and therefore unlikely to be the object's custodian. So we really are speaking of theft after all, but the thief is no longer the trader himself.

The dismaying thing is that we scholars of African art provide collectors with fresh ammunition every time we publish the outcome of our research. It's a well-known fact that traders in Africa and dealers in the West make extensive use of our books and catalogs. Steiner's text describes precisely how this works in Abidjan, where traders delight in showing customers catalog illustrations of masks or figures slightly inferior to the ones they happen to be selling. While in this case the catalog validates the traders' product by comparison, illustrations also function as guidebooks, pure and simple.

As a graduate student in London, I was introduced to a youngish up-and-coming London dealer, a trained artist who, along with a fellow dealer in Paris, had already made one illegal field trip to Idomaland—illegal because Nigeria has a strin-

gent Antiquities Law forbidding most exports. They were "looking forward to reading my dissertation," which they clearly planned to use as a kind of Antiquities Trip-Tick when they went back again. Appalled and fascinated by the sheer hubris of what they regarded as a profitable adventure, I later tracked down the Parisian dealer and discovered that he held a Ph.D. in anthropology from the Sorbonne and considered what he was doing (buying masks and figures for about £5 each and reselling them for about £500 each) an extension of his "fieldwork," complete with little black notebooks and tape recordings. Most Western dealers who claim to collect works in the "field" actually sit in a hotel in Douala or Abidjan for days, making deals with those traders from Foumban or Korhogo. My two interested dealers were an exception, in that they actually hoped to have some kind of validating experience along the way. But make no mistake: they were doing it for the money.

Ivoirian traders have their own terms to rate the exchange value of the goods they are selling, but for these to be useful, they must be roughly congruent with the classifications used by the world art market in which the traders operate. Hence their discourse of authenticity is immediately recognizable, a sliding scale on which old is good and new is bad, at least as far as money is concerned. Objects that appear to be old, that show signs of use, are "top," or *antiquités*. Pieces made in traditional styles and genres expressly for the art market are "copies," even if they don't actually replicate any existing older piece. (They are often artificially aged.) And objects invented for the souvenir buyer (as opposed to the collector of *antiquités*) are known as *nyama-nyama*.

Among the assortment of objects that Steiner describes in this last category are masks and figures based loosely on traditional prototypes, such as the Asante *akua'ba*, but embellished (e.g., with inset beads) and carved in a slightly different style, or on a different scale. These *nyama-nyama* are also called "Kenya" by the traders, to indicate a generic "African" rather than a specific "tribal" style. (In Côte d'Ivoire, Kenya, located at the other end of the continent, sounds exotic; in Kenya, these "improved" objects are thought to come from Ghana, where the Asante prototype originates. Steiner claims they are actually made by Senegalese.) These are the items that turn up regularly on this side of the Atlantic in African American boutiques and street fairs—and perhaps more surprisingly, in museum shops from L.A. to Boston, Chicago to Atlanta.

Only a few "top" pieces make their way in traders' suitcases from West and Central Africa to Nairobi, although the "copies" and *poupeés et masques Kenya* are as ubiquitous there as in Abidjan. The few objects priced above $3,000 or $4,000 are brought there by a handful of itinerant West African traders, who understand the Kenya market to be a venue where the richest safari tourists gather—at Charleton Heston's Mount Kenya Safari Club in Nanyuki, for example. Other potential clients for these pieces are high-level diplomats connected with the embassies and the United Nations, whose headquarters for Africa is located outside Nairobi. As elsewhere in formerly British Africa, local government and business elites rarely spend big money on art objects, preferring more conspicuous forms of public consumption such as houses and luxury cars. In this sense, they are very much the inheritors of the white colonial taste, even going so far as to prefer those very colonial visions of majestic elephants bursting

Tourists inspect art, Bamburi Beach, Kenya

© Sidney L. Kasfir

through the bush to the homegrown imaginings of African artists.

But while it appears that educated Africans make the same assumptions about authenticity as Western dealers and collectors, Steiner found that this was not always the case with the Ivoirian traders. As one explained to him, "At the beginning, there was only one of everything that you now see in the marketplace. When the Europeans came, they took these things with them and put them in the museums and in the books. After that time, everything became a copy." As Steiner points out, this locates

The discourse of authenticity is a sliding scale on which old is good and new is bad

authenticity in a far-off place rather than in Africa: authentic objects, therefore, no longer exist, as they were removed from circulation long ago by the colonials. One would like to know a little more about this trader's business. A trader who sells only "copies" would have an interest in propagating such a totalizing dis-

self. As a result of the interest generated by this combined dialogue/diatribe, *African Arts* decided also to reprint its 1976 "authenticity issue" on fakes and fakery, which reproduces the range of scholarly opinion on the subject prior to the New Art History and the New Ethnography. Finally the *Annual Reviews of Anthropology* for 1993 devoted an article entitled "Exploding Canons" to the matter. The subject is at the heart of debates concerning canonicity, and has become a major annoyance for those who have a stake in denying the commodity status of African art, from the leading auction houses to museums of fine art.

Institutional criteria for determining the authenticity of African art veer between arguments about the object's uniqueness, on the one hand, and its cultural embeddedness on the other. To make the grade under these conditions, an object must be demonstrably one-of-a-kind but also embedded in a tradition, and has to bear evidence of actual use, as opposed to having been made for the market. A work's authenticity, then, is a function of its distance from the "commodity form." Anthropology museums have less at stake in this argument (commodities are, after all, cultural artifacts, even if they're not art), and some have even begun to concertedly collect "commodities." But on balance, almost everyone prefers the "real thing."

It would be hard to overestimate the importance of this framing of what counts as *authentic*, which Steiner identifies with cultural brokerage, and which goes well beyond the transaction in Africa. It informs collecting practice back in Europe and the United States, and has a strong influence on what West-

course. On the other hand, you'd be very unlikely to hear it from a top-of-the-line trader trying to sell "antiquities" at a high price. From him one might expect to hear instead of undiscovered caches of authentic art hidden deep in the bush. (It is this kind of thinking, of course, that induces dealers like my friends in London and Paris to go collecting.)

In the only lapse in an otherwise very prescient book, the author begins with the assertion that "surprisingly little" has been said on the subject of authenticity in African art. In 1992 I published an article in the journal *African Arts* called "African Art and Authenticity: A Text with a Shadow," which elicited twelve rather impassioned and sometimes prickly responses, including one by Steiner him-

ern publics perceive as art, as opposed to souvenir. It also influences cultural production, sometimes quite decisively, as when artists have no direct contact with their clientele. Finally, these traders and dealers, like their counterparts in New York or Paris, have the capacity to affirm or deny the commodity status of the objects that pass through their hands, and in doing so, confirm or deny their claims to distinction.

. . .

By now, there may be more people who have seen the associated film video *In and Out of Africa* (a collaboration between Chris Steiner and filmmakers Ilisa Barbash and Lucien Taylor) than have read *African Art in Transit*. The film, following the fortunes of a single trader, pursues the vexing notion of authenticity as it is applied to African art by Western collectors, observing its deconstruction—or, better, demolition—by pragmatic African traders and African intellectuals. It follows one typical trader from the loading of his container in Abidjan with an assortment of "copies," souvenirs, and crafts (all dumped inside unceremoniously, and without benefit of bubble wrap) to his cramped hotel room in New York (a place patronized by many traders), to his transactions out of the back of a rented van with a dealer on Long Island. Americans tend to be impatient at clinching deals and don't have the time or the skills to practice the art of bargaining the way it is practiced in Africa. Unlike in Korhogo, the transaction time is measurable in minutes instead of hours, and the Long Island dealer doesn't seem to mind that she is being overcharged. She'll just

pass it along to her affluent suburban clients.

The best part of the film consists of interviews with West African intellectuals and European and American collectors and dealers. The latter uphold in varying ways the inviolable standards of authenticity, which are mirrored in the discourse of the traders: use, age, traditional craftsmanship, and so on. The African intellectuals, on the other hand—one an Ivoirian painter and writer, Wewere Liking, and the other the director of the National Museum in Abidjan—insist that authenticity is a Western problem, not an African one. Why, she asks, shouldn't an artist be able to sell his work? In what way does that render it inauthentic? The question serves to locate the authenticity question unambiguously in collecting practice. It is not an artist's question. It can only arise at a considerable cultural distance from the scene of production, whether voiced by a Muslim trader or a department head at Christie's.

Why shouldn't an African artist be able to sell his work? In what way does that render it inauthentic?

One might say that the film is so successful in making its point that it is almost misleading. I once saw it with an audience of anthropologists, nearly all of whom specialized in Native American arts and knew very little about Africa in the 1990s. After seeing *In and Out of Africa*, those with whom I spoke had concluded that all African art has now been successfully commodified, and that "traditional" art, as a class of objects made

and used exclusively within an African community, must now be a thing of the past. This is, of course, not the case; the two conditions coexist and interrelate in complicated ways. That this dialectic is not the subject of either the book or the film does nothing to detract from either. But I do think that the next important study in this field will be one that takes this interplay into account. In doing so, it will shift the focus back toward the producers of African art and their relation to traders and dealers, rather than the brokerage between traders and buyers. This, then, is the other half of a very complex equation.

Blacked Out

Dilemmas of Race, Identity, and Success at Capital High

Signithia Fordham

"Fordham entered the inner-cultural world of African-American adolescents, understood it, and described it as no one has done."—John U. Ogbu, University of California, Berkeley
*Paper $22.95 432 pages

Tomorrow Is Another Country

The Inside Story of South Africa's Road to Change

Allister Sparks

"Sparks has written a gripping, fast-paced authoritative account of the long and mostly secret negotiations that brought South Africa's bitter conflict to its near-miraculous end."—Adam Hochschild, *New York Times Book Review*
Paper $14.95 266 pages

Divided by Color

Racial Politics and Democratic Ideals

Donald R. Kinder and Lynn M. Sanders

"A marvelous accomplishment. . . . [Divided by Color] exhibits a remarkably well-integrated, almost seamless, treatment of diverse literatures. . . . It is unequivocally a stunning piece of work likely to stand for some stretch of time as the most important work in political science on the matter of race."—Lawrence Bobo, University of California, Los Angeles.
Cloth $27.50 344 pages
American Politics and Political Economy series

Giving Offense

Essays on Censorship

J. M. Coetzee

"Coetzee's erudition and intelligence remain truly formidable throughout. And as Coetzee's own experience has shown, censorship ultimately fights a losing battle."
—*Kirkus Reviews*
Cloth $24.95 304 pages

Parish Boundaries

The Catholic Encounter with Race in the Twentieth-Century Urban North

John T. McGreevy

"This superb study illuminates—for the first time—a central aspect of black/white relations in the twentieth century. McGreevy shows that the Catholic response to black migration to the northern cities was more varied and complex than anyone had imagined."—George Fredrickson, Stanford University
Cloth $27.50 368 pages 29 b&w photographs, 4 maps
Historical Studies of Urban America

THE UNIVERSITY OF CHICAGO PRESS

5801 South Ellis Avenue, Chicago, Illinois 60637

YOUNG ADORNO

Alex Ross

Thomas Mann, eerily nicknamed the Magician by his own children, did not hesitate to use the people nearest him in his art. Anyone who crossed his path could be conjured away into fiction's limbo. After completing his final major novel, however, he felt uneasy; one of his literary creations had cast a spell of its own. *Doktor Faustus*, the "novel of music," depended on the prior work and day-to-day counsel of a younger writer so heavily that public acknowledgment seemed due. Mann took the unusual step of issuing a literary memoir in which various borrowings were disclosed. He also gave the "musical adviser" a brief but spectacular cameo in the novel itself. When the doomed Faustian composer, feeling the onset of syphilitic dementia, hallucinates a conversation with the Devil, he sees before him "a member of the intelligentsia, writer on art, on music for the ordinary press, a theoretician and critic, who himself composes, so far as thinking allows him"—Doktor Adorno.

Mann could not have guessed that this obscure "theoretician and critic," a fellow emigré and Hollywood neighbor during World War II, would eventually win an esoteric renown far beyond the pages of *Doktor Faustus*. Returning to Germany in 1949, Theodor W. Adorno became an academic institution in his final years, presiding over the Frankfurt Institute for Social Research. In music, he was the iconic explainer of early Viennese modernism and a buttress for the postwar European avant-garde. After his death in August of 1969, three days before the Manson murders, he unexpectedly emerged as a thinker of general importance, an oft-quoted oracle of the late-modern, post-Holocaust world. His gladiatorial attacks on the "culture industry" (with their biases reversed) form a model for the multidisciplinary "cultural studies" of today. Reprinted in Frankfurt School anthologies, his essays on commodity fetishism and late-capitalist reification cause nightmares on college campuses across the country.

If Adorno has not actually become

Theodor
Wiesengrund
Adorno, 1917,
in Frankfurt

*Theodor W. Adorno
Archive, Frankfurt*

the Devil, he is, at the very least, the great nay-sayer, the father of negations. On the left, he is deeply suspect for his quietistic nihilism. On the right, he is naturally loathed for his deep-grained, though highly attenuated, Marxism. Proponents of pop culture denounce him for the thoroughgoing elitism, bordering on racism, exhibited in his notorious essay "Jazz." Defenders of Western tradi-

Adorno dropped hints of a great music existing outside the realm of the classical altogether, somewhere out in the wailing jungle of the popular

tion denounce his contrary contempt for commercial high culture, which he considered a moribund self-parody falling victim to the same forces driving the popular. Culture itself is going away, he proclaimed, leaving a husk of itself behind. Only a small handful of twentieth-century artistic fragments—Beckett, Kafka, Schoenberg, Berg—survived the catastrophe, floating Voyager II–like through the deep space of Adornian prose. His desolation had an aristocratic air; in Georg Lukács's deadly quip, he looked at the world through the glass floor of the Grand Hotel Abyss.

Adorno's negative delirium undermines most potential applications of his social theory. An all-pervading conception of a "totality" governing social life collapses into picturesque tautology in this work; what matters most is the frisson of the phrase. It might be said that secretly he is style and nothing but. Rhetoric swirls in all directions; the famous arrogantly clanging phrases—"the fully enlightened earth radiates disaster

triumphant," "all poetry after Auschwitz is garbage"—fall side by side with instances of morose self-parody, like the surreal aphorisms on punctuation in *Notes to Literature* ("In the dash, thought becomes aware of its fragmentary character.") Gillian Rose has called his style "eminently quotable, but egregiously misconstruable." Like Mann, like Nietzsche, like Karl Kraus, Adorno practiced an irony so heavy and deep that his whole body of work is an all-or-nothing proposition, a life written out on a limb.

But there are certain areas where Adorno still finds deeper resonances, most notably in the realm of music. His cherished idea of a music in resistance to society—a "passionate protest of convention"—carries weight because the art of music has almost always found itself in resistance to society, in one form or another. Moreover, Adorno brings himself to address a particular music, materially rather than rhetorically defined. What is always forgotten is that music, and the embattled world of musical modernism in particular, served as his professional home ground; all the other murky tributaries flow from the watershed of his musical experience. Academic commentators have generally suffered from only a glancing acquaintance with his musical writings, which lie at the core of his thought and comprise nearly half of the twenty-two volumes of the Suhrkamp Adorno edition. He studied composition with Alban Berg and made an early living as a music critic; as a musicologist, he singularly combined the broad gaze of a cultural thinker with the expert eye of a trained musician. Despite the inevitable idiosyncrasies, we know in music precisely whereof Adorno speaks.

Three recently translated books from the 1960s—*Berg: Master of the Smallest Link, Mahler: A Musical Physiognomy,* and *Quasi una Fantasia*—show Adorno in a surprising light. They are not strained sociological schematizations of music history, but portraits of composers in action; they concentrate on compositional "tone," accents of voice in which individuality evolves from general language. One section of *Quasi una Fantasia* is given the title "Evocations": what is evoked is not only the lost past, but also the possible future, possible paths through the ever-burgeoning and ever-diversifying culture of the same. Seeing the limitations of the classical culture to which he was tied, Adorno dropped hints of a great music existing outside the realm of the classical altogether, somewhere out in the wailing jungle of the popular. He ends up offering us a way beyond the destructive distinction between "high" and "low." But to reach this conclusion requires patience, and, admittedly, a certain amount of imaginative reading.

. . .

Adorno was born to well-to-do bourgeois parents in Frankfurt am Main, toward the end of the Wilhelmine era. His childhood was comfortable; he was coddled for the life of the mind. All his life he remained a noted dandy, a fancier of the better things. He was an excellent dancer. But he did not listen to music in order to relax. Listening, for him, was an active, risky, difficult endeavor. His metaphoric accounts of music's effects are fraught with odd, disturbing images. Take the description of the opening of Mahler's Symphony No. 1: "An unpleasant whistling sound like that emitted by old-fashioned steam engines. A thin curtain, threadbare but densely woven, it hangs from the sky like a pale gray cloud layer." Adorno's books on Gustav Mahler and Alban Berg, written at a time when neither composer had fully entered into the company of the Great Composers, play down their links to tradition; indeed, they stress those aspects of the music that go against the grain of classical tradition, or at least tradition's modern-day aspect.

In the chapter on Mahlerian tone, Adorno describes how a multiplicity of musical languages is absorbed into the composer's individual dialect. Alert to quotations and allusions, he details each element of the general Mahlerian chaos: "His symphonies flaunt shamelessly what rang in all ears, scraps of melody from great music, shallow popular songs, street ballads, hits." He insists that the critic who once charged Mahler with producing "gigantic symphonic potpourris" was right on the mark. The argument culminates in the following passage:

Jacobinically the lower music irrupts into the higher. The complacent gloss of the intermediate form is demolished by the immoderate clamor from the military bandstands and palm court orchestras. . . . The unrisen lower is stirred as yeast into high music. The rude vigor and immediacy of a musical entity that can neither be replaced nor forgotten: the power of naming is often better protected in kitsch and vulgar music than in high music that even before the age of radical construction had sacrificed all that to the principle of stylization. This power is mobilized in Mahler. Free as only one can be who has not himself been entirely swallowed by culture, in his musical vagrancy he picks up the broken glass by the

Discussed in this essay

Berg: Master of the Smallest Link, *Theodor W. Adorno, translated by Juliane Brand and Christopher Hailey, New York: Cambridge University Press*

Mahler: A Musical Physiognomy, Adorno, *translated by Edmund Jephcott, Chicago: University of Chicago Press*

Quasi una Fantasia, *Adorno, translated by Rodney Livingstone, New York: Verso*

Adorno's Aesthetics of Music, *Max Paddison, New York: Cambridge University Press*

Young Mahler:
Gustav Mahler in
Prague, 1911

The Bettman Archive

roadside and holds it up to the sun so that all the colors are refracted.

The translation is awkward, but the force of the thought comes through. Mahler arrays his ragged symphonic army against the dead mass of tradition, against the teeming trivialities of the present, and against a fast-approaching entity identified as "the age of radical construction" —this is, essentially, the dogma of modernism to come. Unformed, untamed things, out of childhood and dreams, march in the vanguard. The symphonist's final sympathy lies with the "social outcast," the solitary voice lost amid the whole.

Mahler was not, ultimately, a radical; his disorder appears within a larger order. The "Tone" chapter ends with a sentence that renders all other writing on the composer superfluous: "Each Mahlerian symphony asks how, from the ruins

of the musical objective world, a living totality can arise." Mahler cast a deep shadow over all composers of the last hundred years because he asked that one tremendous question and then dared to answer it. The "living totality" of his music, personal yet universal, fragmentary yet complete, has found precious few parallels in twentieth-century history. The irony now is that composers have taken to imitating Mahler directly; swooping string lines, ominous marches, and skewy waltz satires have all become familiar devices. But skewy waltzes no longer hold any news, since the waltz is now too rarefied to serve as a popular model. Others have tried to update the Mahlerian project with contemporary popular materials, trying to reconcile a jazz or rock or funk element with pre-existing classical forms. They run the risk of exploitatively appropriating pop genres that have well-developed traditions of their own.

Seeing all of these problems from afar, Adorno paid no serious attention to post-Mahlerian symphonists and allied himself instead with the atonal modernism of the Second Viennese School, which had forsaken Mahler's battleground of the cultural middle and entrenched itself in the new space of the musical avant-garde. Most notably, he spent much ink early in his career defending Arnold Schoenberg, who considered himself Mahler's heir but who was in most ways as un-Mahlerian a composer as could be imagined. When Adorno took an interest in the European avant-garde movement led by Boulez and Stockhausen in later years, he appeared to endorse music that absolved the question of style altogether and replaced it with an aesthetic of pure extremity and difficulty. There was, however, one great exception. He never wavered in his admiration for the music of Alban Berg, who made an obvious and direct extension of Mahler's method. What Adorno hears in Mahler he also hears in Berg: the mining of the past, the elevation of the banal, the arches built across the disparate.

To reach Berg, however, we must first get around the always troublesome figure of Schoenberg, whose link to Adorno (and to anyone else, for that matter) is prone to gross simplification. The oft-repeated epithet identifying Adorno as a "defender of Schoenberg" deserves to be retired. Certainly, Schoenberg played an enormous role in Adorno's musical thought; the mountainous dissonances of post-Mahlerian Viennese modernism (1909–22) definitively illustrated the philosophical imperative of resistance, difficulty, desperate freedom. They fulfilled what Adorno memorably called the "inherent tendency within the musical material"—the continual and irrevocable erosion of the harmonic system that reached its crisis with Mahler. Schoenberg completed the process, and perhaps the task of music itself: "Modern music sees absolute oblivion as its goal. It is the surviving message of despair from the shipwrecked."

Yet a book like *The Philosophy of Modern Music*, for many years the only major musical text by Adorno available in English, shows a profound skepticism about the full sweep of Schoenberg's Ahab-like course. Schoenberg was not only the faithful adherent of a historical process, but also the *victim* of it. Having discovered the unknown plateau of total har-

monic freedom, he became unsure of his footing. The free atonality of *Erwartung*, a direct extension of the Mahlerian late Romanticism of *Pelleas und Melisande*, gave way to the edgy formalism of later twelve-tone works. Eventually, the revolutionary-despite-himself even made a few hesitant retreats to tonal ground, with dodecaphony still dictating his movements. His longing for order brought music onto the shoals of mathematics, and worse yet of invented dogma. Adorno saw in all this the guilty return of burgherly orderliness: the aesthetic criminal called the police on himself. And it could not have happened any other way: "Twelve-tone music is truly the fate of music."

To echo Schoenberg's own critique of John Cage, the composer became a mere inventor. Schoenberg was the better composer and the lesser inventor. The twelve-tone notion led not only to technical disasters, to gray music in empty halls, but to a historical collapse that horribly paralleled the larger cultural tendencies the composers were supposed to resist. Even in 1940, Adorno noted how "progressive" music depended helplessly on support from patrons, foundations, universities, and other clammy institutions; it chained itself to "absolute intellectualization," to a "blind existence." The method itself became a sort of astrological chart for composers lost in the cosmos of the new. A further indignity arrived later in the century: dissonance in new music became a universal cliché in film scores, a monochrome signal of terror and sci-fi strangeness. As Adorno scathingly noted, the Schoenberg who pinpointed the ethereal abstraction of Stefan George's "I feel the air of other

ARNOLD SCHÖNBERG

MIT BEITRAGEN VON ALBAN BERG
PARIS VON GÜTERSLOH · K. HORWITZ
HEINRICH JALOWETZ · W. KANDINSKY
PAUL KÖNIGER · KARL LINKE
ROBERT NEUMANN · ERWIN STEIN
ANT. V. WEBERN · EGON WELLESZ

R. PIPER & CO · MÜNCHEN 1912

ARNOLD SCHÖNBERG
Nach einer Amateur-Aufnahme

planets" in his Second Quartet found himself glossing the piece decades later as a prophecy of space travel.

The Schoenberg case obsessed Adorno because it embodied, in passing phases, the triumph and the failure of the new music. With these later works on Mahler and Berg, it becomes clear that Adorno saw another way through the musical landscape of his time: beside the straight path of historical necessity, Schoenberg's doomed lunge for new sound, there was a more obscure route that went forward sometimes by going back, that registered resistance by subverting stylistic elements already in circulation—"expressing the truly unprecedented with a traditional vocabulary," as Adorno put it in the Mahler book; what he called "music built out of ruins" in an essay on Stravinsky. Only later did he formulate his precise regard for Berg, for several decades considered the regressive and out-of-date member of the Second Viennese School. In the terms of aesthetic value that Adorno developed toward the end of his life, amid the bleak meanderings of the fifties and sixties avant-garde, Berg belatedly arrived as the paragon of twentieth-century modernism.

Berg's musical ruins were organic. They were not the dancing skeletons of neoclassicism, nor the unidentifiable bone-shards collected by Anton Webern, but chunks of musical history transplanted into the modernist organism. Even when he applied the twelve-tone method with some degree of thoroughness, as in the *Lyric Suite* and the unfinished opera *Lulu*, Berg preserved the unrestrained freedom of atonality's initial period. Moreover, he left his textures open to a wide range of sounds and influences. The conductor Jascha Horenstein once remarked that Schoenberg and his circle were all Viennese provincials to the core, with the notable exception of Berg. Suave and remote, exuding a cosmopolitan languor that reminded many observers of Oscar Wilde, Berg took an interest in everything that crossed his path, from Puccini to Sibelius to jazz. He was the first to apply the new Schoenbergian language to extended forms, but in so doing he refused to give up the tonal centers that Schoenberg planned to abolish.

Among the musical values left behind by the previous century, Berg sampled those things that seemed most dated: ambiguous progressions of middle Romantics like Schumann and Liszt, the heaving orchestration of the New German school, Mahler's mournful pulse. The most famous instance is the grand orchestral interlude just before the end of *Wozzeck*, that sudden explosion of plush, semi-Puccinian music that Adorno characterizes as *Der Dichter spricht*, "The Poet Speaks" (a Schumann title). Through this exercise in Romantic nostalgia, which for many decades cost him the support of the avant-garde, Berg performed the most amazing feat of all: holding on to the audience that abandoned Schoenberg and all who followed him. Adorno does not endorse accessibility per se, of course, but he tacitly signals its importance by noting the sensuous, enrapturing, sheerly gorgeous quality of Berg's sound; and perhaps also in highlighting, as with Mahler, his sympathy for the outcast.

The other side of Berg's achievement is his vulnerability to the present, and to the possible future. He faced the challenge of the high-low gulf and incorpo-rated bits of present pop culture into many of his later scores. The practice was, of course, rampant in the twenties; every hip composer of the period sat down to write a wacky jazz piece, an insolent tango, a dissonant foxtrot. But Berg did not merely experiment on the side: ragtime, saxophone jazz, even a miniature film score invade the fabric of his most ambitious composition, the grand opera *Lulu*, in a process that Adorno calls "synthesizing the incompatible, the disparate, and letting them grow together." As with Mahler, the composer is praised rather than exposed for his lapses, his vulgarity, his disjoint eclecticism: "Where Berg verges on kitsch he also approaches the sublime." Such moments appear in desperate relief against a constant and contrary slippage toward extremist dissonance, toward those final, terrible lashings of violence that come sailing in from the avant-garde musical future.

This synthesis of past and future is an immensely complex process, one that partakes of both daring and nostalgia. Adorno isolates the core of the process in Berg's passive personality, his self-dissipating, melancholy, utterly Viennese renunciation of musical ego. Worldly renunciation had, of course, been standard practice in German music and literature since Schopenhauer, Liszt, and Wagner— a self-redemptive tone not free of what Adorno calls "self-glorification." Berg's surrender was not a withdrawal but an engagement with and abandonment to elements from the outside: pop-cultural fragments were damaged and transfigured as they took hold in the other sphere. In contrast to his teacher, Berg never took a polemical tone or put a premium on innovation. Adorno wrote:

Alban Berg
The Bettman Archive

taking in which signs of dialectic doom are discovered in the Dvorak *Humoresque*, Rachmaninoff's Prelude in C-Sharp Minor, Tchaikovsky's Fifth Symphony, and the Mozart sonatina that became a novelty pop hit in the thirties; and "Natural History of the Theater," a spatial sociology of the German opera house in which the rigid class codes and ritualistic gestures of a high-culture mob are neatly skewered. (In the same spirit he elsewhere aimed sharp jibes at Arturo Toscanini, who achieved mass popularity in the 1930s and 1940s with his broadcast performances of the Viennese classics on NBC radio.)

At the heart of *Quasi una Fantasia* is a weird essay in homage to Franz Schreker, the nonradical Viennese composer of heavily scented fin de siècle operatic farragoes, the purveyor of outmoded Wagnerian impressionism. Adorno takes a guiltless pleasure in Schreker's self-conscious decadence and art nouveau style. Even while confessing it as a lingering enthusiasm from his teenage years, he argues an opera like *Der ferne Klang* shows a fabulous richness of orchestral invention, its diaphanous sound becoming an autonomous musical voice. As with Berg, regression and innovation are densely interwoven, hovering in a stylistic neverland—"music that puts down roots in mid-air." And Adorno then delivers another surprising announcement on the subject of the high-low divide, parallel to the "Jacobinic" passage in the Mahler book:

"The question of specific relevance to Berg is how it can be possible for an act of constant yielding, listening, a gesture of gliding, of not asserting himself, to culminate in something like a large-scale form." The best example of this process is the March from the *Three Pieces for Orchestra*, which begins with murmuring and ends in detonation.

Quasi una Fantasia, a late collection of essays lucidly and lyrically translated by Rodney Livingstone, marks the outer limits of Adorno's horizons. It gathers bewitching satiric fragments from early in Adorno's career—"Commodity Music Analyzed," a grimly hilarious under-

The sharp dichotomy between highbrow and lowbrow music has been erected by the administrators of musical culture into a fetish

*which neither side may question. In conse-
quence the guardians of highbrow music are
shy of sounds that have found a home in lowbrow music and might discredit the lucrative
sanctity of the highbrow variety, while the fa-
natical supporters of lowbrow music wax in-
dignant at the mere suggestion that their music could have claims as art.*

A fondness for Schreker led Adorno to
admit the unthinkable—not only that
high culture might have brought itself to
the brink of bankruptcy, but that some
substantial wealth might be hidden on
the other side of the divide. He would
never indicate, of course, what "lowbrow
music" might have "claims as art," but
the ethics of his musical thinking forced
him to allow the possibility.

It is no coincidence that the celebration of the messy, the kitschy, and the
semi-tonal in Mahler, Zemlinsky, Schreker, and Berg came well after each composer had died. Whenever Adorno addressed the living music of his day, armor
snapped in place; his pronouncements
took a cautious, political character, as in
the propagandistic *Philosophy*. Among
contemporary composers he conspicu-
ously endorsed those who appealed to
him first and foremost on an intellectual
level, those whose rhetoric he could
echo with confidence—first Schoenberg, later Stockhausen and Boulez. He
was more wary of praising composers
simply on the basis of visceral identification with their sound. He dismissed out
of hand composers such as Richard
Strauss, Britten, and Shostakovich, each
of whom paralleled or echoed significant
strands of his Mahlerian-Bergian worldview. His views on the subject of Stravin-

sky are a mess of prejudice and paradox,
although the essay in *Quasi una Fantasia*
makes more sense than the Stravinsky
section of the *Philosophy*.

The remarkable, frustrating final essay
of *Quasi una Fantasia* is entitled "Vers
une musique informelle"—"Toward an
Informal Music." It makes gestures of
moving past Schoenbergian pieties, dis-
carding the template of process: "I have
never understood the so-called need for
order. . . . It is illuminating that after the
collapse of the tonal schemata . . . music
should stand in need of organizing powers so as not to lapse into chaos. But the
fear of chaos is excessive, in music as in
social psychology. It results in the same
short-circuiting as is found in the schools
of neo-Classicism and twelve-note technique, which in this respect are not all
that far apart from each other." Postwar
experiments with chance, inaugurated
by John Cage, promise a revolutionary
new state of possibility; but Adorno finds
chance-controlled music to be just as
numbingly systematic as twelve-tone
music, and no more intriguing to the
objective ear. In their place, Adorno
trumpets "informal music," free of a
"false reliance on both an alien necessity and an alien chance." These are stirring words. One leans forward, anticipating parameters of the new sound, or
citations of its use—but the essay (and
the book) comes screeching to a halt.

But we can add something to this in-
complete manifesto if we read between
the lines of *Doktor Faustus*, the story of a
German composer who makes a pact
with the Devil and writes increasingly
difficult music as his nation sinks into
Nazi madness. Despite the simplistic na-

**Alban Berg
with portrait of
Alban Berg by
Arnold Schoenberg**

*Arnold Schoenberg
Archives, Los Angeles*

ture of Mann's scheme, Adorno enthusiastically embraced his role as "musical adviser" to the novel. He not only supplied Mann with background details of the twelve-tone method, which the fictional composer Adrian Leverkühn is said to have invented (Schoenberg threw a tantrum when the novel came out), but he also affected the thematic and stylistic substance of the book. Adorno's voice enters as Mann inserts long quotations from *The Philosophy of Modern Music* into the dialogue between the composer and the Devil; it also colors descriptions of individual works. The rigorously detailed and completely plausible Leverkühn output follows the whole Adornian sweep of modernist musical development, including music that in the late 1940s had yet to be composed.

The most extreme of the Leverkühn works is the *Apocalypse* Oratorio, for which Mann needed "*specific* detail"— "what sort of music," he wrote to Adorno, "would [you] write if you were in league with the devil?" What emerged was a musical fabric incorporating "barbarism" and "bloodless intellectuality," glissandi and volleys of percussion, howling and shrieking choruses that accompany the opening of the seventh seal, "graded whisperings, antiphonal speech," and, most strikingly, an incongruous blend of styles high and low—"a gehanan *gaudium*, sweeping through fifty bars, beginning with the chuckle of a single voice and rapidly gaining ground, embracing choir and orchestra, frightfully swelling in rhythmic upheavals and contrary motions to a *fortissimo tutti*, an overwhelming, sardonically yelling . . ." (It goes on.) This is music that combines elements of the interwar avant-garde, the

postwar avant-garde, and a sort of meta-music that had not even been conceived —and that would only arrive twenty years later, in the music of Bernd Alois Zimmermann, Luciano Berio, William Bolcom, and most especially Alfred Schnittke, for whom the novel has been a direct inspiration.

In his final work, *The Lamentation of Dr. Faustus*, Leverkühn journeys further into "a free language of feeling," a "reconstruction of expressiveness," one final "breakthrough." A parodic element persists in the "grand-ballet music" of Faust's descent into hell, but the piece is dominated by a tone of serene lamentation—"repetitions, . . . the lingering out of syllables, falling intervals, dying-away declamations." It balances bleakness and hope, standstill and hovering redemption; it revokes Beethovenian joy but rediscovers lyric expressivity. The final measures are described as follows: "One group of instruments after another retires, and what remains, as the work fades on the air, is the high G of a cello, the last word, the last fainting sound, slowly dying in a pianissimo fermata . . . but that tone which vibrates in the silence, which is no longer there, to which only the spirit hearkens, and which was the voice of mourning, is no more. It changes its meaning; it abides as a light in the night." This famous passage is, in fact, a paraphrase of Adorno's description of Berg's *Lyric Suite*, written several years before the novel and reprinted in *Master of the Smallest Link*: "One instrument after another falls silent. The viola alone remains, but it is not even allowed to expire, to die. It must play for ever; except that we can no longer hear it."

Leverkühn came to a bad end: "We

point: music emptily talking to itself, shuffling through dead archives of style. But the faintly luminous coda of *Lamentation* represents a second hope, a "hope beyond hopelessness." At a time when all the great composers made gestures of being the last, at a time when an incomprehensible din of commercial art was rising around him, Adorno knew that music would not give in, would play on forever—even if he could not hear it.

. . .

Adorno's best-known work on popular music is the essay "Jazz," contained in the collection *Prisms*. It was one of the first Adorno works to be widely read in English; with the infamous treatment of the "Culture Industry" in the *Dialectic of Enlightenment*, it has shaped contemporary assumptions of what Adorno thought of postclassical culture. It is some of his worst writing, and some of his most uncharacteristic. What is incensing about his treatment of the subject, besides the racist characterizations of jazz players as jungle animals, is his across-the-board dismissal not merely of extant elements in the field but of all imaginable possibilities, whether past, present, or future. He attacks devotees of "pure" jazz for making what he considers a false distinction between commercial and noncommercial varieties of the same commodity product. Jazz is entirely captive of the total system of commodity culture that he attacks on all fronts, whether in Hollywood, television, or glossy print media, as "uniform as a whole and in every part."

But it should be made clear exactly what kind of jazz Adorno was talking about. In his far-ranging study of Ador-

Thomas Mann

The Bettman Archive.
Photo: Roy Bernard Co

saw tears run down his cheeks and fall on the keyboard, wetting it, as he attacked the keys in a strongly dissonant chord. At the same time he opened his mouth as though to sing, but only a wail which will ring for ever in my ears broke from his lips." In Mann's scheme, the composer embodied the degenerative insanity of German politics and aesthetics. But through the very tantalizing realism of the Adornian compositions, the novel becomes less a morality tale of Germany than a parable of the history of music itself. It foresees one possible end-no, *Late Marxism*, Fredric Jameson has summarized the limits of Adorno's popular horizons as follows: "The products of Adorno's Culture Industry must now be identified as standard Hollywood Grade-B genre film (before the latter's reorganization by *auteur* theory), as radio comedy and serials of a thirties and forties variety ("Fibber McGee" and "Molly," for example) and, in music, as Paul Whiteman (the proper referent for what Adorno calls 'jazz' which has little to do with the richness of a Black culture we [*sic*] have only long since then discovered); it has something to do with Toscanini as well . . . and arguably also anticipates the first television programs of the late 1940s (such as Milton Berle)." He concludes: "The 'Culture Industry' is not a theory of culture but the theory of an *industry*, of a branch of the interlocking monopolies of late capitalism that makes money out of what used to be called culture." So Adorno's hostility was directed not so much at a particular kind of music as at its commercial system of distribution, to which both high and low could fall victim.

Similarly, in a lucid new study entitled *Adorno's Aesthetics of Music*, Max Paddison highlights the following passage in Adorno's *Introduction to the Sociology of Music*: "The social function of jazz coincides with its history, the history of a heresy that has been received into the mass culture. Certainly, jazz has the potential of a musical breakout from this culture on the part of those who were either refused admittance to it or annoyed by its mendacity. Time and again, however, jazz became a captive of the culture industry and thus of musical and social conformism. . . ." Paddison observes that this passage "shows Adorno for once applying his own dialectical principles with admirable rigor to a music he clearly dislikes." Far from attacking jazz's African American origins as an instance of quasi-musical barbarism, Adorno was annoyed precisely by the facile appropriation of the "African" by white culture. What he disliked most in popular music was the *illusion* of barbarism, the manufactured whiff of the primitive—the *faux-sauvage* tone he heard as early as Stravinsky's *Rite of Spring*.

How far off was he, in the long view? One need not insult the intelligence of individual consumers to concur that the American lowest-common-denominator process of cultural selection erodes creative individuality. With a sympathetic ear, one can argue further that popular music is a general field of mediocrity in the way that classical music has always been a general field of mediocrity. (For every Beethoven there are a hundred Boccherinis.) Within such fields, to a greater or lesser degree, the passionate protest of convention persists. Adorno did not recognize the resistant note that bebop and free jazz sounded in a complacent postwar culture, but sound it did. Here was music free of constraints, yet monastically severe, an ecstasy of dissonance. Cecil Taylor's coruscating piano is the sound that the classical avant-garde dreams fitfully at night. Read "Vers une musique informelle" in this light, and it becomes an eloquent manifesto for the entire achievement of free jazz. It is worth noting that this art does not subsist merely on a fetishistic pursuit of the new; like Berg, it also partakes of nostalgia, as when the sonorities produced by Taylor's larger ensembles wheel back toward an Elling-

**Theodor Adorno
with mother and
aunt**

*Schillernationalmuseum,
Marburg, Germany*

ton sound, or when David S. Ware rings variations on "Autumn Leaves." In Austria, Franz Koglmann has produced jazz scores that achieve an uncanny synthesis of Anton Webern and swing.

It might also be argued, however provisionally, that certain isolated zones of rock music have practiced the same refusal of the world that Adorno celebrated in new music. "[Adorno's] few analyses of popular music," writes Robert Walser in *Running with the Devil: Power, Gender, and Madness in Heavy Metal Music*, "are so vague, vitriolic, and transparently racist that one wishes he had limited the scope of his analytical attentions even more than he did. So for those working in the area of popular music, the need to recoup that music from Adorno's damning criticism has taken precedence over the possibilities of adapting his methods to other ends." Greil Marcus, in *Lipstick Traces*, daringly specifies those other ends: "Probably no definition of punk can be stretched far enough to enclose Theodor Adorno. As a music lover he hated jazz, likely retched when he heard Elvis Presley, and no doubt would have understood the Sex Pistols as a return to Kristallnacht if he hadn't been lucky enough to die in 1969. But you can find punk between every line of *Minima Moralia*: its miasmic loathing for what Western civilization had made itself by the end of the Second World War was, by 1977, the stuff of a hundred songs and slogans."

This claim is not quite so ridiculous as it might seem on first glance. The various art-school students and college dropouts who headed many of the first punk bands were often familiar with the general cant of the Frankfurt School, if not with Adorno himself. ("The mass

media have homogenized the popular taste in music. . . . There is now a standard sound for all popular music idioms," writes Joe Carducci in an underground-rock manifesto entitled *Rock and the Pop Narcotic*. "There are neither mistakes of execution, nor accidents of tone or tonal harmonics between instrumental voices. Every element is harmonized, chorused and digitally brought to pitch.") Punk was sometimes advertised as a return to rock's roots, but more often it was an insistence on a peculiar or parodic vocabulary of its own devising. One can see what Marcus meant about *Minima Moralia* in a passage such as this:

Progress and barbarism are today so matted together in mass culture that only barbaric asceticism towards the latter, and towards progress in technical means, could restore an unbarbaric condition. No work of art, no thought, has a chance of survival, unless it bear within it repudiation of false riches and high-class production, of color films and television, millionaire's magazines and Toscanini. The older media, not designed for mass-production, take on a new timeliness: that of exemption and of improvisation. They alone could outflank the united front of trusts and technology. In a world where books have long lost all likeness to books, the real book can no longer be one. If the invention of the printing press inaugurated the bourgeois era, the time is at hand for its repeal by the mimeograph, the only fitting, the unobtrusive means of dissemination.

Here, if one squints, one can see a rough map of the world of 1970s and 1980s underground rock, in which music was improvised in suburban garages, cultivated by inquisitive small labels, printed on out-

Young Adorno

Schillernationalmuseum, Marburg, Germany

dated 7-inch singles, and marketed with xeroxed fliers and fanzines, all outside the reach (at least for a few years) of major musical corporations. Whether Adorno would have retched to hear the result is beside the point; he codified a mode of musical resistance that has spontaneously replicated itself through the decades.

Noise, as the enemy of perfectly engineered pop products, has become a last refuge of social protest in music. Political messages in pop lyrics are all too easily manipulated and reversed: witness the myriad nonsubversive uses to which Brecht and Weill's "Mack the Knife" has been put, or the rapid dissipation of sixties radical ideals in the pop counterculture. But the vague, unsettling rawness of punk and postpunk music has never

been completely absorbed, and a few bands have maintained their careers while declining the enticements of commercial production. If many others simply faded from view as the decade of the eighties wore on, the dumb power of noise surfaced in other contexts. "Bring the Noise," Public Enemy enjoined on their second album; rap's thick, discordant, splintered, buzzing texture surfaced from another spontaneous network of independent record labels. The turntable, a technology already well on the way out of fashion, was mobilized for its musical possibilities. Modern styles of rave, dub, and techno exist in a spaced-out, continuous, noise-saturated world beyond the grasp of formal definition. Every decade, *Minima Moralia* finds fresh unconscious fulfillment—however short-lived, however misguided.

All this goes to demonstrate, I think, a certain cryptic youthfulness in Adorno's writing. He has come down to posterity as a curmudgeon, but *Quasi una Fantasia* and other books have an undertow of unforgotten adolescent discontent. No one else would have dared to praise Franz Schreker for his "incorrigible immaturity" or Erik Satie for his "pert and puerile piano pieces," and no one else could have written this epitaph for Berg: "He successfully avoided becoming an adult without remaining infantile." Adorno was never fully adult himself. In a magnificent passage in "Commodity Music Analyzed," some 1930s pop lyrics are quoted—"Hear their two hearts softly beat, / one moment more and their lips will meet. / What a sweet and charming picture, / love in glory, love in bloom, / don't you wish that we were in an eighteenth-century drawing room?"—and then answered: "No." It has the vehemence of a disgruntled teenager running up to his room and slamming the door.

Adorno's punkish, devilish negations are still needlesome to the culture of idiotic savoir-faire. They are the spiky fantasies of an unreconstructed aesthete, imagining "paradigms of a possible music" in Schoenberg and conveying "unheard melodies" through the medium of Mann. The possible went underground as the improbable; Adorno dreamt of what could be, and then explained why not. His possible or ideal music had deep, unbreakable, constraining relations with the past. But this was all of a piece with his peculiar realism, his appraisal of music's outcast status in an unlistening world. His true poetic counterpart was Wallace Stevens's aesthetician of evil, writing paragraphs on the sublime under the shadow of Vesuvius: "Under every no / lay a passion for yes that had never been broken."

OF GENES AND GENITALS

Richard Lewontin

About six years ago a political storm arose in Canada surrounding the person of a professor of psychology who made himself notorious with a theory of racial superiority and inferiority, supported in part by tantalizing data on the length and angle of penises. Indeed, if it were not for their excessive fascination with the phallic, his academic colleagues and the press probably would have ignored J. Phillipe Rushton as just another hitchhiker on the bandwagon of biological determinism. But Professor Rushton, like all successful propagandists, understood his public. It is said that a famous trainer of mules hit his subjects over the head with a two-by-four, because, he explained, the first trick was to get their attention. Professor Rushton found that even a smaller rod would do. Prurient interest aside, the Rushton phenomenon deserves attention as a revealing moment in the historical development of ideological weapons in the war between those who have and those who do not. It makes no sense unless it is seen in that context.

The central social agony of American life for the last two hundred years has been the problem of equality—the motivation for a bloody civil war, urban uprisings, and many of the domestic political structures of the United States and Canada. It is an agony because of the stark contradiction between the ideology of equality that lies at the heart of the legitimating myth of America (indeed of all European society), and the enduring inequalities of status, wealth, and power between individuals and groups. The ideology of *Liberté, Egalité, Fraternité,* of the "self-evident" truth that "all men are created equal, that they are endowed by their Creator with certain unalienable Rights, that among these are the Rights to Life, Liberty and the Pursuit of Happiness," simply does not correspond to the facts of our social existence. It never has.

The solution offered over and over again to this apparent contradiction is that equality was never meant to be equality of status, but only equality of

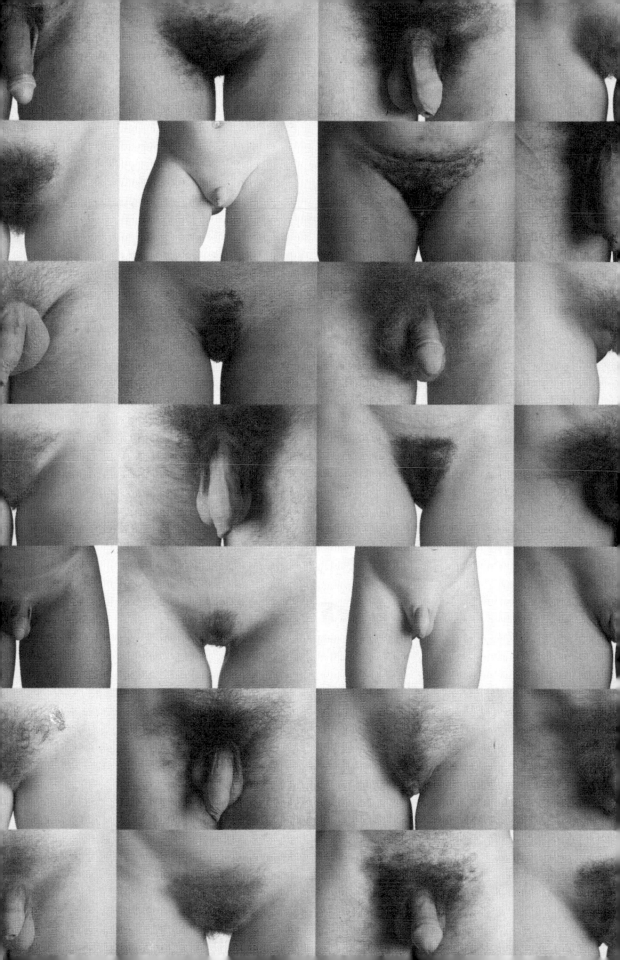

opportunity. Our revolutions, it is said, replaced an unfair, and so unjust, aristocracy with a just meritocracy. Ecclesiastes notwithstanding, the race indeed belongs to the swift, the battle to the strong, bread to the wise, and riches to the man of understanding. Democratic societies have maximized the social entropy, eliminating artificial inequalities and leaving the natural and intrinsic inequalities between individuals, races, sexes, and nations as an ineradicable residue. In vain do we struggle through social programs to decrease the aggressiveness and increase the marital stability and law abidingness of the lesser breeds. People are just doing what comes naturally.

The claim that inequalities of status, wealth, and power between nations and races are a consequence of natural and intrinsic differences in behavior, which, in turn, are the result of different anatomical and physiological properties, has been the dominant explanation offered for the prevailing social structure for the last two centuries. The view that environmental explanations of equality have been the orthodoxy, opposed only by a hardy few objective scholars, is a bit of self-serving propaganda asserted by the supporters of the biologistic claim. It nonetheless enjoys a broad currency. Charles Murray claimed that part of his motivation in writing *The Bell Curve* was to say publicly what everyone he knew believed in private—that blacks were on the average intellectually inferior to whites. Murray's assertion that "environmentalism" has been our intellectual paradigm can only be credited by those with severe generational myopia.

Biologistic explanations of social power and success were the unchallenged con-

Discussed in this essay

Race, Evolution, and Behavior: A Life History Perspective, J. Phillipe Rushton, New Brunswick: Transaction Publishers

sensus of the nineteenth century, not only in zoology, anthropology, and statistics, but in English and French literature from Dickens to Zola. Indeed, Zola's Rougon Macquart novels dramatizing the dominance of inner nature over external circumstance were consciously constructed as what he called "experimental novels" based on the latest findings of criminal anthropology. With the rise of modern genetics after the rediscovery of Mendelism in 1900, geneticists became virtually unanimously biologistic in their explanations of human group and individual differences. Sir Ronald Fisher, a founder of both modern statistics and population genetics, put a genetic gloss on the nineteenth-century biological determinism of Sir Francis Galton, with as little evidence. It was a rare geneticist indeed who would deny the dominance of genes over intellect and temperament.

The Nazis changed all that. During and immediately after the Second World War, as a consequence of the revelations of the German program of genocide based on claims of the biological inferiority of Jews, Gypsies, blacks, gays, and other "degenerate groups," there was a revulsion against theories of intrinsic inferiority. Most theorists of human variation emphasized the historical contingency of the present differences in social power between groups, pointing to the accomplishments of civilizations that had been destroyed by European colonizations. Intellectual and temperamental differences were seen as largely the consequence of different family environments and of the experience of social discrimination. But the revulsion against biological theories of inferiority was of short duration, and by 1967 it was again respectable to claim that the socially disruptive behavior of some groups was anatomical rather than circumstantial in origin. Professors Vernon Mark, William Sweet, and Frank Ervin enlarged on the "Role of Brain Disease in Riots and Urban Violence" in the *Journal of the American Medical Association*, and this explanation led them to the suggestion that the only way to secure social peace was by cutting out some of the offenders' brains!

The memory of Nuremberg had lasted a mere two decades. With the exception of that brief twenty years of dreadful memory, there has been a constant production of works of propaganda and advocacy whose purpose is to justify social inequality as the inevitable consequence of intrinsic inequality of individuals. At their subtlest these take on the appearance of Baconian induction (in which the causes of human inequalities emerge out of collections of objective data, forcing us to a conclusion), or as exercises in Popperian hypothesis-testing (in which we state, purely in a hypothetical mode, some social theory that is then excluded by the brute facts). The most famous exemplar is Arthur Jensen's "refutation" of the hypothesis that equal education makes an equal society. At their most transparent and crude they appear as faintly crackpot compilations of odd bits and pieces of information, all of which support the thesis of biological inequality, rather like a collection of varied stories of contact with space aliens. The most recent example is *Race, Evolution, and Behavior* by J. Phillipe Rushton.

• • •

In 1969 Arthur Jensen's "How Much Can We Boost IQ and Scholastic Achievement?" gave renewed currency to the theory that differences in social and economic power between blacks and whites were ineradicable because they were genetic. Rather than making him an intellectual outcast, his "unorthodox" claim made Jensen a celebrity. He appeared to distance himself from the prewar propagandistic literature of race and class inferiority by using the scientific technical apparatus of quantitative genetics and modern statistics to establish the innate intellectual superiority of whites over blacks. Some older arguments of innate racial superiority were based on doctored evidence and nineteenth-century naïveté about human anatomy and physiology. For example, Harvard's Louis Agassiz claimed that the skull sutures of black babies closed earlier than those of white babies, so that black brains could not expand to accommodate great knowledge. The bulk of the early-twentieth-century literature on mental ability simply documented the better performance of American-born whites of northern European ancestry on the various tests of "intelligence" produced by educational psychologists, taking it as uncontroversial that these differences were innate and unchangeable. Lacking any "scientific" pretensions, this older literature was transparently political, although it was not therefore less convincing to its public. It was essentially a supporting literature, illustrating the consequences of an unchallenged truth.

Jensen's review of the literature on psychological testing appeared to break with that older tradition. Coming in a period when the inherent superiority of Europeans was no longer a public orthodoxy, Jensen's tract had a tougher row to hoe. He could not simply document the poorer social performance of the lower orders, but needed to put the claim of inevitability in a modern, objective, "scientific" frame. Using published studies of IQ test scores that compared biological relatives of varying closeness, including studies of twins raised together and raised apart, he employed the statistical apparatus of quantitative genetics to calculate the *heritability* of IQ performance, a quantity that he estimated as about 80 percent. His argument then flowed smoothly: social success depends upon an intrinsic property of individuals, intelligence; intelligence is measured by IQ test performance; IQ test performance is very highly heritable; what is heritable is not susceptible to change by external circumstances; blacks, on the average, have lower IQ scores than whites;

With Jensen, claims which had previously been entirely works of advocacy and propoganda became scientific claims.

therefore it follows that blacks' lower social and economic status is a natural and unchangeable consequence of their biology. To the rhetorical question posed in the title of Jensen's article, "How Much Can We Boost IQ and Scholastic Achievement?" the answer was unambiguously given, "Not much!"

Jensen's article was specifically commissioned by the *Harvard Educational Review*, and was the longest piece it had ever published. The respect with which it was greeted, even among professional scholars of quantitative genetics and educational psychology, placed his argument at the center of the ideological struggle over equality. A set of critiques in subsequent issues of the *Harvard Educational Review* discussed the adequacy of some of his experimental designs, or disagreed about the appropriate estimators of heritability, or called into question biases in the test instruments. Even Leon Kamin's *The Science and Politics of IQ* (1974), which placed the studies Jensen used firmly in their historical and political frame, and established their intellectual continuity with the older demagogic literature, nevertheless devoted its critical thrust to demonstrating the methodological inadequacy of published heritability studies. Kamin uncovered massive and consistent fraud by the English educational psychologist Sir Cyril Burt, in which data and analyses were simply made up; yet as unsettling to the forces of hereditarianism as this revelation was, it proved not to be fatal to their project. After all, there were all the other data pointing in the same direction, and anyway, new honest and careful studies could always be done. The Social Sciences Research Council put the seal of scientific legitimacy on the question by commissioning what was meant to be a definitive study of race and IQ by a team of unimpeachable psychologists and human geneticists. Their report, *Race Differences in Intelligence*, appearing in 1975, written by the eminently respectable John Loehlin, Gardner Lindzey, and James Spuhler while at the Center For Advanced Studies in the Social Sciences in Palo Alto, provided no definitive answers but established the legitimacy of the problematic: How heritable are IQ differences, and how much freedom does this leave us to create a society founded on equality?

This, then, was the real work of Jensenism: claims about the biological, and therefore unchangeable, differences in status, wealth, and power between races, which had previously been entirely works of advocacy and propaganda, had now become *scientific* claims, to be debated on purely *technical* grounds of statistical adequacy and experimental design. What was previously in the sphere of ideology had moved to the sphere of science. Yet this shift was entirely illusory. Jensen's argument, and those of his epigones like Hans Eysenck and Richard Herrnstein, were entirely consistent with the aprioristic advocacy of their intellectual ancestors, and their claim to scientific legitimacy has given license to a revival of a more patently vulgar literature in the tradition of prewar scientific racialism.

Scientific investigation is set off from propaganda in two ways. First, there is the matter of the canons of evidence. Works of advocacy are generally characterized by a mishmash of anecdotal evidence, large claims about history, "common sense," qualitative judgments, some observational statistics, and a smattering of well-established facts about the natural world, all summoned up to "prove" some a priori assertion about the world. Scientific claims, on the other hand, are supposed to adhere to certain clear demands on evidence, including controlled experiments, independent testing of instruments, unbiased sampling of data, and standard principles of statistical inference. It was on these grounds that Jensen succeeded in assuming the

mantle of science. Kamin's correct and devastating criticisms of the adequacy of the evidence cited by Jensen (even excluding the fraudulent claims of Burt) only demonstrated the rather lax standards of experimental design and analysis that characterize educational psychology and much of human genetics, standards that would make, say, corn breeders snort derisively. While we can demand that these fields as a whole clean up their act, it has to be admitted that the studies of the heritability of IQ performance cited by Jensen fall clearly within the range accepted by the established practitioners. I might not want to accept educational psychology and human behavioral genetics as sciences, but the American Association for the Advancement of Science does.

The second, deeper, demand of works of scientific investigation is that the evidence offered, whatever its quality, must fit into a coherent conceptual framework in such a way that it tests that framework and is in a clear logical relation to the questions being asked about nature. It is in this respect that Jensen and his imitators reveal themselves as pure ideologues who have tried to appropriate the conceptual apparatus of a science but have gotten it all wrong where it counts. They are poseurs.

There are two fundamental errors that pervade modern genetic determinism. First there is the confusion between *heritability* and *changeability*. The question "How Much Can We Boost IQ and Scholastic Achievement?" cannot be answered by asking, "How heritable is IQ?" As explained repeatedly to Jensen, Herrnstein, and their coconspirators, heritability is not the opposite of changeability, and a trait may be 100 percent heritable in a population, yet trivially changeable. It may be discovered that the various anatomical deformations of the eyeballs that lead to myopia, presbyopia and astigmatism are entirely the consequence of genetic differences, but optometrists will still make a living. The equation of the statistical quantity "heritability" with fixity makes use of a long tradition of everyday misunderstanding of the notion of "inherited" characteristics. The only way to find out how much one can boost IQ is to try it. And indeed it has been tried. Despite the high estimates of heritability of IQ performance obtained in the adoption studies cited by Jensen, *those same adoption studies* show that adoption of infants, usually by middle-class parents of babies born to working-class or unemployed parents, produces children whose IQ scores and scholastic achievement is considerably above that of their biological parents and unadopted biological siblings. Thus the demonstration, whether convincing or not, of a high heritability of IQ is simply irrelevant to the question being asked about malleability.

Second, the demonstration, whether convincing or not, of a high heritability of some trait *within* a group (say, among whites) provides no information about the causes of differences *between* groups (say, between whites and blacks). Within-group and between-group differences may have quite different causes, such that all of the variation within a group may be genetic, yet none of the difference between groups; and, conversely, all of the variation within a group may be environmental, yet the differences between

groups may be entirely genetic. On this score as well, then, information about heritability of IQ within white populations or within black populations reveals nothing about the causes of racial inequality in status, wealth, and power. If one wants to know whether the swarthy can have cultural, political, and economic hegemony over the pale, one need only consult the history of Europe for the half millennium following the Hegira.

• • •

The conceptual incoherence of Jensen and his imitators is the unambiguous sign of their status as propagandists rather than investigators. By a massive emission of statistically analyzed data they succeeded in sending their pursuers off on a false scent, distracting attention from their conceptual confusions and, more important, giving renewed life and respectability to a literature of advocacy in a more vulgar and transparent form.

Every scientist whose name has appeared outside the academy has received more than one ten-page manifesto from someone with a heterodox vision of the truth. Such writings are usually distinguished by a familiarity with the vocabulary of some recent scientific development, but, in a kind of secular glossolalia, the words spill out in an unrecognizable logic, making syntactical but not semantic sense. The authors know how to play all the notes, but they can't get the tune right. By combining a semblance of theory with a heterogeneous assemblage of supporting "data," they become, in their own eyes, the reincarnation of Charles Darwin. When produced by a lonely paranoid-schizophrenic bent over his word processor, this is a harmless exercise that elicits some sympathy as it slides into the wastebasket. When it is created by a professor of psychology at a respectable academic institution—a former Guggenheim fellow with access to publishers—and sports dust jacket blurbs from most of the determinist establishment (Arthur Jensen, Hans Eysenck, Thomas Bouchard, Richard Lynn, and Michael Levin), it cannot be ignored.

Race, Evolution, and Behavior is a classic of its genre. It takes a trendy theoretical construct that can be used to organize population data, reifying it and universalizing it beyond its original scope. It then completely misconstrues the theory, turning it on its head so that, by using the wrong explanatory variable, it makes exactly the opposite prediction from what the theory intends. It then compiles an immense and heterogeneous collection of claims, conjectures, data of varying degrees of reliability, and unsubstantiated guesses characterized as "estimates," all of which are supposed to provide overwhelming evidence for the erroneously constructed theory. This entire apparatus is, of course, in the service of an argument with powerful political and social implications.

The theory Rushton misappropriates is the *r-K* selection theory of Robert MacArthur and Edward O. Wilson, as set out in *The Theory of Island Biogeography* (1967). Mendelian genetics provides a simple set of guidelines that give rise to exact specifications of the changes that will occur in the genetic constitution of populations as a result of various evolutionary forces. Evolutionary genetics is

thus an exact science in its theoretical formulations, although there are more or less serious problems in measuring the parameters of the theory in natural populations.

In contrast, there are no simple mechanical rules for the growth in size of populations. Beyond saying that in sexual populations it takes two to tango, and that there must be some (unknown) limit to the amount of living flesh that can exist at any time, there are no universal regularities in demography. As a result, there is no set of lawlike mathematical formulations for the growth of population size. Instead, population ecology and demography have created formulations that are intended to be the simplest mathematical *forms* that can describe the fact that organisms give birth to other organisms and that populations do not grow infinite in size. There is no

We are not offered any data on the relation between penis size, testis size, and fertility, the author depending only on the adolescent fantasy that being well hung means greater virility

commitment to the biological reality of these formulations. The simplest equation that can be produced for the rate of change per unit time of population numbers can take several mathematically equivalent forms with arbitrary parameters, and one of these, the so-called "logistic growth equation," has two parameters, r and K. These can be interpreted respectively as the rate of growth of the population when there is no limit to available resources (r), the so-called "intrinsic rate of natural increase," and the maximum size to which the population can grow in a given resource situation (K), the so-called "carrying capacity" of the environment for that kind of organism. Neither the equation nor the names of the parameters in it should be reified, giving them some underlying independent causal efficacy. Exactly the same growth relation can be written in an equivalent mathematical form with parameters that appear in a different way and that cannot be given the same metaphorical interpretation.

MacArthur and Wilson reasoned that in different sorts of externally imposed regimes, different patterns of reproduction would be favored by natural selection. If resources fluctuated in an uncertain way from time to time, so that there were years of feast and years of famine, then genetic types that could take immediate advantage of the good years by having a high reproductive rate when resources were plentiful (high r) would increase in frequency in the population. If, in contrast, resources were predictably constant (whether abundant or not) from reproductive period to reproductive period, then genetic types that could maintain the largest numbers under that constant resource level (high K) would be favored by natural selection. It is easy enough to distinguish species that lay very large numbers of eggs with short development times from species that produce only a few slowly developing offspring that require considerable expenditure of parental energy for their care. One can *call* these "r-maximizing" species and "K-maximizing species," but no one has ever suggested how we would go about reconstructing the environments in which they evolved and whether these differences in reproductive patterns were really selected as responses to environmental stability. After all, the North Atlantic is home both to the codfish, which lays huge numbers of eggs and leaves them to chance, and the eelpout, which is viviparous and broods its few young within its own body cavity. Organizing metaphors should not be confused with scientific fact.

Rushton has taken r-K selection theory to explain differences that he says characterize different major races. The first problem for his theory is that there need to be major races. That is, the differences between "Oriental," "Black," and "White" need to be more than skin deep. In claiming that these old racial categories correspond to large biological differences, Rushton moves in the opposite direction from the entire development of physical anthropology and human genetics for the last thirty years. Anthropologists no longer regard "race" as a useful concept in understanding human evolution and variation. There has been, as a consequence of worldwide sampling, an immense accumulation of data on the differences in frequencies of different allelic forms of human genes within and between geographical populations. There is now no question that the major geographical groups, distinguishable by skin color and hair form, differ in virtually no other respect genetically. Of the total human genetic variation, about 85 percent is within any local population, another 7–8 percent is between local nationalities or tribes within major "races," and the remaining 7–8 percent of frequency variation lies between these major "races." We know of no single case where one "race" has a set of allelic forms of a gene that do not overlap with those of other "races." There are no known "race-differentiating" genes, with the exception of the (as yet genetically unmapped) genes that distinguish the range of African skin colors from the range of Asian or European skin colors. There is also a different col-

Rushton really wants to argue that Africans are genetically dumber, less prudent, and sexier, because living in the tropics is less demanding and leaves more leisure time for screwing.

lection of heritable statures and body conformations in the different geographical regions, but variations between local groups—between Swedes and Greeks, or between Watutsi and Batwa—make any attempt to characterize major geographical groups as a whole hopeless. "Race" is simply not a category that biologists and anthropologists still take seriously, although as a social phenomenon race still has a compelling reality. While providing his own capsule history of older ideas of biological race in chapter 5, Rushton is curiously reticent about the current status of the concept.

Having finessed the problem of whether race is a useful biological distinction, Rushton is now free to use r-K theory to explain the origin of claimed typological differences between races. According to him, while all humans are at the K end of the spectrum, "Orientals" were more K selected than "Whites,"

who in turn were more K selected than "Blacks." This, he says, is a consequence of the history of human migrations out of the original species home in Africa 100,000 years ago. First came the Caucasians, who left the comparatively soft life of tropical Africa to occupy the harsher climate of temperate Europe, and so were more K selected. The "Orientals" then split off from the "Whites" to occupy the frozen wastes of Siberia, and so were even more K selected. The manifestations of this K selection were bigger brains, smaller genitals, and a middle-class temperament. True to form, Rushton has got the theory upside down. First, r-K selection theory is about the temporal *predictability* of a resource, not its abundance. So the question is not whether goodies were harder to come by in the frozen wastes, but whether their season-to-season and year-to-year abundance was more or less *constant*. Second, since temperate continental environments are more variable than tropical environments, both from season to season and from year to year, we would predict that the "Orientals" and "Whites" would be *less* K selected, not more. It is the Asians and Europeans who need to make hay while the sun shines. In his desire to align himself with a trendy biological theory, Rushton has confused it with the argument he really wants to make—namely that Africans are genetically dumber, less prudent, and sexier, because living in the tropics is less demanding and leaves more leisure time for screwing. "Because groups migrating out of Africa into the colder climate of Eurasia encountered more challenging environments, including the last ice age, which ended just 12,000 years ago, they

From Race, Evolution, and Behavior, by J. Philippe Rushton.

TABLE 1.1
Relative Ranking of Races on Diverse Variables

Variable	Orientals	Whites	Blacks
Brain size			
Autopsy data (cm^3 equivalents)	1,351	1,356	1,223
Endocranial volume (cm^3)	1,415	1,362	1,268
External head measures (cm^3)	1,356	1,329	1,294
Cortical neurons (billions)	13.767	13.665	13.185
Intelligence			
IQ test scores	106	100	85
Decision times	Faster	Intermediate	Slower
Cultural achievements	Higher	Higher	Lower
Maturation rate			
Gestation time	?	Intermediate	Earlier
Skeletal development	Later	Intermediate	Earlier
Motor development	Later	Intermediate	Earlier
Dental development	Later	Intermediate	Earlier
Age of first intercourse	Later	Intermediate	Earlier
Age of first pregnancy	Later	Intermediate	Earlier
Life span	Longer	Intermediate	Shorter
Personality			
Activity level	Lower	Intermediate	Higher
Aggressiveness	Lower	Intermediate	Higher
Cautiousness	Higher	Intermediate	Lower
Dominance	Lower	Intermediate	Higher
Impulsivity	Lower	Intermediate	Higher
Self-concept	Lower	Intermediate	Higher
Sociability	Lower	Intermediate	Higher
Social organization			
Marital stability	Higher	Intermediate	Lower
Law abidingness	Higher	Intermediate	Lower
Mental health	Higher	Intermediate	Lower
Administrative capacity	Higher	Higher	Lower
Reproductive effort			
Two-egg twinning (per 1,000 births)	4	8	16
Hormone levels	Lower	Intermediate	Higher
Size of genitalia	Smaller	Intermediate	Larger
Secondary sex characteristics	Smaller	Intermediate	Larger
Intercourse frequencies	Lower	Intermediate	Higher
Permissive attitudes	Lower	Intermediate	Higher
Sexually transmitted diseases	Lower	Intermediate	Higher

were more stringently selected for intelligence, forward planning, sexual and personal restraint, and a *K*-parenting strategy." Stripped of the demographic sleight of hand, this is pretty old-fashioned stuff. The theoretical part of Rushton's tract seems to serve the purpose of legitimizing the rest, to provide an excuse for pouring out a mass of "data" that show that blacks are biologically inferior in every sense that civilized people care about. It is the "facts" that do the work. The theory is window dressing, so perhaps it doesn't matter so much whether he gets it right.

The "facts" that Rushton wants to validate are summarized at the very beginning (his Table 1.1) and consist of the "Relative Ranking of Races on Diverse Variables." The variables include brain size, intelligence, physical maturation rates (including age of first intercourse and pregnancy), personality traits like aggressiveness, impulsivity, and sociability, social traits like law abidingness and administrative capacity, and, of course, size of genitalia. "Orientals," "Whites," and "Blacks" are characterized as "higher" ("larger"), "lower" ("smaller"), or "intermediate." Close inspection reveals that "Blacks" are at the uncivilized and oversexed end of the scale for every trait, without exception, while "Orientals" are uniformly the most desirable, with Europeans intermediate in every case. Sometimes the results of survey data seem to disagree with the big picture, as when "Tanfer and Cubbins (1992) found that twenty- to twenty-nine-year old single black women cohabiting with a sexual partner reported only 4.3 occasions of intercourse in the previous four weeks as compared with 6.9 among co-

habiting white women." Once a week? So much for the oversexed black male! But never fear, the exception proves the rule. "The authors suggest that these black women's partners had other sexual partners as well and were less available than white women's partners. Another possible reason was that more of the black sample were pregnant."

The literature from which this extraordinary summary table is derived is, as might be expected, an undifferentiated collection of sample surveys and back-of-the-envelope calculations, and Rushton makes no attempt to judge their adequacy or reliability. So Table 6.6, which gives the data for brain size, includes an 1865 measurement of "5 Negro men," an 1874 study of "10 Japanese men executed by decapitation," a 1911 sample of an "unspecified number of men and women (probably Russian) aged 20 to 80 years," up to Rushton's own 1994 compilation of twenty-eight "world samples" comprising "tens of thousands of individuals." But they all tell the same story. Using a guess that the human brain has about 100 billion neural cells, and supposing, just for fun, that "there may be 100,000 billion synapses," then based on cranial measurements, "hundreds of millions of cerebral cortex neurons differentiate Mongoloids from Negroids" which are "probably sufficient to underlie the proportionate achievements in intelligence and social organization." We are not told what formula is used to calculate this proportionality, or what scientific theory allows us to predict intelligence from brain size. Why is it, for example, that although women have absolutely smaller brain sizes than men on the average—more than the difference

From Race, Evolution,
and Behavior,
by J. Philippe Rushton.

TABLE 4.3
Heritability Estimates and Similarity Between Friends on Conservatism Items
(N = 76)

Item	Heritability estimate	Friendship similarity score	Test-retest reliability	Similarity score corected for unreliability	Similarity score corrected for age, education, and occupation
1. Death penalty	.51	.28	.87	.30	.38
2. Evolution theory	–	.08	.95	.08	.20
3. School uniforms	–	.20	.99	.20	.42
4. Striptease shows	–	.13	.97	.13	.24
5. Sabbath observance	.35	.08	.91	.08	.09
6. Hippies	.27	.03	.97	.03	.15
7. Patriotism	–	.10	.89	.11	.13
8. Modern art	–	.02	.93	.02	.09
9. Self-denial	.28	.08	.79	.09	.12
10. Working mothers	.36	.07	.83	.08	.13
11. Horoscopes	–	.23	.92	.24	.20
12. Birth control	–	.04	-.01	.00	.19
13. Military drill	.40	.10	.96	.10	.22
14. Coeducation	.07	-.05	.74	-.06	-.05
15. Divine law	.22	.25	.82	.28	.20
16. Socialism	.26	.08	.83	.09	.14
17. White superiority	.40	.22	.68	.27	.11
18. Cousin marriage	.35	.04	.89	.04	.24
19. Moral training	.29	.07	.77	.08	.16
20. Suicide	–	.08	.86	.09	.08
21. Chaperones	–	.00	.94	.00	.11
22. Legalized abortion	.32	.13	.96	.13	.29
23. Empire building	–	.02	.85	.02	.05
24. Student pranks	.30	-.02	.88	-.02	.07
25. Licensing law	–	-.20	.85	-.22	-.13
26. Computer music	.26	.02	.91	.02	.16
27. Chastity	–	.00	.76	.00	.13
28. Fluoridation	.34	.08	.86	.09	.04
29. Royalty	.44	.15	.92	.16	.16
30. Women judges	.27	.03	1.00	.03	.08
31. Conventional clothes	.35	.31	.83	.34	.29
32. Teenage drivers	.26	.02	.78	.02	.20
33. Apartheid	.43	.14	.69	.17	.10
34. Nudist camps	.28	.08	.85	.09	-.09
35. Church authority	.29	.08	.86	.09	.21
36. Disarmament	.38	.07	.96	.07	.19
37. Censorship	.41	.03	.81	.03	.10
38. White lies	.35	.06	.76	.07	-.01
39. Caning	.21	.14	.83	.15	.11
40. Mixed marriage	.33	.25	.79	.28	.29
41. Strict rules	.31	.25	.81	.28	.19
42. Jazz	.45	.42	.77	.48	.40
43. Straitjackets	.09	.00	.85	.00	.00
44. Casual living	.29	.18	.63	.23	.55
45. Learning Latin	.26	.03	.97	.03	.10
46. Divorce	.40	.03	.92	.03	.09
47. Inborn conscience	–	.20	.70	.24	-.11
48. Colored immigration	–	.06	.88	.06	.10
49. Bible truth	.25	.30	.95	.31	.47
50. Pajama parties	.08	.08	.91	.08	.24

between racial groups—they neverthe-less do just as well as men on IQ tests?

Like all biological determinists, Rushton is impelled to show that the characteristics he cares about are *genetically* different between groups. He shares with Jensen the error of supposing that heritability of variation within groups tells him something about the causes of the differences between groups, but he makes an error of taste that Jensen would never make, and so brings the whole crackpot enterprise down. In a fit of silliness, Rushton tries to convince his reader that *everything* is heritable in some nontrivial sense, and that the numerically low heritabilities of each socially constructed attribute are collective evidence of an important genetic difference between "races." We learn, for example, from a sample of seventy-six pairs of friends surveyed by Rushton, that the heritabilities of attitudes toward the death penalty, jazz, the royal family, apartheid, censorship, military service, white superiority, and divorce are all between 40 percent and 50 percent, while much lower heritabilities were found for attitudes toward caning, nudist camps, and pajama parties. He was, curiously, unable to calculate the heritabilities for opinions on evolution, modern art, and striptease shows. The probability of serving in Vietnam had a heritability of 35 percent.

In the absence of any direct evidence on the causes of variation among individuals and groups, one can always ask the opinions of people who are supposed to be knowledgeable. So we learn that of 661 scientists in relevant disciplines who were surveyed, 94 percent thought there was a significant genetic component for variation in intelligence

Figure 1.1: Galton's (1869) Classification of English and African Mental Ability

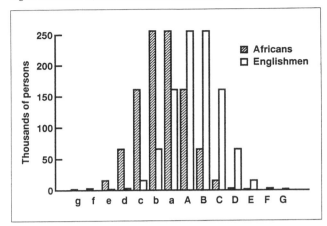

From Race, Evolution, and Behavior, *by J. Philippe Rushton.*

among individuals, with a mean intuition of heritability equal to 60 percent, and 52 percent thought that a part of the black-white difference was genetic. (No estimate for the heritability of this difference was offered.) "The case for genetic determination is even more strongly felt for socioeconomic status differences."

Sometimes what look like quantitative results are, in fact, made up out of someone's head. Rushton makes a considerable point of claiming Francis Galton, the nineteenth-century theoretician of statistics, heredity, and the superiority of Anglo-Saxons, as his intellectual ancestor. To illustrate Galton's statistical insights into variation in human intelligence he presents a frequency histogram of the proportion of all persons falling in various intelligence grades, showing that the distribution of grades for "Englishmen" has the same shape as that for "Africans," except that the African distribution is shifted three grades downward. This figure is based on "estimates given by Galton" (1869) and "on his opinion," but the figure, despite its quantitative look, is wholly the product of the combined imaginations of Rushton and Galton, since IQ testing (and educational psychology) had not yet been invented.

Finally, like all works of its genre, *Race, Evolution, and Behavior* has a hard time distinguishing between speculations and proven causal relations. At one point, Rushton admits that what he is describing is "the *possible* family life and social organization of *Homo*" (my emphasis), but then slips into a forwardly assertive mode, assuring the reader that "competition leads to enlarged penises and testes to make deeper and more voluminous ejaculations possible." We are not offered any data on the relation between penis size, testis size, and fertility, the author depending only on the adolescent fantasy that being well hung means greater virility. Rushton also tells us that "brain size, even more than body size, is the key factor, acting as the biological constant determining many variables." How he knows that brain size determines other variables biologically is not revealed. What he really wants to say is that he thinks "Orientals" and Europeans are smarter and better behaved than blacks, and that he wants us to believe, as he does, that the other differences that he claims exist between "races" are a consequence.

Race, Evolution, and Behavior exhibits all the characteristics of classic prewar racist tracts like Madison Grant's *The Passing of the Great Race*, but it differs in one interesting particular. It does not claim that Europeans are the highest stage of humanity. Rather, they are in the middle, second to "Orientals" but superior to Africans. This is a masterstroke; on this basis Rushton can claim not to be racist, at least not generally. He defines racism as "hatred or intolerance of an-

other race. The treatment of all members of another race as though they were all the same, usually in order to do them harm." But he has declared no hatred of other races, nor can we catch him out trying to do them harm. He is just an objective observer, *describing* the differences between races and providing a theory of how they got that way. There is no value attached to being smarter, more temperate, less inclined to criminality, more prudent, less promiscuous. His lack of racism is proven by the fact that he does not describe his own race as superior to all others. It is clear what Rushton's advocacy position gains from positing the superiority of the Asians. But what is he forced to give up? Not much.

It is here that we must confront the relations between race and class and the effect of the hegemony of European culture on the history of racism. In the nineteenth century, North American anti-Asian racism was as strong as antiblack. Asian immigration, mainly Chinese, was pronounced in the decades after the Civil War, and they were considered the lowest form of unskilled labor. Asians were felt to be dirty, devious, and degenerate, both in Canada and the United States. The sexual overtones of that racism can be seen in the film versions of Sax Rohmer's *Fu Manchu* stories, when the evil Oriental doctor holds the unconscious body of a beautiful English girl before a crowd of drug-crazed Chinese, exclaiming, "You'd all like to have one of these for your very own, wouldn't you?"

Meiji, MacArthur, and Mao Tse-Tung changed all that. The appropriation of European culture and the accumulation of great resources of finance and industrial capital by the Japanese and by refugees from the Chinese revolution in Taiwan, Hong Kong, the United States, and Canada have created a trans-racial upper-middle and upper class, whose class position trivializes petty differences in skin and hair in the eyes of most Americans. It is still possible that in places like California the immense success of Asians as students and in the professions, and the weight of their numbers, will make Europeans regret their own constant trumpeting of the meritocratic ideal. But for now, class remains anterior to race in white Americans' perceptions of Asians.

The predominant white vision of blacks, on the contrary, is of a class of unskilled workers or, more frequently, of an unemployed lumpenproletariat, threatening, inassimilable, excluded from both production and consumption, whose very existence is to be wished away.

The current situation of Europeans, Asians, and Africans in North America is the best demonstration that one can have that race is a proxy for class. The existence of large numbers of economically and socially marginalized people has been, and will remain, a necessary feature of the economic and political system to which we are bound. Biologizing the marginality of peasants and factory workers allowed Europeans to live with the ideological contradiction between the myth of equality and the realities of class power. But Americans added a more intuitively appealing element to the nineteenth-century belief in blood, namely race—a legacy of the North American history of conquest, slavery, and immigration. By loading marginality onto particular physically and historically distinguishable groups, it becomes far easier to biologize inequality both in theory and in practice. Given the perception of obvious physical differentiation coupled with a history of domination, nothing could be easier than to spin out a theory of the inherent inferiority of some that does not seem to contradict the promise of a good life for all. At the same time, economic and social discrimination becomes far simpler when an ineradicable physical difference can be used to mark out the oppressed; superficial anatomical differences are fetishized, taking on a life of their own. As "race" becomes real, endowed with causal efficacy in producing the structure of society, so too is *racism* made into an aspect of "human nature," an innate xenophobia that is claimed, as in E. O. Wilson's *Sociobiology*, to be coded in our genes, a consequence of our evolution.

The demand to abolish the illusion of race is a demand to abolish the conditions that require illusion.

MONGREL AMERICA

The multicultural malaise

Michael Lind

One of the most striking developments in recent American intellectual and political life is the critical reevaluation, by liberal and left thinkers, of the multicultural enterprise that dominated left-of-center discourse in the 1980s. In part this reflects the success of conservatives in turning multiculturalism and racial preferences into weapons in the arsenal of Republican "culture-war" politics. But there is more to the reconsideration of multiculturalism than electoral strategy. After a generation in which various racial, ethnic, and sexual particularisms have tended to triumph, in the American academy if not in American politics, over an older liberal humanism with universalist aspirations, the philosophical inconsistencies and illiberal tendencies of the multicultural project have become increasingly evident.

David A. Hollinger's *Postethnic America* is a lucid, insightful, and important contribution to what may prove to be the central debate of the 1990s. Hollinger, who teaches history at the epicenter of the culture wars at the University of California at Berkeley, seeks to answer the question: "Does the United States have an ethnos of its own, or is the nation best seen as a container of cultures defined largely by ethno-racial communities?" Hollinger's answer to the question of whether the United States is a nation-state is a qualified but definite yes.

Before arriving at this conclusion, Hollinger takes the reader through a thoughtful if frequently abstract discussion of contemporary American approaches to race and culture. He has coined the memorable term "ethno-racial pentagon" for the current five-group classification system formalized by the Office of Management and Budget's Statistical Directive 15 in 1977: "On application forms and questionnaires, individuals are routinely invited to declare themselves to be one of the following: Euro-American (or sometimes white), Asian American, African American, Hispanic (or sometimes Latino), and In-

digenous Peoples (or sometimes Native American)." The ethno-racial pentagon, Hollinger suggests, "might also be called a 'quintuple melting pot,' replacing the 'triple melting pot' made famous by Will Herberg's book of 1955, *Protestant-Catholic-Jew.*"

Nietzsche once cynically suggested that democracy gives one a choice of conforming to one of several official orthodoxies, rather than merely one. A similar remark might be made about the five-race theory of the American people. By assimilating diverse white Americans to a single category, Hollinger observes, the pentagon "has symbolically erased much of the cultural diversity within the Euro-American bloc." Similarly, the five-race scheme lumps together "Americans whose ancestors were Koreans, Cambodians, Chinese, Vietnamese, and Japanese

Nietzsche once cynically suggested that democracy gives one a choice of conforming to one of several official orthodoxies rather than merely one. A similar remark might be made about the five-race theory of the American people

by calling them all Asian Americans" and shoehorns immigrants and descendants of immigrants from "Argentina, Cuba, El Salvador, Mexico and Puerto Rico" into the Hispanic or Latino category.

Hollinger notes the irony of left-liberal enthusiasm for redefining America on the basis of slightly updated versions of old white-supremacist categories: "The blocs of the pentagon, whatever

their shifting labels, have come to replicate the popular color-consciousness of the past: black, white, red, yellow, and brown." Hollinger also suggests that the attention to minority history motivated by multiculturalism may inevitably undermine the five-bloc schema with which multiculturalism is now identified: "The more these differences [between groups] have come to be recognized, the more difficult it has become to convincingly represent American society in classically pluralist fashion as an expanse of internally homogeneous and analogically structured units, each authorized by an ancestral charter and each possessed of a singular mythology of diaspora. The historical experiences of African Americans, Mexican Americans, Korean Americans, and Norwegian Americans do not fit the same abstract model."

How have Americans come to classify one another by this dubious scheme? Those seeking a detailed history of the evolution of American racial ideologies and classifications will not find one here. Hollinger's discussion of history is limited to changes in fashion within the relatively small community of American left-liberal intellectuals in the twentieth century. Hollinger writes that by the early 1970s the universalism or "species-consciousness" of midcentury American intellectuals had given way to "a newer ethnic-consciousness." The result, in intellectual life and in politics, has been "a collectivization of the subjective" of the sort associated with the group-centered perspectives of multiculturalism.

Hollinger notes that the term *multiculturalism* itself conceals "a variety of persuasions and counterpersuasions." In

particular, contemporary multicultural-ism—like early-twentieth-century cul-tural pluralism—comprises two tenden-cies or schools of thought, "pluralism" and "cosmopolitanism." Hollinger ex-plains the difference thus: "While cos-mopolitanism is willing to put the future of every culture at risk through the sym-

Nativism and liberal nationalism have been far more important in shaping American society than multi-culturalism or cultural pluralism

pathetic but critical scrutiny of other cultures, pluralism is more concerned to protect and perpetuate particular, exist-ing cultures." The tension is embodied in the two patron saints of American cul-tural pluralism in the World War I era, Horace Kallen and Randolph Bourne. Kallen's "celebration of group differ-ences" placed him at the pluralist end of the cultural pluralist-multiculturalist spectrum, while Bourne, Kallen's ally against Anglo-Protestant nativism, "em-phasized the dynamic mixing that would change the immigrants as well as the de-scendants of the Pilgrims and the Found-ing Fathers." Having made this distinc-tion, though, Hollinger undermines it by suggesting that sometimes "Bourne spoke in a pluralist rather than a cosmopolitan mode, endorsing the integrity of immi-grant cultures and lamenting their dilu-tion in the mass of American society." Though Hollinger does not, an unfriend-ly critic might conclude that this shows that Kallen at least was a consistent think-er, and Bourne confused.

Whether Kallen and Bourne were as important as their prominence in cen-

ter-left discussions of American identity would suggest may be doubted—as Hollinger admits. "Cultural pluralism," Hollinger writes, "had been a minor movement in the history of the Ameri-can academic and literary intelligentsia. By contrast, multiculturalism has proved to be a major preoccupation in Ameri-can life as registered in the deliberations of local school boards and in the profes-sional journals of the humanities and so-cial sciences." But Hollinger's account of the history of controversies over Amer-ican identity tends to reduce it to de-bates among professors. At times the pa-rade of thinkers largely unknown even inside the academy—literary theorist Tobin Siebers, historian Linda Kerber, legal scholar Bruce Ackerman, political philosopher Jeremy Waldron—baffles the lay reader.

Outside the academy, racial-religious nativism and melting-pot liberal nation-alism have been far more important in shaping American society than multi-culturalism or cultural pluralism. It is un-derstandable that a left-of-center intel-lectual like Hollinger would refrain from discussing nativism, except as a threaten-ing constituency "made up of a great va-riety of Middle Americans, evangelical Christians, advocates of family values, and supporters of Newt Gingrich and of Rush Limbaugh." He spends too little time, however, on the melting pot ideal he identifies with J. Hector St. John de Crevecoeur, Ralph Waldo Emerson, Herman Melville, and Israel Zangwill (Frederick Douglass and Jean Toomer are not mentioned), with its emphasis on "the diversity not of the final product but only of the materials going into it." This is all the more puzzling, because

*Winold Reiss
(German, 1886-1953).
Portrait of the Artist's
Son in New York
(W. Tjark Reiss).
1938. Pastel on board.
Mr. and Mrs. W. Tjark
Reiss.*

Hollinger's conception of a "postethnic" America would seem to be more in the melting-pot tradition than in the cultural pluralist and cosmopolitan traditions upon which he bestows so much respect and attention.

Hollinger joins other left-liberal revisionist critics of multiculturalism in suggesting that "the value of civic nation-states in protecting rights and protecting basic welfare is undervalued by proponents of postnationality." According to Hollinger, the "American nation-state is being pulled in different directions by three formidable constituencies." These are a globalist "business elite," groups of "diasporas" that view "the United States more as a site for transnational affiliations than as an affiliation of its own," and a conservative nationalist constituency devoted to a white Christian America. He defends "the notion of a national culture as an adhesive enabling diverse Americans to see themselves as sufficiently 'in it together' to act on problems that are genuinely common."

Hollinger accepts the contrast between "ethnic" and "civic" nations, but he incorporates—one might almost say

When it comes to the most important questions of social life, one's identity as "an American" trumps all the rest

smuggles—cultural nationalism, if only of a benign and inclusive sort, into his definition of civic nationalism: "Insofar as there is an ideal nation from a postethnic point of view, it is a democratic state defined by a civic principle of nationality in the hands of an ethno-racially diverse population and possessed of a na-

tional ethos of its own. This last element —a national culture—is too often belittled . . . but without it the promise of postethnic nationality can be too easily swept aside by the forces of transnational capitalism and ethno-racial particularism." Hollinger argues that "it would be a mistake to conflate America's version of the battle between the ethnic and the civic nation with the versions of this battle now being fought in Kurdistan, Bosnia, and most of the other parts of the world that generate today's headlines about nationalism." The United States, he suggests, "has maintained a greater measure of cultural particularity of its own . . . than have most of the other, comparable entities."

All of this makes Hollinger sound very much like a liberal nationalist. So, too, does his insistence that many of the most important social reforms in the United States—the Civil Rights Revolution, the welfare state—have been justified by American nationalism: "The appeal to a common destiny—to a sense that we, as Americans, are all in it together—has been a vital element in the mobilization of state power on behalf of a number of worthy causes." Hollinger harshly criticizes thinkers on the left for whom "the question of the national culture has become a popular search-and-destroy sport." He quotes former Modern Language Association president Barbara Herrnstein's sneering dismissal of the idea of a common American culture: "Wild applause; fireworks; music— *America the Beautiful*; all together, now; *Calvin Coolidge, Gunga Din, Peter Pan, spontaneous combustion.* Hurrah for America and the national culture! Hurrah!" Hollinger observes:

WINOL
REIZ

It is doubtful that Smith would similarly parody the educational programs associated with Black History Month, where basic facts about the accomplishments of African Americans are made accessible. Were she to do so, it might sound like this:

Wild applause; fireworks; music—We Shall Overcome; all together, now: Father Divine, Ralph Bunche, Chicago Blues, the NAACP, double consciousness. Hurrah, hurrah, for the African American culture! Hurrah!

"If people do need to belong, and if there is no escaping the drawing of boundaries, these insights can apply to the national community of the United States as well as to more global or more local solidarities," Hollinger writes. He calls for the United States "to maintain its own public culture—constantly contested and critically revised, to be sure—against which the demands of various particularisms shall be obliged to struggle within a formal constitutional framework."

Hollinger writes, "In a postethnic America someone of Ishmael Reed's color could march in a St. Patrick's Day parade without anyone finding it a joke"

Hollinger's conception of a "postethnic America" in which a common, primary American national identity coexists with a variety of ancestral, religious, and partisan affiliations, is appealing. It is difficult, though, to distinguish this "postethnic" conception from the "melting-pot" theory (properly understood as cultural syncretism and racial amalgamation, not as coercive assimilation to an Anglo-Protestant or Euro-Christian norm). Perhaps the difference is Hollinger's replacement of the concept of "identity" (shared by liberal melting-pot nationalists with illiberal nationalists and particularists of various kinds) with the idea of multiple "affiliations" in a postethnic or cosmopolitan America: "How much weight at what particular moment is assigned to the fact that one is Pennsylvania Dutch or Navajo relative to the weight assigned to the fact that one is also an American, a lawyer, a woman, a Republican, a Baptist, and a resident of Minneapolis?" With all due respect, it might be suggested that this is a trivial point. When it comes to the most important questions of social life—citizenship, civil rights, taxation, conscription, defense—one's identity as "an American," as a citizen of a particular state, trumps all the rest. The American political community can not only tax Americans, but execute them for crimes and conscript them and compel them to kill members of other political communities in wars. The Pennsylvania Dutch, female, Republican, and Baptist communities cannot.

To discuss U.S. citizenship as a voluntary "affiliation" rather than as an inherited identity is also rather academic, for the simple reason that the overwhelming majority of American citizens today, as throughout American history, are citizens as the involuntary result of being born on U.S. territory. The United States, indeed, belongs to a minority of democracies that grant citizenship on the basis of place of birth, rather than descent from citizen parents. (Though this is sometimes touted as a manifestation of a morally superior

"territorial" or "civic" rather than "ethnic" or "nationalist" approach to identity, it is really nothing more than a historical accident resulting from the need to retroactively grant U.S. citizenship to former slaves born in the United States by means of the Fourteenth Amendment.) At any rate, only voluntary immigrants— a minority in every generation—can be said to have *chosen* American citizenship in any meaningful sense. For most native-born Americans of all races, indeed, citizenship in most other countries is not an option, because most states make it difficult if not impossible for Americans or for that matter any foreigners to become naturalized citizens. Americans cannot "choose" Japanese citizenship; Japan will not allow it.

Hollinger himself notes that "choices are made in limiting, specific circumstances, some of which are ancestral. . . . One does not easily choose to be a Japanese American in the absence of an element of Japanese ancestry to begin with." Hollinger's primary concern, it quickly becomes clear, is to promote the blurring of ethno-racial boundaries *within* the larger American community. In Hollinger's ideal America, the categories of the ethno-racial pentagon would become as permeable and fluid as are contemporary European-American ethnicities, or religious denominations. Noting Ishmael Reed's acknowledgment that his ancestors include Irishmen as well as Africans, Hollinger writes, "In a postethnic America someone of Reed's color could march in a St. Patrick's Day parade without anyone finding it a joke." Noting that intense religious commitment is compatible with "the right of exit, and also the dynamics of entry"

from and to religious communities, Hollinger suggests that there are lessons in this for the way we think of "ethno-racial affiliations." "A truly postethnic America would be one in which the ethno-racial component in identity would loom less large than it now does in politics as well as culture, and in which affiliation by shared descent would be more voluntary than prescribed in every context. . . . This ideal for the American civic community is, indeed, just that—an ideal, embodying the hope that the United States can be more than a site for a variety of diasporas and of projects in colonization and conquest."

The suspicion many readers may have that Hollinger's "postethnic" or "cosmopolitan" ideal is an updated version of the melting-pot ideal will only be strengthened by the fact that Hollinger, in the epilogue, returns to the theme of the blurring of ethno-racial categories by intermarriage: "The extraordinary increase in marriage and reproduction across the lines of the ethno-racial pentagon presents a fundamental challenge to the authority of descent-derived categories." Though some wish to "turn the pentagon into a hexagon" by adding a mixed-race category, "the logic of mixed race actually threatens to destroy the whole structure." Though Hollinger does not draw it himself, the logical conclusion of his argument would seem to be that the U.S. government's crude ethno-racial classifications (without which racial preference policies cannot be implemented) ought to be abolished. Hollinger hints that race-neutral, class-based reforms should take precedence over race-conscious approaches to social policy: "The disadvantages of class and of

race are deeply entangled in history, but the chances of diminishing racial inequalities are now limited by obvious class inequalities." As he notes, "Changing our vocabulary will not do much to diminish unequal treatment, but it might at least keep us aware of the direction in which antiracists want to be heading. Racism is real, but races are not."

The American caste system has been the most rigid and dichotomous in the Western Hemisphere. But the most rigid things are often the most brittle

Hollinger makes it clear that this is a liberal proposal, not to be confused with conservative "root-hog-or-die" approaches to color-blind public policy: "Critics who simply denounce ethnoracial separatism and call upon ethnoracial minorities to "just say no" would do well to focus more attention to the rigidification of the class structure."

Hollinger's measured and thoughtful book is a valuable contribution to the debate about American identity. At least one of his coinages, the "ethno-racial pentagon," deserves to pass into common usage. His proposal to replace "identity" with "affiliation" is less persuasive, and I admit to having even graver reservations about the term "postethnic." I hasten to add that I criticize Hollinger with a respectful awareness of the difficulties of proposing changes in the way we talk about these matters; my own tentative proposal, in my recent book *The Next American Nation*, that the term *Trans-American* be used to denote members of the transracial cultural majority in the United States was passed over in con-

temptuous silence by friendly and hostile reviewers alike. Still, it would be useful if American intellectuals could agree upon the terms to be used in the never-ending conversation about identities and cultures. As employed in public discourse, the word "ethnicity" confuses three quite distinct things—nationality, ancestry, and race (caste). As Hollinger's example of black Americans with Irish ancestors shows, Americans of similar ancestries may be assigned, by the arbitrary, pseudoscientific rules of the North American caste system inherited by multiculturalists from white supremacists, to different racial castes. The terms *ethno-racial* and *postethnic* are not very helpful, because they incorporate the ambiguity of "ethnicity." It might be best if we dropped the term *ethnicity* altogether.

It is much easier to expunge "ethnicity" than "race" from the consciousness of Americans. Hollinger is correct to argue that today's notion of "white" or "Euro-American" makes it easier to blur the "ethnic" or ancestral-subcultural differences among immigrants from Europe and their descendants in America. It needs to be stressed, though, that this is hardly a recent phenomenon, nor one for which the multicultural left is chiefly responsible. Indeed, as scholars from W. E. B. Du Bois to Alexander Saxton have pointed out, white racism has always provided a means for members of disadvantaged and despised European-American minority groups, like Irish and Italian Americans, to make claims on the majority while gaining a sense of collective superiority over Americans defined as nonwhite.

The American caste system has been the most rigid and dichotomous in the

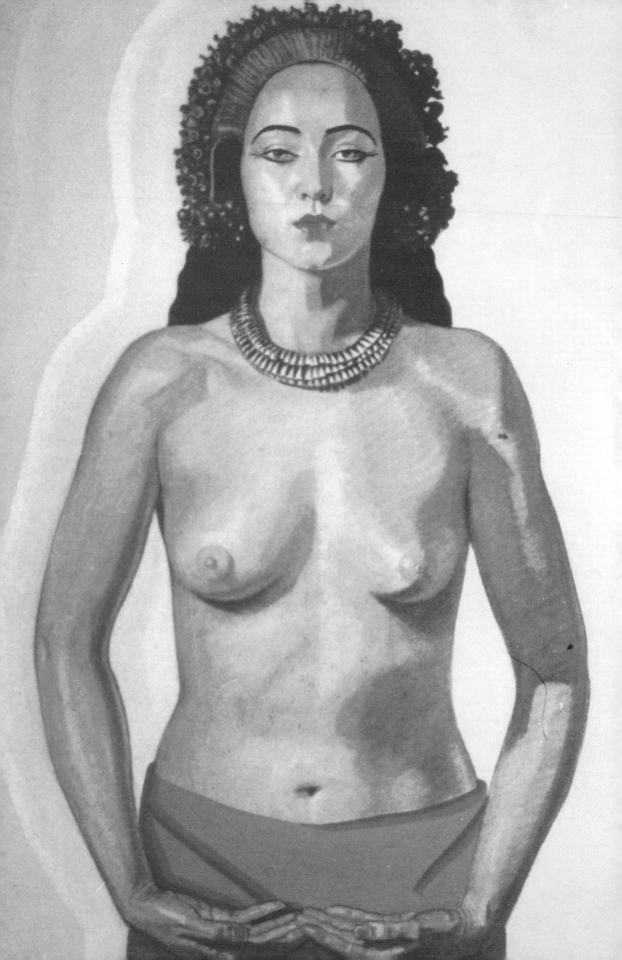

western hemisphere. Though apartheid was real enough for Asian Americans and American Indians (Hispanics having been the victims of social but not formal legal discrimination), the "racial problem" in the minds of most Americans remains the question of relations between "whites" and "blacks." This reflex was evident in journalistic accounts of responses to the verdict in the O. J. Simpson trial, which almost never mentioned Hispanic or Asian reactions.

The growth in the number of mixed-race Americans will not necessarily alter this ancient dichotomy, inasmuch as intermarriage rates among whites, Asians, and Hispanics are much higher than those between black Americans and Americans of other races. It is conceivable that the white-black dualism might be succeeded, in the twenty-first and twenty-second centuries, by a mixed-race/black dualism, like the colored/black distinction in Haiti, or the mestizo or ladino/Indian divide in much of Central and South America. On the other hand, an optimist might suggest that the very absence of distinct historic subcultures based on gradations of "color" between white and black in the United States might render the final crumbling of the old caste system as certain as it will be sudden. The most rigid things are often the most brittle.

Whether one is optimistic or pessimistic about the future, it is difficult to disagree with Hollinger's conclusion: "We may never have a postethnic America. But whatever chances there may be for such a commitment will amount to nothing if the ideal is not articulated and defended."

TRANSITION

Extremely good read. Subscribe now and save 40% off the newsstand price.

○ Please enter my one-year subscription (four big issues) to *Transition* at the low subscriber rate of $24 (a savings of $16 off the newsstand price). Subscribers outside the US: Please add $12 for postage. Canadian subscribers: Please add 7% GST to the subscriber rate, in addition to outside-US postage.

○ Enclosed is my check made payable to Duke University Press.

Please charge my   ○ MasterCard   ○ VISA

Account Number

Expiration Date   **Signature**

Name

Address

City/State/Zip   TR96BN

Send your order to the Journals Fulfillment Department, Duke University Press, Box 90660, Durham, NC 27708-0660. http://www.duke.edu/web/dupress/

Extremely good read. Subscribe now and save 40% off the newsstand price.

○ Please enter my one-year subscription (four big issues) to *Transition* at the low subscriber rate of $24 (a savings of $16 off the newsstand price). Subscribers outside the US: Please add $12 for postage. Canadian subscribers: Please add 7% GST to the subscriber rate, in addition to outside-US postage.

○ Enclosed is my check made payable to Duke University Press.

Please charge my   ○ MasterCard   ○ VISA

Account Number

Expiration Date   **Signature**

Name

Address

City/State/Zip   TR96BN

Send your order to the Journals Fulfillment Department, Duke University Press, Box 90660, Durham, NC 27708-0660. http://www.duke.edu/web/dupress/

IIIII

BUSINESS REPLY MAIL

FIRST CLASS MAIL   PERMIT NO. 1000   DURHAM, NC

POSTAGE WILL BE PAID BY ADDRESSEE

Duke University Press
Journals Fulfillment
Box 90660
Durham, NC 27708-9987

IIIII

BUSINESS REPLY MAIL

FIRST CLASS MAIL   PERMIT NO. 1000   DURHAM, NC

POSTAGE WILL BE PAID BY ADDRESSEE

Duke University Press
Journals Fulfillment
Box 90660
Durham, NC 27708-9987

Come back to _Transition_. Four big issues for only $24.

O Please restart my subscription to _Transition_ for one year at the $24 rate.
(Subscriptions will begin with Issue 70.)

O Please restart my subscription for two years at the current rate, for a total of $48.

O Subscribers outside the US: Please add $12 per year for postage.

O Canadian residents: Please add 7% GST to the subscription rate in addition to postage charges.

O Enclosed is my check payable to Duke University Press.

Please bill my   OMasterCard   OVISA

Acct. no. _____   Exp. date _____

Signature _____   Daytime phone _____

Duke University Press, Journals Fulfillment,
Box 90660, Durham, NC 27708-0660.
To restart your subscription by phone,
call 919-687-3613, Monday–Friday, 8 AM–5 PM EST
http://www.duke.edu/web/dupress/

Name _____

Address _____

City/State/Zip _____   TR96RN

THE PINK AND THE BLACK

Race and sex in postwar Britain

Chris Waters

Discussed in this essay

New Right Discourse on Race and Sexuality: Britain, 1968-1990, *Anna Marie Smith, Cambridge: Cambridge University Press*

The author would like to thank Robin Kilson for her assistance with this article.

Margaret Thatcher, 1979

Archive Photos

In 1945, Clement Attlee led the Labour Party to victory in one of the most impressive electoral landslides in twentieth-century British history. Promising to build "a new Jerusalem in England's green and promised land," Labour radically transformed British society—nationalizing basic industries, effecting a thorough reform of existing welfare services, and establishing others, such as the National Health Service. So popular were these programs that the opposition Conservative Party adopted them as their own; when Winston Churchill returned to power in 1951 the stage was set for what has since been termed the "postwar consensus," the shared commitment of both major parties in Britain to Keynesian economic principles, the mixed economy, planning by "experts" from above, and the principles of the welfare state.

By the 1960s, it looked as if the postwar consensus had become an immutable fact of British political life. When, under the leadership of Harold Wilson, the

Labour Party returned to power in 1964, state investment in technological development, the extension of welfare state benefits, and the massive expansion of state-funded higher education became the order of the day. Moreover, in that decade consensus politics gave rise to what has since been dubbed Britain's "permissive moment"—the passage of a series of legislative acts in the moral sphere that, in the wake of the sensational trial of Penguin Books for publishing D. H. Lawrence's *Lady Chatterley's Lover*, ended state censorship of the theater, liberalized divorce and abortion laws, and decriminalized homosexuality. Members of both the Conservative and Labour Parties supported this legislation; even Margaret Thatcher, despite her rhetorical opposition to permissiveness in the 1980s, never fully reneged on her commitment to the social reforms she had supported twenty years earlier.

By 1979 the bubble had burst. "Permissive" child-rearing practices, popularized during the postwar "age of afflu-

Dangerous Queers

From Ten. 8

raveling of Britain's economy, the money simply ran out. Now it was the *British* government that was forced to go, cup in hand, to the International Monetary Fund, and to begin to curtail public spending. All of this culminated in the Winter of Discontent (1978–79), a season of widespread militant strikes, when nothing seemed to work anymore. Britain had become, as the saying went, "ungovernable."

Nothing captures the disillusion of that decade better than John Schlesinger's film *Sunday Bloody Sunday*, released in 1971. In 1965, Schlesinger had directed *Darling*, an extraordinarily upbeat film in which Julie Christie screwed her way through "swinging" London, shocking some moral sensibilities but essentially confirming the vibrant possibilities of that decade. (She won an Academy Award for her performance.) Six years later, Schlesinger's tone in *Sunday Bloody Sunday* was much more subdued. Despite valiant attempts to enjoy their newfound freedoms, Peter Finch and Glenda Jackson, in love with the same feckless bisexual artist, seemed utterly lost. Moreover, their passions and anxieties were charted against a backdrop of economic decline, in a London uncertain of the way forward and full of ominous signs of what was to come. "Don't let the economic crisis ruin your weekend," advised one character somewhat facetiously. But the economic crises of the 1970s ruined almost everybody's weekend, and the Conservative Party, under the leadership of Margaret Thatcher, was elected in 1979 to set things right, to restore confidence and begin the process of national renewal.

ence," had provoked considerable conservative backlash even in the 1950s (witness the moral panic over juvenile delinquency); by the late 1960s New Right figures like Mary Whitehouse and Enoch Powell made Britain's "moral decline" the centerpiece of a revitalized conservative movement. Welfare state sympathies, along with the commitment to increasingly unprofitable public sector industries, were still part of the ruling consensus, but after the Arab oil embargo in 1973 and the consequent un-

The only British prime minister in the twentieth century to lend her name to an entire movement, Margaret Thatcher was determined to break with the postwar consensus, which she believed was wholly responsible for Britain's postwar decline.

Thatcherism posed an ideological challenge not only to the welfare state, but to its defenders among the historians. The postwar consensus had generated a number of positive historical narratives about 1945 and its aftermath. In these narratives, Labour's post-1945 policies, whether viewed as the final flowering of Victorian philanthropy, the institutionalization of a moral commitment to aid the less fortunate, or as a gesture toward a new socialist Britain, were unequivocally praised. Thatcherites told a different story. They described a Britain that, having turned leftward in 1945, teetered on the verge of final collapse. In this story, Margaret Thatcher was the redeemer, the one figure who could rescue Britain from decline by dismantling the wrongheaded policies of the postwar past, thereby restoring the nation to its historical destiny.

Both stories view 1979 as a watershed. Whether Thatcher was attacked or praised made no difference: while each side told a markedly different story about 1979 and what came before and after, both agreed on the importance of Thatcher's electoral victory in changing the course of British history. But did 1979 really mark a rupture? Were New Right discourses opposed to the permissive order of the postwar consensus, or might they have been logical developments of the very order that they actively repudiated and claimed to dislodge?

• • •

Most scholars of the period have explained the presumed rupture of 1979 by focusing on Thatcherism as an economic doctrine that stressed monetarist policies and the privatization of state industries. In *New Right Discourse on Race and Sexuality: Britain, 1968–1990*, Anna Marie Smith argues that these inter-

Good Immigrant, 1960

Studio Portrait, Birmingham. From Ten. 8

preters have impoverished our under-standing of Thatcherism as theory and practice by ignoring Thatcher's statements on race, national identity, the family, multiculturalism and morality. Smith intends to take these pronouncements seriously—to show how Thatcher's project of renewal depended not only on fiscal restraint but also on an idea of the British nation threatened by "alien" invasions, from both within and without. Smith argues that Thatcher's "revolution" took the form of a moral crusade at least as much as the economic one, and one of her book's virtues is its elucidation of that crusade's sometimes ob-

Subversive immigrants, it was feared, would "congregate together" in areas that might soon become "English Harlems."

scure logic. In doing so, she notes hitherto unremarked connections between the revitalized racism of the 1970s and the homophobia of the New Right.

Smith's text is only the latest to examine what Martin Barker called, in a 1981 book of the same name, "the new racism": the cultural ideas of race and racism promulgated by Enoch Powell in the late 1960s, as against crude, "old" assertions of biological superiority. Following the work of Barker, Stuart Hall, and Paul Gilroy, Smith argues that Powell's genius was his ability to create a populist bloc out of Britons disenchanted with the permissive society. In blaming virtually every aspect of the perceived national crisis on black immigration, Powell suggested that the essence of Britishness was whiteness. White natives

needed to recover their "true" identity by excluding blackness from the nation—through ever-stricter immigration controls. The Powellian legacy of guilt-free nationalism, racially constructed, increasingly took hold as the seventies wore on: as Smith writes, race "played a crucial role in the formation of the Powellian movement, and Powellism was one of the most important precursors to Thatcherism."

Despite its excesses, however, Powell's racism was not simply exclusionary. Blacks willing and able to assimilate to white British values were acceptable; those who could not adapt to British values, or who actively subverted them, were the real target of his animosity. "The new racism," as Smith deftly suggests, "defines the blackness which it wants to exclude not as that which is non-white and therefore inferior, but as that which is inherently anti-British. This 'cultural' definition of race opens up the disciplinary differentiation of blackness." Thatcher's Conservative Party continued to play upon images of assimilated, or assimilable, blackness in order to exclude others from the national imaginary. Smith, citing Gilroy, analyzes a 1983 Conservative election poster in which a solitary black male in a respectable business suit is framed by the caption, "Labour says he's black. Tories say he's British."

Smith argues that Thatcherite sexual discourse followed a similar logic. Section 28 of the Local Government Act of 1987–88 outlawed the "promotion" of homosexuality by local government. It specifically prohibited local authorities from giving any kind of assistance, financial or otherwise, to individuals or

With the Conservatives, there are no 'blacks', no 'whites', just people.

Conservatives believe that treating minorities as equals encourages the majority to treat them as equals.

Yet the Labour Party aim to treat you as a 'special case', as a group all on your own.

Is setting you apart from the rest of society a sensible way to overcome racial prejudice and social inequality?

The question is, should we really divide the British people instead of uniting them?

WHOSE PROMISES ARE YOU TO BELIEVE?

When Labour were in government, they promised to repeal Immigration Acts passed in 1962 and 1971. Both promises were broken.

This time, they are promising to throw out the British Nationality Act, which gives full and equal citizenship to everyone permanently settled in Britain.

But how do the Conservatives' promises compare?

We said that we'd abolish the 'SUS' law.

We kept our promise.

We said we'd recruit more coloured policemen, get the police back into the community, and train them for a better understanding of your needs.

We kept our promise.

PUTTING THE ECONOMY BACK ON ITS FEET.

The Conservatives have always said that the only long term answer to our economic problems was to conquer inflation.

Inflation is now lower than it's been for over a decade, keeping all prices stable, with the price of food now hardly rising at all.

Meanwhile, many businesses throughout Britain are recovering, leading to thousands of new jobs.

Firstly, in our traditional industries, but just as importantly in new technology areas such as microelectronics.

In other words, the medicine is working.

Yet Labour want to change everything, and put us back to square one.

They intend to increase taxation. They intend to increase the National Debt.

They promise import and export controls.

Cast your mind back to the last Labour government. Labour's methods didn't work then.

They won't work now.

A BETTER BRITAIN FOR ALL OF US.

The Conservatives believe that everyone wants to work hard and be rewarded for it.

Those rewards will only come about by creating a mood of equal opportunity for everyone in Britain, regardless of their race, creed or colour.

The difference you're voting for is this:

To the Labour Party, you're a black person.

To the Conservatives, you're a British Citizen.

Vote Conservative, and you vote for a more equal, more prosperous Britain.

LABOUR SAYS HE'S BLACK.
TORIES SAY HE'S BRITISH.

CONSERVATIVE ☒

Conservative Party election poster, 1983

Conservative Party, Saatchi and Saatchi

**Lesbian nurses
protest
Section 28, 1988**

*Gavin Crilly,
Impact Visuals*

groups who "promoted" homosexuality, and made the teaching of homosexuality as an acceptable "pretended family relationship" illegal. Claiming that militant homosexuals had taken over local educational programs, and that overly permissive local authorities were funding lesbian and gay political events, Conservatives demonized homosexuality as part of their attack on the (predominantly Labour) local councils—bodies led by what the tabloid press derided as the "Loony Left."

In the parliamentary debates that took place around Section 28, against the backdrop of the emerging moral panic over AIDS, supporters of the legislation made a crucial distinction between the good homosexual and the dangerous queer. They ignored lesbian sexuality but were willing to accept gay men, as long as they were law-abiding, disease-free, and closeted. They accepted this imaginary figure as a legitimate member of British society, and argued that they merely wished to restrict the activities of a different kind of person, the dangerous queer, whom Lord Halsbury described as angry, exhibitionistic, "promiscuous," and "proselytizing." In short, Section 28 entailed a disciplinary strategy that "promoted the domestication of difference by differentiating difference against itself and by inciting self-surveillance." Promiscuous homosexuality was equated with disease, an alien invasion that threatened the heart of the nation and appeared to be promoted by permissive local authorities.

What's more, Smith ingeniously argues, supporters of Section 28 drew extensively on New Right racial rhetoric. The attack on the local councils and the homosexuality they allegedly supported depended on "already normalized racist metaphors around disease, foreign invasions, inassimilable 'other' cultures, dangerous criminals, excessive permissiveness and so on." In short, "radically new discourse on homosexuality was represented within already normalized racist structures." Like Powell's subversive immigrant, whose very presence undermined the essential unity of the nation, the queer posed a challenge to the heterosexual family, itself the bedrock of the nation. Thatcherite homophobia thus rested to a large extent on a reconstitution of "the Powellian image of the nation under siege through the substitution of the dangerous queer for the black immigrant." Queers and immigrants alike threatened the stability of the nation itself.

· · ·

Smith's book points to important similarities between Powellite racism and Thatcherite homophobia, notably that both discourses attempted to stabilize the boundaries of national belonging in Britain. But too often the book does little more than showcase analogous rhetorical structures. We are informed that Powellite racism operates *like* Thatcherite homophobia, but seldom are the *effects* of the former on the latter adequately mapped. Moreover, Powellite racism is only rarely traced forward to its more polite Thatcherite manifestations, while Thatcherite homophobia is not linked in a precise historical manner to earlier expressions of antigay sentiment in Britain. Indeed, Smith seems to view mid-eighties homophobia as a "radically new discourse," with a slight historical antecedent in Powellite racism. A more expansive consideration of twentieth-century British history might have helped explain why New Right discourses in Britain have come to enjoy such widespread support.

Supporters of Section 28 were willing to accept gay men, as long as they were law-abiding, disease-free, and closeted.

Although Powell's diatribes against subversive immigrants were indeed a departure from "polite" notions of what was acceptable to say about race in public, and while his "cultural" racism was a new take on an old hatred, the anxiety about the "dark stranger" was actually a staple of liberal writings in the postwar period. In the attempt to repudiate prewar discourses of scientific racism in the wake of Nazi atrocities, consensus intellectuals in the 1950s and 1960s had already established elaborate criteria of *cultural* belonging to distinguish the white British native from newly arrived black and Asian immigrants from the outposts of the Commonwealth. These criteria were those employed by Powell and other "new" racists.

Boy and friend protesting Section 28, 1988

Impact Visuals

Young Englanders,
1971

Associated Press

Powell once argued that the "West Indian or Asian does not, by being born in England, become an Englishman. In law he becomes a United Kingdom citizen by birth; in fact he is a West Indian or Asian still." In his 1959 study, *White and Coloured*, the white liberal scholar Michael Banton made a very similar point about cultural difference. Citing George Santayana's claim that the English are "glad if only natives will remain natives and strangers," Banton argued that if immigrants could gain social acceptance as easily as they could immigration papers (which, he claimed, they could not), then "being British would be much less worth." A decade before Powellism, Banton both noted and helped to consolidate popular beliefs about Britishness and blackness. Banton and his liberal colleagues were already mapping the cultural distinctions between "insiders and outsiders" (to use a phrase current at the time), between white Britons and dark strangers. While their work repudiated racist sentiments in British society, it was motivated by a similar desire to chart the boundaries of national belonging. Moreover, as with Powell's writings and speeches, consensus race relations writers distinguished between good and bad, assimilable and subversive immigrants. The latter, it was feared, would "congregate together" in areas that might soon become "English Harlems."

Demonstrators
in Brixton, 1981

The Bettman Archive

If assumptions about cultural difference that were central to the New Racism had antecedents in Britain's postwar consensus, so too did the distinction between the good homosexual and the dangerous queer. That distinction, as Smith implies, was made in the *Wolfenden Report*, the government document published in 1957 that called for the decriminalization of homosexuality, or at least for the legalization of consensual sexual activity between two responsible adults in private. Two years earlier, Peter Wildeblood, a journalist imprisoned for engaging in consensual homosexual activity with another man, published his own plea for social tolerance and legal change, *Against the Law*. A modern coming-out narrative, Wildeblood's study distinguished the "normal" homosexual (like himself) from the effeminate "queer," attempting to gain sympathy for the former by repudiating the latter. In a similar vein, the prosecutor at Wildeblood's trial in 1954 had asked Wildeblood if he was an "invert" or a "pervert," deploying the early-twentieth-century rhetoric of Havelock Ellis and anticipating the distinctions made by the supporters of Section 28.

Over a decade later, when the 1967 Sexual Offences Act decriminalized male homosexual behavior, the distinction between the dangerous queer and the good homosexual remained in full force. Lord Arran, who had successfully defended the Act in the House of Lords, argued that homosexuals should strive to become decent, upright citizens out of gratitude to those who had struggled on their behalf: "Any form of ostentatious behaviour, now or in the future," he argued, "would be utterly distasteful and would ... make the sponsors of this Bill regret that they have done what they have done." Lord Arran would be quickly disappointed, for in the wake of the 1967 Act a flourishing gay subculture emerged in Britain. Moreover, the subsequent appearance of militant organizations, from the Gay Liberation Front to Outrage, and the popularization of gay

Black Power advocate speaks in Hyde Park, 1968

The Bettman Archive

styles throughout the glam seventies and techno eighties, fed into the anxieties over the spread of homosexuality. These were exploited by Conservatives in their attacks on the local councils in the 1980s.

In short, the New Right did not have a monopoly on culturalist definitions of race and sex. The set of binary oppositions in which British conservatives trafficked—subversive and assimilable immigrants, good homosexuals and dangerous queers—were very similar to tropes that structured liberal discourses in the 1950s and after. Questions of belonging, of identity and difference, came to the fore in the decades after World War II. Increasing waves of nonwhite immigration were read as threatening to the social cohesion of the nation, provoking intense national introspection and the desire to consolidate the boundaries of the nation against perceived enemies, internal and external. Thatcherism, then, was not simply the antithesis of the postwar consensus, but embodied the many uncertainties and contradictions that were at the heart of the postwar consensus itself.

The postwar consensus was neither the golden age much admired by some observers, nor the moment when Britain took a disastrous "wrong turn," the story its critics love to tell. It was instead a period of deep anxiety about Britain's rapidly changing place in the world. The retreat from empire, uncertainty about Britain's role in postwar Europe, the eclipse of the nation as a world power (pointedly illustrated by the Suez crisis in 1956), anxieties about the effects of American mass culture on British society, and even the contradictory feelings generated by the advent of the "affluent society," led to intense questioning about what it now meant to be British. These uncertainties reactivated the myth of The War as a powerful locus for feelings of national pride. They also generated new fears about imagined threats to the cohesion of the nation, whether they came from juvenile delinquents, mass culture, Brussels bureaucrats, immigrants, or queers.

This is not to claim that there is a fundamental continuity between British history, pre- and post-1979. It is to suggest, however, that much of what we consider to be the enabling dynamic of the New Right needs to be traced back to earlier periods, to earlier crises in the national imaginary. As Thatcherism, in its kinder, gentler Majorite incarnation, seems increasingly winded, and as John Major veers from one defeat to another,

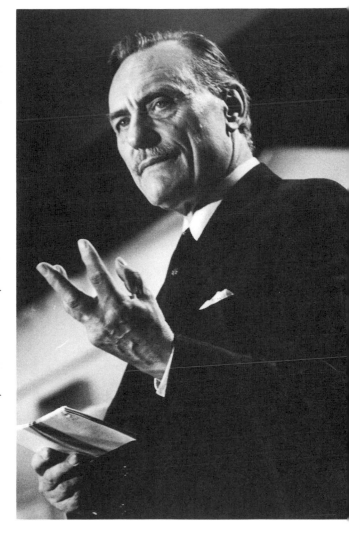

Enoch Powell, 1976

The Bettman Archive

paving the way for what most observers believe will be a Labour victory in the next general election, it is perhaps time to reconsider the periodization of postwar British history. Only then will we be able fully to understand the origins, meaning, and impact of New Right discourses on race and sexuality.

THE DOUBLE BIND

America and the African diaspora

Stanley Aronowitz

Some ten years ago, I was invited by the Afro-American Studies program at Yale to give a talk about Richard Wright's political writings. I argued, among other things, that a coherent and reasonable —admirable, even—vision animated Wright's writings from early to late. I was unprepared for the storm of controversy that followed.

My focus was on Wright's 1954 political travelogue, *Black Power,* subtitled *A Record of Reactions in a Land of Pathos.* Written seven years after his permanent departure from the United States, the book seemed distant in topic and tone from the writings on black America that had propelled Wright to fame. *Black Power* is a controversial study of Nkrumah's Ghana (then "Gold Coast"), exploring the conflict between modernization and tradition that faced all developing countries on the verge of independence. At a time when the decolonizing societies of Asia and Africa were often dazzled by the lure of tradition, Wright entered the

debate on the side of modernity, urging Nkrumah to refuse the tribalist temptation as well as the prevailing anti-Western ideology of the period and to pursue a program of relentless political, economic, and *cultural* modernization.

Wright was fully aware that the success of such a campaign would depend on the capital and expertise of the colonial powers, and the risks that would entail. But, while admitting a limited role for indigenous traditions, he outlined a clear-eyed course for emerging African nations that incorporated the benefits of modernity: democracy, industrialization, and personal freedom. My interest in talking about the later Wright was to show that his refusal of cultural nationalism was nonetheless a vision of black liberation, and that his cosmopolitanism represented a genuine alternative to what I perceived as a tendency in the 1970s and 1980s of black intellectuals and sympathetic whites to embrace one or another variant of ethnocentricity. I

*Aaron Douglas
(1899-1979).
Building More Stately
Mansions, 1944.
Carl Van Vechten
Gallery of Art, Fisk
University*

suggested that Wright's "cosmopolitan-ism" represented an eclipsed tradition in black intellectual culture.

My listeners included some of the leading scholars in the field, and they were not particularly sympathetic to the idea of resuscitating this notorious side of Wright's corpus. For them, Wright's political writings had no place in the emerging canon of African American literature, if only because he had, more or less explicitly, renounced that designation for what he considered its misguided nationalist connotations. His unapologetic restatement of the virtues of the Enlightenment, including the much-criticized humanisms of both liberalism and Marxism, was an embarrassment. The Wright of the political writings was swimming against a current for which modernity itself was in question.

After my lecture, the late Charles Davis suggested that, although he appreciated my account of the political writings, Wright's work was not only seriously flawed, it was little short of blas-phemy. Others wondered why I had bothered to bring these discredited views to their attention. In an environment in which the black "tradition" was being constructed along the lines of an ethnically based vernacular and folk culture—a turn dictated by the quest for a usable past—Wright's later writings were nothing less than an affront to the projects of Afrocentricity and African Americanness itself. Arnold Rampersad, the editor of the New American Library's definitive edition of Wright's works, agreed: his version of the Wright canon closes in 1953, with the novel *The Outsiders*, leaving the political writings out of the Library of America altogether.

. . .

Even before his death in 1960, Richard Wright was best known for *Native Son* (published in 1940, and the first Book-of-the-Month Club selection by a black writer) and for *Black Boy* (1945), his stunning autobiographical essay. Both were heralded at the time of their publication as among the most important narratives of black American life. With the establishment of black studies departments in American universities, these works, along with his short stories and newly discovered writings from his early years (including *American Hunger*, the second, unpublished half of the original manuscript for *Black Boy*) have been given a central place in the African American canon.

Despite the evident Marxism of Wright's writings from this period, texts like *Twelve Million Black Voices* (1941) have retained a certain academic élan. That book, an account of the social, economic, and psychological complexities of black life in the wake of the Great Migration, has been praised for telling the story of blacks outside the respectable, middle-class bounds of the Talented Tenth. Michel Fabre, one of Wright's biographers, has argued that *Twelve Million Black Voices* made an important contribution to sundering racial stereotypes by depicting the diversity of blacks and their communities.

But Wright's self-imposed exile to Paris in 1947 struck his contemporaries as a kind of apostasy. As Paul Gilroy notes in the Wright chapter of his remarkable book, *The Black Atlantic*, "The consensus stipulates as far as his art was concerned the move to Europe was disastrous."

This argument takes several forms. . . . It dismisses Wright's entitlement to hold a view of modernity at all and has grave implications for how we place his work in debates about black modernism(s). It is claimed that after moving to France Wright's work was corrupted by his dabbling in philosophical modes of thought entirely alien to his African- *American history and vernacular style. Secondly, it is argued that the interest in psychiatry and psychoanalysis which had, in any case, preceded his transatlantic move got out of control in the European milieu. Third, it is suggested that, once resident in Europe, Wright was simply too remote from the vital folk sources which made his early work so uniquely powerful.*

Wright's "Paris" novels—*The Long Dream, Savage Holiday*, and especially *The Outsider*—revealed the powerful influence of Jean-Paul Sartre and French existentialism on his writing. The Paris books were neither commercially nor critically successful in the United States (*Savage Holiday*, a paperback original, went unreviewed), in part because these works broke with the naturalist conventions of black fiction that Wright himself had helped establish. After *Native Son*, black writing was supposed to reveal the degradation of black everyday life through uncompromising narratives that reveal the depth and scope of black oppression in White America.

Savage Holiday, in fact, breaks an unwritten rule: not only does it not concern itself with poverty and the withering realities of black life, it doesn't have a single black character. Informed by Wright's increasing attraction to existential themes, it's a story of *white* oppression in White America. Its protagonist is a midlevel insurance executive, age forty-three, who is dismissed after twenty-five years of faithful service, and who proceeds to murder his wife. Like all of Wright's fiction, early and late, *Savage Holiday* concerns the crisis of social and psychological identity in the face of capitalist modernity. Remarkably, it antici-

Laurent. Marché
d'esclaves.
*Copper engraving.
Courtesy of the
Bibliothèque nationale,
Paris.*

prevents African Americans from enjoying the fruits of modernity understood
not simply as economic well-being, but
as a sense of being at home in the world.

Wright's abiding concern remained,
of course, the fate of blacks on an international scale. In *The Black Atlantic* Gilroy takes Wright's permanent expatria-
tion from the United States as a sign, not
of betrayal, but of a broadening of his
commitment to black freedom: as Wright
wrote in his journals, "I took my subject
matter with me in the baggage of my
memory when I left America." His non-
fiction of this period, especially *White
Man, Listen!*, *The Color Curtain*, and *Black
Power*, are serious, albeit unorthodox, attempts to come to grips with the question raised at the opening of Gilroy's
book: The "transverse dynamics of racial
politics . . . [and] the broader questions of
ethnic identity" linked to the project of
"striving to be both European and black."
(And, one might add, American.) In
Gilroy's thoughtful attempt to address
the complex questions of modernity,
race, and ethnic identity, Wright appears
(with W. E. B. Du Bois) as the most
courageous pan-African intellectual of
the last half of this century.

• • •

Wright's legacy, fully resumed by Gilroy
in *The Black Atlantic*, is to acknowledge
the contradictory ambitions of the quest
for an autonomous black identity in the
face of inescapable modernity. Gilroy
constructs a new and alternative narrative of the past five centuries of black
politics and culture, heavily indebted to
Wright's (and Du Bois's) insistence that
the black diaspora is globally indivisible,
and on the implicit call for a commu-

pates the fate of many middle managers
in the corporate merger and acquisition
fever of the early 1990s. By invoking a
white "victim" of the corporate culture
that nurtured him, revealing the precarious position of even relatively privileged inhabitants of the mainstream, the
creator of Bigger Thomas raised universal issues of identity and belonging. What
does a person do when he or she is no
longer integrated by a culture? What remains of the self when the corporate
self—our contemporary experience of
community, however degraded—evap-
orates? That these are questions for
everyone—we are increasingly interpel-
lated by our jobs—violates the still-
prevalent notion that *only* the color line

nity of black expressive cultures. As we have seen, he reiterates Wright's forthright defense of modernity as a desirable (or at least, inescapable) aspect of black identity.

To begin with, the title itself signals two departures from the mainstream of African American cultural studies. Gilroy uses the term *black* to make clear his rejection of ethnocentric perspectives represented by terms such as *African American, black British*, and *Afro-Caribbean*, as well as nationalist accounts that would deny the discrete existence of the African diaspora; for him, "black" is a transverse signifier that subordinates nationality to a more or less common history. The word evokes the scattering of already differentiated and diverse African peoples via their enslavement, from the sixteenth through nineteenth centuries. Moreover, as the "diaspora" of the title implies, their dispersal to the Americas, the Caribbean, and Europe parallels the Jewish diaspora, both in its geographic breadth and in its economic and political, if not cultural, unity.

That there are differences of circumstance between blacks and Jews, differences of settlement and of degree of cultural assimilation and exclusion (and, therefore, "race" consciousness), Gilroy does not deny. But he insists that the analogy between the Jewish and black diaspora is more than a literary elegance: it describes two peoples systematically deprived of their homelands and, for this reason, condemned permanently to negotiate with "host" societies for whom they remain ineluctably "other." He writes:

In the preparation of this book I have been repeatedly drawn to the work of Jewish thinkers [notably Walter Benjamin] in order to find both inspiration and resources with which to map the ambivalent experiences of blacks inside and outside modernity. I want to acknowledge these debts openly in the hope that in some small way the link they reveal might contribute to a better political relationship between Jews and blacks at some distant future point. Many writers have been struck by some of the correspondences between histories of these groups, but thinkers from both communities are not always prepared to admit them, let alone explore any possible connections in an uninhibited way.

By awarding pride of place in his own analysis to the concept of diaspora, Gilroy signifies his intention to be less inhibited. As Gilroy notes, pan-Africanism was significantly modeled on Zionism. Just as the Zionists adopted, after much consideration, the biblical designation of Palestine as the Jewish homeland, Marcus Garvey and Martin Delany sought, in various ways, to unite the dispersed people of Africa to a project of "return."

Gilroy's acknowledgment of the continuing influence of nationalism should not be confused either with cultural nationalism or with the integrationist dissolution of ethnic identity into patriotism within a single country. His own vision of black nationalism, indebted to Du Bois, is a kind of ethnic particularism without a country, a "nation" in permanent exile. His central argument is that while nationality plays a significant role in black and Jewish historical formation, the crucial event was that of *dispersal.* Following Du Bois, he claims that blacks throughout Europe and the Americas were forced into a position of "double consciousness." This dual awareness, of being black and a citizen of a white-majority liberal democratic nation, placed a heavy burden on programs of complete assimilation as well as those of pan-Africanism. Contrary to some neo-Marxist efforts (including Du Bois's own *Black Reconstruction*) to model blackness on the image of the nineteenth-century proletariat, "in, but not of, society," Gilroy suggests that the black Atlantic is culturally modern *and* possesses its own unique racialized identity within Western culture. In his chapter on Wright, Gilroy observes a crucial interaction, a conversation between Wright, already in exile in the French country-

Gesturing to a shelf of Kierkegaard, Wright exlaimed, "You see those books there? Everything that he writes in those books I knew before I had them."

side, and the great Trinidadian critic and activist C. L. R. James. Gesturing to a bookshelf full of Kierkegaard, Wright exclaimed, "Look here, . . . you see those books there? . . . Everything that he writes in those books I knew before I had them." Gilroy cites James' gloss on the event: "'What [Wright] was telling me was that he was a black man in the United States and that gave him an insight into what today is the universal opinion and attitude of the *modern* perspective" (emphasis added).

One of Gilroy's striking contributions to the theory of black identity is his pro-found exploration of the interiority of black consciousness. Following Raymond Williams's injunction that critical theory find the ways in which cultural expressions plumb "structures of feeling," Gilroy references black music as often as more traditional forms of "high" culture like the novel and the essay. In *The Black Atlantic* the juxtapositions between the treatise and the song are always apposite. The chapter on Toni Morrison, for example, sports twin epigraphs: one a famous quote from the "Theses on the Philosophy of History" of the Frankfurt School fellow traveler Walter Benjamin, the other a sensitive reflection—"Slavery was a terrible thing, but when black people in America finally got out from under that crushing system, they were stronger. . . . I admire that kind of strength. People who have it take a stand and put their blood and soul into what they believe"—from Michael Jackson, the King of Pop. To open his complex chapter on Du Bois, whose characteristic statement was the scholarly tract, the memoir, the manifesto, Gilroy finds that "in the space and time that separate Robert Johnson's 'Hellhound on My Trail' and the Wailers' exhortation to 'Keep on Moving,' and the more recent Soul II Soul piece with the same name, the expressive cultures of the black Atlantic world have been dominated by a special mood of restlessness."

These songs, according to Gilroy, reverse the usual designation of homelessness or exile as a "curse." Diasporic dispersal becomes an affirmation, a repossession of a condition usually exclusively associated with subordination. This "restless sensibility" comes to characterize Gilroy's vision of the black At-

*Aaron Douglas
(1899-1979).
Aspects of Negro
Life: Song of the
Towers, 1934.
Oil on canvas.
Photo:
Manu Sassoonian.
Schomburg Center
for Research in Black
Culture, The New
York Public Library*

lantic, a corrective, one infers, to "rooted" particularisms like Jesse Jackson's "African American" or even Albert Murray's "Omni-American." Gilroy acutely observes that "the appeal to and for roots became an urgent issue when diaspora blacks sought to construct a political agenda in which the ideal of rootedness was identified as a prerequisite for the forms of cultural integrity that would guarantee the nationhood and statehood to which they aspired." This historicizing method displaces the conventional ethnicism of many writers who take the search for roots as a transhistorical feature of self and group affirmation. Gilroy instead understands it as a response to the *specificity* of black dispersal under determinate historical conditions. In this respect he names racism as an agent in configuring black political identity as a *national* project.

It's at this point, however, that Gilroy's transatlantic vision runs aground. Missing from his text is any extended treatment of the differentiated economic and cultural position of blacks within Western nations. He observes that black double consciousness is modernity's secret sharer: "Racial subordination is integral to the processes of development and social and economic progress known as modernization." This, of course, has been the contention of such eminent scholars as Orlando Patterson, Eric Williams, C. L. R. James, and Du Bois himself. Recall Williams's claim, drawn from the extensive Caribbean experience, that slavery was the bedrock of the entire structure of social and political domination characteristic of Western capitalist societies. Patterson has argued that slavery remains an intrinsic feature of Western culture, and it is more than symbolic; contrary to the conventional wisdom, capitalism has never wholly dispensed with slavery. Racial subordination, and its impoverishment of the majority of U.S., Latin-American, and Caribbean blacks, remains one of the conditions of accumulation.

If these analyses are correct, one may not take racism as an aberrant or anomalous feature of modernity. Nor is racism entirely subject to legal remedy. Rather, the position of blacks in both economically developed and underdeveloped societies suggests that racial formation is at once relatively autonomous from class formation and a crucial aspect of it—and that, as Gilroy recognizes, is the dirty secret of modernity. All the more interesting, then, that *The Black Atlantic* does not fully address the legacy of slavery and its political and economic consequences. Gilroy cites James's magisterial *Black Jacobins* and refers briefly to *Black Reconstruction*, but he mostly avoids consideration of the later Du Bois and the massive Caribbean contributions to the modernity debates.

· · ·

Gilroy's predicament is itself completely modern, and again points toward an affinity with the thinkers of the Frankfurt School. For if capitalism, slavery, and modernity are irrevocably linked, then one might well question the very ideals of the Enlightenment—democracy, industrialization, and personal freedom—extolled by Wright in the 1950s. This is precisely the problematic that generated Max Horkheimer and Theodor Adorno's *Dialectic of Enlightenment*, a critical interrogation of what we might call the "double consciousness" of the Enlightenment.

Written during World War II, the book attempted to grapple with the implications of the rise of National Socialism in Germany, one of the most revered of Western cultures. German fascism seemed to give the lie to the very idea of the West, revealing the interpenetration of civilization and barbarism. The core of Adorno and Horkheimer's argument was that the age-old project of mastery over nature, which had promised human liberation, had also made possible the wholesale destruction of human life. Rather than serving human ends, the machinery of progress signaled the end of humanity.

Modernity and its cognates—freedom, democracy, progress—depend, in part, on the externalization of their own inner contradictions. For the Enlightenment of the eighteenth century it was science, that magnificent warrior against religious superstition, which, in showing us how to strip nature of its mystery, had wreaked havoc on ecological systems the world over. Even as the Germans led the world in science and the arts, they also perfected the "technology" that would enable the Nazis to run the Jewish death camps with a supremely efficient bureaucracy. The New World, with its individualism, industrialization, and explicit rhetoric of human rights, was no less dependent on the otherness of black slaves and mass industrial workers, of Mexicans and other Latinos, and of various foreign enemies—first the Germans, in two world wars, and then the "gooks" of Japan, Korea, and Vietnam. In *Black Reconstruction*, twelve years before the publication of *Dialectic of Enlightenment*, Du Bois had argued that the black *worker*, laboring under slave and then near-slave conditions in factories and industrialized farms, provided the basis for American modernity—the surplus labor needed for capital accumulation and the development of manufacturing, as well as the leisure necessary to the creation of culture.

One may interpret these contemporary critiques of modernity as expressing the contradictions of progressive reason. The political construction and economic exploitation of otherness appears be to be an unresolved, and perhaps unresolvable, aspect of modernity. While

Dialectic of Enlightenment suggests the weight of this contradiction—that Enlightenment and barbarism are coterminous, but that Enlightenment remains our only hope—it was unable to provide a satisfactory answer to the riddle of the modern. Adorno never did find a way to project that hope beyond series of indeterminate negations. In one of his last works, *Negative Dialectics*, he declared the inevitability of *difference*, a signal that Hegelian reconciliation was utopian, in the bad sense.

It's here, perhaps, that Walter Benjamin's cautious invocation of agency, a product of his study of Jewish mysticism and Cabalistic thought, can be understood as the hope of the hopeless. Benjamin's idiosyncratic melding of Marx's insight that "men make their own history" and the Jewish command to redeem the unfinished tasks of the past by creating a new world was dismissed by Adorno as an unacceptable concession to tradition. Yet Benjamin stood for a critical modernism, critical because it was acutely aware of modernity's poten-

While "the black Atlantic" may describe a more comprehensive reality than "African American," it's difficult to rally behind its as-yet amorphous banner

tial for inhumanity. Where Adorno lamented that "after Auschwitz, all poetry is garbage," Benjamin (and after him Marcuse) suggested that despite all the atrocities that had been committed in the name of progress, we cannot help but make history (if not Universal history) by engaging in local struggles to make life better.

In *The Black Atlantic* Gilroy makes a new application of Benjamin's claim that "there is no document of civilization which is not at the same time a document of barbarism." But in his totalizing conception of a black diaspora consciousness, Gilroy is less attentive to the way that the fact of New World slavery localized black struggles for freedom and happiness as *national* projects.

• • •

Gilroy's avoidance of the historical problem posed by slavery in the Atlantic world might also explain something about the weakness of his analyses of specific, nationalized experiences of double consciousness—the unique trajectories of "integrationist" projects in the Caribbean (where Creolistes strive to be both Martinican and black) and the United States. For the aspiration to American citizenship is a red thread that runs through the history of the black freedom movement in the twentieth century; despite a steep decline in the past twenty years, it may not yet have reached its historical limit. Although varieties of black nationalism from Martin Delany and Alexander Crummell, to Marcus Garvey and Louis Farrakhan, have had considerable influence over the black "masses," political and economic integration, if not cultural assimilation, remains the endpoint of struggles for civil rights in this country. While the "the black Atlantic" may describe a more comprehensive reality than "African American," it's difficult to rally behind its as-yet amorphous banner.

For most of this century, movements for civil rights have been strongly Americanist in orientation. The career of W. E. B. Du Bois, and Gilroy's interpretation of it, is instructive here. Gilroy makes Du Bois the leading black Atlantic figure by having him shed his American "roots":

Du Bois' analysis of modernity also expressed his turn away from the United States. That country ceased to be the locus of his political aspirations once it became clear that the commitments to private rectitude and public reason for which he had argued so powerfully would not be sufficient to precipitate the comprehensive reforms demanded by black suffering in the North as well as the South.

In light of Du Bois's restless journey—from a middle-class New England childhood to Harvard, on to Europe, back to America to teach in black colleges in the South and thence to Ghana—this is a highly selective claim. *The Souls of Black Folk* was published in 1903. A few years later Du Bois spearheaded the Niagara movement, which was shortly thereafter institutionalized as the National Association for the Advancement of Colored People, still the leading civil rights organization in the country.

To be sure, Du Bois became less inclined to rely exclusively on domestic reform. After decades of dedication to altering the legal and economic conditions of American blacks (a project that led him to support Woodrow Wilson and American entrance into World War I), he joined with George Padmore and others in the incipient pan-African movement. But he returned in *Black Reconstruction* (1935) to a consideration of the fate of the black worker in the postbellum South, and, in a shift from his socialist sentiments, joined the Communist Party, of which he remained a member until his death, in Nkrumah's Ghana, in 1963. The interpenetration of these consciousnesses—black, American, pan-Africanist, Communist—was complex, and Du Bois's "turn away from America" was never as definitive as Gilroy would have it.

Struggles for "civil rights" have always been about more than the assertion of narrowly political rights; in marching on Washington, blacks have always been expressing a determination to tie their economic fortunes with those of other Americans. "Washington" became a metaphor for the power that could deliver blacks not only from social, political, and *economic* servitude. The crucial event was the New Deal. Roosevelt's activist state was commited to redistributive policies aimed at alleviating poverty, as well as job creation. The Democrats, once viewed as the party of the lynch mob, segregation, and the plantation aristocracy, were now in a position to appeal to blacks, some of whom were already entering the new industrial unions, on the promise that they would break from the old Jim Crow policies of the American Federation of Labor.

Wright's *Twelve Million Black Voices* was, in part, a popular front document of the times. Gilroy reads it convincingly as an early example of the conflict between Wright's interests in psychoanalysis and Marxism. But the book fairly bristles with the accusation that blacks may be excluded from the economic prosperity already on the horizon. As the historian Harvard Sitkoff has shown, it was a moment in which the objections of Southern Democrats were causing Roosevelt to hold back on pursuing social and economic equality for blacks.

Under these conditions, it was A. Philip Randolph, the black leader of the Brotherhood of Sleeping Car Porters (AF of L), who emerged as the most powerful exemplar of double consciousness: as a thinker and organizer he was deeply and practically committed to black people *and* their place in the American project. With war clouds looming, he threatened a potentially embarrassing mass march to force Roosevelt to open the gates of war industries to blacks—a threat sufficiently credible for Roosevelt to issue an executive order barring employers who would do business with the federal government from discriminating against blacks.

As a socialist and war opponent, Randolph couldn't have cared less about Roosevelt's political dilemma. But, perhaps unwittingly, he provoked the Democrats into a qualitatively new alliance with blacks, one that had the long-term effect of encouraging the development of a mass civil rights movement whose fundamental aim was integration. Indeed, in the quarter century after Randolph's bold initiative, black nationalism fell on hard times. Many blacks and whites believed in the possibility that blacks could one day evolve into just another ethnic group.

Talk about modernity. No oppressed people in human history has more thoroughly embraced the leading features of modernity than American blacks. In the 1960s the most militant and radical contingent of the Black Power movement declared voter registration its supreme aspiration. With the murder of Martin Luther King, Jr., the nation lost the quintessential figure of American modernity; nobody was more loyal to the American Dream. Even after, many blacks responded by even more fervently dedicating themselves to the integrationist principles for which he gave his life. They entered electoral politics with new energy, won a wide array of public offices, and, by the 1980s, when many white blue-collar workers deserted to the suburbs and to the Republicans, they had become the bedrock of the Democratic Party.

Ironically, the fires of black nationalism would flare again in the midst of the most rapid economic gains since Reconstruction. A new internationalism excited the collective imagination of young blacks. After the 1967 war, there was new enthusiasm for the Palestinian struggle, and a few years later American blacks reached out to South Africa. As the struggle against apartheid gained momentum in the 1980s, American blacks initiated and led an astonishingly effective boycott against American companies doing business with South Africa.

For an articulate minority, the assassinations of Martin and Malcolm, the urban riots of the 1960s, and the success of race-tinged "Southern strategies" in national presidential politics since 1968 confirmed the bankruptcy of the integrationist ideology of the bulk of black leaders. While Jesse Jackson's Rainbow Coalition injected some life into the old liberal faith, his rejection by a newly minted "centrist" Democratic Party provided further evidence that a broad-based civil rights movement was now history.

This, then, may be the ultimate meaning of Farrakhanism. The success of the Million Man March may well prove that the integrationist hegemony has finally been broken. Surely, the failure of Jackson or the NAACP to call for a different kind of march reveals the bankruptcy of the old liberal alliance to galvanize the black masses, even in the face of the most sustained assault on

No oppressed people in human history has more thoroughly embraced the leading features of modernity than American blacks

their living standards and basic human rights since the Great Depression. Without making a single demand on a political power structure that had announced open season on the welfare state, the march gathered *as if* it could still deliver.

In the end, Gilroy's brilliant, flawed book leaves the unhappy double consciousness intact. Karl Marx once criticized Hegel's dialectic of master and slave (one of the most famous sections of the *Phenomenology of Spirit*) in which the bondsman, through his struggle with the lord, attains reflexive *self-consciousness* but not liberation. Gilroy, too, has deferred a discourse of emancipation, one that supersedes ethnic particularity for some universal project. He is unable to find a way out of perhaps the most troubling contradiction of modernity: the two souls of nationality. His often brilliant readings seem to cancel the enormous impetus for reform bound up in nationalist projects. If nationally based liberal reform has failed the black Atlantic as well, alongside that other modernist ideology of liberation, communism, the path ahead awaits a new affirmative vision.

AUTOPSY OF TERROR

A conversation with Raoul Peck

Clyde Taylor

Raoul Peck never set out to become the preeminent chronicler of Haiti's ordeal with tyranny, but in making five films that excavate Haiti's recent memory he has done just that. Born and educated in Haiti, with additional schooling in Zaire, Germany, France, and the United States, Peck has invented a Haitian cinema virtually from scratch. At once visually sophisticated and deeply engaged with the nation's history of dictatorship, Peck's films seek to perform an "Autopsy of Terror"—the title of his recent five-film retrospective in Haiti.

The films explore unthinkable political brutality through a focus on the everyday. Peck's eye for detail and economical storytelling style give his films a visceral force. In *Haitian Corner* (1989) a man who was once tortured in Haiti spots his assailant on the streets of Brooklyn, where both of them now live. Though his friends and relatives tell him it is best to forget, he becomes obsessed with thoughts of vengeance, searching the streets for the man who destroyed his

life. When he finally finds his tormentor and confronts him with a pistol, the man cringes before him, begging for mercy. Should he kill him or just spit on him and walk away?

Though it follows a fictional character, *Haitian Corner* opens with actual torture victims speaking directly to the camera about their experiences. Peck uses the same technique in the documentary *Desounen: Dialogue with Death* (1994). Made for the BBC, *Dialogue with Death* personalizes the displacements, postponements, and griefs of everyday Haitians, allowing them to tell their life stories to the camera as if to a patient and sympathetic friend. Among the most memorable is the story of how one mother implored her youngest son not to join his siblings in a boat headed for America; how she received word of a shipwreck, and of his death; and how she came to hear the news, many months later, that he had survived.

The critically acclaimed *Lumumba: Death of a Prophet* (1991) frees itself from

Patrice Lumumba with General Mobutu, 1960, from *Lumumba: Death of a Prophet*

California Newsreel

Raoul Peck

Mel Wright

the literalism of "straight doc" in favor of a poetic, improvisational film idiom. The documentary uses home footage of the director as a young boy growing up in Zaire and reflective commentary from his mother on Patrice Lumumba, the prophet of the liberation movement in the Belgian Congo. Through the use of these startlingly personal sequences, the film evokes a more full-bodied image of the mythical hero of Zaire's independence. In Peck's presentation, Lumumba's legend resonates with similar stories from other former colonies. In particular, his film suggests an analogy between the charismatic first premier of the postcolonial Republic of the Congo and the first president of postdictatorship Haiti, Jean Baptiste Aristide.

Peck's most recent feature, *Man by the Shore* (1993), follows the life of Sarah, an eight-year-old girl whose parents have fled the terror of the Duvalier regime, leaving her behind in anticipation of a safer time to travel. Sarah lives in hiding above the family store, guarded by her grandmother. Movingly portrayed by Jennifer Zubar, Sarah's gawky resistance to this smothering environment comes to symbolize the banality of political repression—the angst of Haiti waiting for peaceful existence, free of the threat of abuse. To watch Sarah window-peeking at a world denied to her is to renew one's understanding of freedom.

Peck understands the emotional gauge that can make the menace to one human completely palpable, while news of the massacre of thousands dulls the mind. The threat in this movie comes from a Tonton Macoute who swaggers through the provincial town terrorizing anyone who dares to hold on to human dignity, a man more than willing to use rape as an instrument of intimidation. In its intensity this film seems a mirror of the present moment, but it is also a document of human crisis anywhere. Some might be reminded of the ordeal of Anne Frank. Others will think of the seven years Harriet Jacobs spent hidden in a garret over her mother's house, watching through cracks in the wall as her children grew up without her. For Peck, Sarah's plight must also have a personal meaning, since he left his homeland with his parents at the same age, into exile in Zaire.

Man by the Shore was more topical than Peck had intended. The film was released in the same week that General Raoul Cedras overthrew the fledgling Aristide government. It was intended as an assessment of the emotional damage of Papa Doc's reign of terror; Peck conceived of the project during the brief interregnum between the two dictatorships.

Man by the Shore showcases Peck's assured style. The poise and finesse of the cinematography and acting make the silence that greeted the film in the United States all the more remarkable. How is it that this movie, with its insight into the human cost of the Haitian situation (for which U.S. policy was in certain ways undoubtedly responsible), has had only modest circulation on U.S. screens? The film was seen, Peck insists, by all the major American distributors at Cannes, and passed over by all of them. It was widely and successfully screened in France and other European countries but continues to go unlit here, where its issues affect national policy and American lives.

Peck has had similar problems screening his films in Haiti. During the exhibition, the company that owns most of the theaters initially refused to show *Haiti: The Silence of the Dogs* (1994), a candid documentary about the political maneuverings of March 1994 in which Aristide and Prime Minister Robert Malval are both exposed to a critical gaze. When the company finally agreed to the screenings, it also aired an unusual taped disclaimer assuring audiences that the views expressed in the movies are those of the filmmakers and not of the theater owners.

Man by the Shore makes its U.S. debut in New York City and Miami this May. Meanwhile, Peck has several projects in the works. He plans a fictional Lumumba film, a documentary on Cuban artist Wilfredo Lam for French television, and a version of Jean-Claude Charles's novel *Manhattan Blues*. But his major preoccupation is a film based on Russell Banks's novel *Continental Drift*. The film features Willem Dafoe as a white American involved in an operation to smuggle Haitians across the Caribbean waters.

CLYDE TAYLOR: Haiti does not have many filmmakers. How is it that you are one of the exceptional people, one of the few Haitians who have been able to launch a filmmaking career?
RAOUL PECK: I think I was very privileged to be out of the country for my whole youth. I left Haiti when I was eight years old for Africa, and then I did most of secondary school in France. So I had access to a lot more things than did the few colleagues I have in Haiti. The situation in Haiti doesn't really encourage that kind of project. There is no film school, of course. The state television and the private television stations are not very well developed. You really have to learn everything by yourself. A few other

Young people in Haiti have dreams like everybody else, but they are basically lost

people were lucky enough to go to the United States and get some training, but basically there is no possibility for a young person to say, "Well, I want to be a filmmaker." They have dreams like everybody else, but they are basically lost.

CT: Do you have a particular sense of destiny for yourself as a filmmaker? What is it you're trying to accomplish?

RP: I never saw this as my profession. In my mind it was always something that I was going to do on the side. I come from a rather bourgeois family—not so much in their way of thinking, but certainly in comparison with most people in Haiti, my parents were living very well. My father was a professional, an agronomist. So coming from this type of family, any artistic career is really unre-

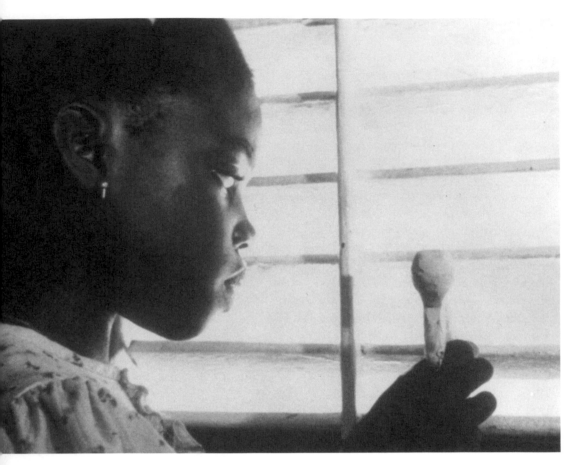

alistic. Artists are not taken very seriously and in our tradition, whether you are a writer or a singer or a painter, it's something you do on the side. You always have another job. It's something you do when you finish your regular job, your money-earning job.

It was the same for myself. Even after I had already started working in this field with friends and with the woman I was living with, who was a filmmaker, I never really thought about it as something I would do full time. Still, I grew up with a camera always in the house. Later my father bought an 8-millimeter camera and then a Super 8 camera, and I would use it with him. I would carry it around,

I would use it when we were traveling to Europe or other places. It was just a way of playing, of having fun and looking at people through a camera. There was a kind of magic for me but it was always a fun thing, it was never like, "When I grow up I want to be a filmmaker." I probably didn't even know what a filmmaker was.

CT: So how did you learn about filmmaking?

RP: After I received my high school diploma, I went to Berlin at my father's insistence to study industrial engineering. I studied that for seven years, but I realized that it was not going to be my life, so I started a Ph.D. in development policy. At one time, I was accepted for a position at the United Nations Development Project in New York City, but after I had already arrived they stopped hiring for a while. So I drove a cab for eight months in New York, writing between fares, before finally returning to Berlin to study film.

CT: Were you always drawn to writing and literature?

RP: Well, reading was my passion. I remember one day I was very sad, I didn't really know why, and I had to write an essay for homework, so I sat down and wrote this personal essay. It was the first time that I had made my intimate thoughts public, and it was one of my first good grades.

CT: Do you remember what the essay was about?

RP: Unfortunately, I don't. But I remember the feeling that it gave me very precisely. I remember sitting in the playground afterwards with my back against the fence, looking at the other children playing, and I felt so powerful. I felt like I had something that the other children didn't, and I could have some impact on the world if I wanted to.

My political awakening was very similar. When I was younger, I had the naive belief that no white boy could fight me, because in Haiti we thought that white people were weak. I remember this French school I went to, on the first day groups of older students had a ritual of attacking the younger boys. About ten of them circled around me and started to push me. Very calmly and slowly I took my leather jacket off and said, "Well, who is first?" [Laughs.] There was a mo-

ment of silence and then one of the guys came to me and said, "Oh, no, we're just joking, we're just having fun."

It was a very strange moment. I think it was the moment when I first had an understanding of what power is, what it is to come from another civilization, another country. I was always very conscious of being from the Third World. I still have that consciousness today: it's very hard to neglect your background, to neglect your whole history. I could not just sit down right now and write a comedy. I would love to make a film where I would only have fun, but I could not be responsible for that. I cannot make a film that I would be ashamed to show in Haiti.

CT: It seems to me that there may be an imperative in your social situation that determines the kind of films you make. I feel that a lot of African filmmakers feel the same way you do because they come from a context where issues are very serious and they must make films in accordance with those realities.

RP: You know, I would say the contrary. I think *every* filmmaker is like that, but the difference is, in places like the United States and Europe, filmmakers have the opportunity to escape this moral responsibility. This profession being also an industry, you can always say to yourself, "Well, it's a job," or "People want to see comedy," or "People want to see easy things." I think most filmmakers start out wanting to give back something, to transform the reality you have absorbed around you—but because of the environment you can easily lose your most inner motivation.

CT: That's interesting, since you would assume that coming from Haiti, where there is no film industry, you would be free to make whatever kind of movie you want.

RP: We are too close to our country, our people, our families, to be free in that respect. To be free is to be without a community that grounds you. If I spend too much time away from Haiti or Haitians, especially when I spend a lot of time with my colleagues in Paris going from cocktail party to cocktail party and following the festival circuit, I can feel myself changing. I start to forget that people are dying in my country, that there is a virulent racism in Paris. You lose contact with your reality and then you feel you're going to try to do something easier. But there's always something, some little incident to remind me who I am and where I come from. That's what I mean when I say we are not free. We are bound.

To me, it's a joke when people try to identify what is specifically Haitian in my films

CT: You have an extraordinary international filmmaking record. You've made films in New York, Santo Domingo, Paris, and Germany. How do you feel about that cosmopolitanism? What's "Haitian" about that?

RP: That's something I'm always fighting against. Journalists ask me if I'm a Haitian filmmaker, but that's not the way I relate to my work. The films I make never start with Haiti; they start with an issue or with a feeling, and then I look for a story. It ends up as a Haitian story, but that's only because I know that location well—it's inside of me. To me, it's a joke when critics and the public try to identify what is specifically Haitian in my films. How can I make Haitian films when I have no examples of Haitian films? How do you film your own community when you have never seen an image on the screen of this community? I can easily sit down and write a western without doing research because I've seen hundreds of westerns, but I can't do the same for a scene set among Haitians in Flatbush, Brooklyn. I'm influenced by Charles Burnett, by German cinema, by Cassavetes, Godard. When I look at a film like *Haitian Corner*, I see a quintessentially German film.

CT: A quintessentially *German* film? How do you mean that?

RP: Cinematically, *Haitian Corner* is totally German; it references the filmic language of German directors like Fassbinder—the "coldness" of it. The city you see in Haitian Corner is a very cold city; there are very few shots of it. It's more imagined than seen.

CT: When I look at, say, *Haitian Corner*, I feel an affinity with other populations who have been repressed and tortured, so I feel the concern with a human dilemma that anyone can respond to. Simultaneously, however, I *do* feel that a specifically Haitian dimension is present. It comes from a number of places: Sometimes from the look of the scene or the sound of the language or—

RP: I do think the humanity of it—the way of dealing with emotions and trauma—is somehow very Haitian. As well as the poetry.

From
Man by the Shore

CT: *Desounen: Dialogue with Death* had what seemed to be particularly Haitian poetry. I thought that there was some accidental cultural definition going on, that the central theme of the film had to do with a particular situation of Haitians dealing with their crisis. The way you approached it reminded me of what the Australian aboriginal filmmaker, Frances Peters, once said. She did not want to define people solely in terms of "issues." Since they are complete people, she would ask them about their everyday lives—how they liked work and school and so on—and they would reply with stories of repression lived through these everyday experiences.

RP: Exactly. There is no difference for me when I encounter a Haitian peasant or a New York businessman or whatever, it's just a person and I react to the person on their terms. I'm interested in what they have to tell me, what they experience as a human being. In *Desounen*

I didn't ask the people specific questions about contemporary Haitian politics, I asked them about the feelings in their lives: How did they feel today? Do they feel like they have succeeded in life? Do they feel that their life was worth it? Do they feel that they have a future? I asked very general, humanist questions. That's how you represent them as humans, not victims. It's interesting that *Desounen* was the first film I shot in Haiti: it was my first real confrontation with my people, and of course, I did not want to go in there and make a film about exotic people or victims. The BBC sent a photographer to take stills of the shooting for the publicity package for a program they were producing, and I was amazed that the photos he took were exactly the images I'm fighting against: you know, a little boy with a torn shirt looking sentimentally at the camera, with big eyes, or peasants working under the hot sun. I don't see my people like this.

From

Man by the Shore

CT: Did you consciously avoid the imagery of voodoo?

RP: Yes, of course. Voodoo is something I respect too much. Hollywood "invented" voodoo—how can you fight Hollywood with only one film? Any way I present voodoo, it will be exotic, it will fit into all the clichés. It's too complicated to fit into one film, so I consciously take it out of my work. There are some moments where I touch on it, and Haitians might feel it, but it's not something that I will confront openly.

CT: I remember Senegalese director Ousmane Sembene saying that he never wanted tom-toms or people dancing in his films because he saw it as too "folkloric."

RP: It's very hard *not* to do a folkloric film in Haiti. That's one of the problems I had with *Man by the Shore*. How do you shoot a rape scene of a little girl in an environment which is obviously touristic? I mean, when you see a beach and palm trees and all those colors? There's always an additional difficulty when you're creating in a world full of clichés—not clichés because we live like that, but because people have seen us as clichés. I'm not fighting against my people, but the views of others, sometimes the views of the people putting money into the film.

CT: Tell me about the audiences' responses to the films.

RP: There were a lot of very different reactions. Audiences outside Haiti were mostly shocked by *Man by the Shore*, because they didn't expect a dictatorship to be like that. People have certain ideas about what a dictatorship is and the film caught them off guard. The film also surprised audiences with its humanity. It's easy to identify with the characters—the grandmother reminds you of your grandmother, the little girl is your little girl— so you don't have the distance to say, "Those are black people," or "Those are Haitians." You are forced to get into the story, and you can be pretty shocked by it since you learn what it is to be afraid, to endure torture and repression. The torture scene in *Haitian Corner* is, for me, one of the film's biggest accomplishments. At the time I was writing it, although I've seen hundreds of films that depicted torture, only a few were convincing.

When *Man by the Shore* played in Paris, during the first few days of its run I talked to the people working at the theater. One of the ladies selling tickets told me how after the film ended, the audience wouldn't come out right away. They would sit inside, almost as if they were afraid of going out. I was told that in Canada, strangers—Haitians and Canadians—would go to cafés near the theater to talk, like they wanted to continue something. Sometimes, when I was at a screening, people would stand up and say, "This is my story. I remember hiding at my grandmother's house. I remember when they came and took my father." That's happened all over—the United States, France, Germany. I hear from Haitians, as well as Latin Americans and Asians. It's so strange. After seeing the rape scene in *Man by the Shore*, a Turkish woman told me that that had happened to her, but in Germany. An American said the same thing. And sometimes people would patiently wait for everyone to leave and then come up to me and say, simply, "Thank you." I'm so surprised by how general those feelings are.

When they were screened in Haiti, I was very curious to see how people there would react. I sometimes think the films are very abstract. I was afraid they might dismiss the films as not being "real" since I'm trying to create an *emotional* reality. I showed the film to schools and had discussions with the students afterwards. Those screenings were incredible, the students were unbelievably responsive. At first, I was suspicious of their ability to understand the films, but not only did they understand them, they were totally involved with them. One fourteen-year-old boy desperately wanted to know what he could do, how we can prevent it from happening again. We had schools in the best neighborhoods and schools in the slums and the questions were the same. The only difference was that if the bourgeois students saw a corpse in the street, they would dismiss it by saying it was the body of a thief, whereas the children from the slums knew who the dead were and what their reality was.

The director of the elite French school in Port-au-Prince obliged all the classes from the sixth grade up to go and see the movies. There were children of the former military, children of the putsch, children of Cedras, and children of the former prime minister in exile, and they fell into cliques representing these same political categories. I heard that there were fights within families because of the questions the children asked their parents after seeing the film. They wanted to know why their parents had been lying to them all those years. Parents told me that for the first time, students were talking about Haiti's history and questioning their teachers—and the teachers were forced to put the issues on the table.

CT: Do you think it's possible that the screenings collectively represented one important confrontation of Haitians, at least in Port-au-Prince, with their history?

RP: Oh, yes. It was really a catharsis. One scholar wrote an article on the effects of those films on Haitian society. He called them milestones—you cannot go around them, you cannot now ignore our history. I believe it's important to have a public consciousness of our history from which to start a process of renewal. It's a tough thing to ask; in Haiti now people who have blood on their hands are mixing with people who have had blood shed in their family. We can have reconciliation, but I don't think that we have to sit at the same table and eat together as if nothing has happened.

Man by the Shore was conceived at a moment where I was wondering, after twenty years of dictatorship—more if you go by the Duvalier era—what is going to be left as a record of that period? My initial motivation was to create a document that would keep us from repeating that past. But just a few weeks before shooting began there was a military coup. I said to myself as I told everyone else, "Don't worry. This is going to last one week." That's how naive we were. And it took three years. Deadly years. It was tragic: the film was supposed to be a monument to a time *passed*.

CT: How do you see your trajectory in the documentary film? In the United States documentaries have a certain character: they seem to be very nonfictional, very realistic, for the most part, involving very little aesthetic play, but yours seem to incorporate those elements.

RP: People sometimes say that my documentaries are "strange" because they are Haitian, or from a Haitian filmmaker. But they are strange as documentary, period! [Laughs.] Although I make documentaries and fictional narratives, my approach is the same with both: my documentaries try to be as fictional as possible and my narratives try to be as "real" as possible. I'm trying to create an active viewer that is both submerged and standing outside of it. I try to do that, in part, by creating nonlinear narratives that draw attention to themselves. But it's difficult to do when contemporary audiences are so jaded: so what language can I choose in my film to reach a viewer? *Lumumba: Death of a Prophet* is typical of this. I asked myself, how am I going to tell this serious story without boring people, and how can I succeed, at the same time, in touching people? One of the "tricks" that I used was to insert this very personal story of this little boy in it so that it would be easier to accept the political parts. At the beginning of each project I ask myself how I can say things in such a way that it will change people. I'm not saying the film is going to change your life, but I'm hoping that a little thing will stay in your head or in your heart—maybe only a question or a thought, but nowadays, that's a lot.

NOTES ON CONTRIBUTORS

STANLEY ARONOWITZ is professor of sociology and director of the Cultural Studies Program at the Graduate Center, City University of New York. He is the author of *Roll Over Beethoven, The Crisis in Historical Materialism, The Jobless Future* (with William DiFazio), and *The Death and Rebirth of American Radicalism* (forthcoming).

MICHAEL BÉRUBÉ is professor of English at the University of Illinois at Champaign-Urbana. He is the author of *Public Access* and *Life As We Know It* (forthcoming). His review of Houston A. Baker, Jr.'s *Rap, Black Studies, and the Academy*, "Bum Rap," appeared in *Transition* 64.

STEPHEN BURT is a PhD candidate in English at Yale University. He has written for *PN Review, The Times Literary Supplement, Thumbscrew*, and *Popwatch*, and is the editor of *Adventure Playground*, a fanzine.

RUSSELL JACOBY is author most recently of *Dogmatic Wisdom: How the Culture Wars Divert Education and Distract America* and co-editor, with Naomi Glauberman, of *The Bell Curve Debate*. He teaches history at UCLA.

SIDNEY L. KASFIR is a professor of art history at Emory University and former manager of the Nommo Gallery in Kampala, Uganda. She is the author of *West African Masks and Cultural Systems* and *Colonial Transformations in African Art and Warriorhood*. Her essay, "Taste and Distaste," appeared in *Transition* 57.

RICHARD LEWONTIN is Alexander Aggasiz Professor of Zoology and Professor of Biology at Harvard University. He is the author of *The Genetic Basis of Evolutionary Change* and *Biology as Ideology: The Doctrine of DNA*.

MICHAEL LIND is senior editor at *The New Republic* and the author of *The Next American Nation: The New Nationalism and the Fourth American Revolution*.

ALI A. MAZRUI is Albert Schweitzer Professor in the Humanities and director of the Institute of Global Cultural Studies at SUNY-Binghamton. He is the author of *The African Condition* and *Political Values and the Educated Class in Africa* and a former associate editor of *Transition*.

ROBERT REID-PHARR is a professor of English at Johns Hopkins University. He is the author of *Conjugal Union: Gender, Sexuality, and the Development of an African-American National Literature* (forthcoming).

ALEX ROSS writes on music for the *New York Times*. His essays and reviews have appeared in *The New Yorker, The New Republic, Lingua Franca* and the *WHRB Program Guide*.

ILAN STAVANS, a novelist and critic, teaches at Amherst College. His latest books include *Bandido, The One-Handed Pianist and Other Stories* and *Art & Anger: Essays 1986–1995*. He is currently editing *The Oxford Book of Latin American Essays*.

WOLE SOYINKA, winner of the 1986 Nobel Prize in Literature, is the author most recently of *The Open Sore of a Continent: A Personal Narrative of the Nigerian Crisis*. He was the editor of *Transition* from 1974 to 1976 and is currently chairman of the editorial board.

CHARLES SUGNET's essays have appeared in *In These Times, The Nation, The Village Voice*, the *Utne Reader*, and *d'Art*. He is the editor, with Alan Burns, of *The Imagination on Trial*. His essay, "Vile Bodies, Vile Places" appeared in *Transition* 51.

CLYDE TAYLOR is Fletcher Professor of Rhetoric and Debate in English at Tufts University. He is the author of *Breaking the Aesthetic Contract* (forthcoming).

LUCIEN TAYLOR is co-director, with Ilisa Barbash, of *In and Out of Africa*, a documentary, and co-author, again with Barbash, of *(Cross-) Cultural Filmmaking* (forthcoming). He is the editor of *Visualizing Theory*.

PAUL THEROUX is the author of numerous travelogues and novels, including *The Mosquito Coast* and *The Old Patagonian Express*. His most recent book is *The Pillars of Hercules: A Grand Tour of the Mediterranean*.

CHRIS WATERS is a professor of history at Williams College. He is the author of *British Socialists and the Politics of Popular Culture 1884–1914* and a forthcoming book on national identity and working class culture in 20th century Britain.

Transition *(ISSN 0041-1191)*
is published quarterly by Duke
University Press, 905 West Main
Street, Suite 18-B, Durham NC
27701 and is an official publication
of the W. E. B. Du Bois Institute.
The editorial offices of Transition
are located at 1430 Massachusetts
Avenue, 4th Floor, Cambridge MA
02138.

Manuscript submissions
Manuscripts should be sent to
the Editors, Transition, *1430*
Massachusetts Avenue, 4th Floor,
Cambridge MA 02138, and
should be submitted typed, double-
spaced, and in triplicate. Unsolicited
manuscripts can be returned only
if accompanied by a self-addressed,
stamped envelope. In general the
journal follows the recommendations
of The Chicago Manual of
Style. *For specific instructions on*
style, contact the editorial office.

Advertising
Correspondence regarding
advertising should be sent to
Journals Advertising Department,
Duke University Press, 905 West
Main Street, Suite 18-B, Durham
NC 27701.

Book reviews
All copies of books to be considered
for review should be sent to
Transition, *1430 Massachusetts*
Avenue, 4th Floor, Cambridge
MA 02138.

Indexing
Transition *is indexed/abstracted*
in A Matter of Fact, Index to
Black Periodicals, Periodica
Islamica, Media Review Digest,
Consumers Index, *and* Current
Index to Journals in Education.

Photocopies and quotations
This journal is registered with the
Copyright Clearance Center
(222 Rosewood Drive, Danvers
MD 01923). Permission to
photocopy items for personal or
classroom use can be obtained from
CCC. Permission to photocopy or
quote items for classroom use or
any form of republication, including
general distribution, advertising,
resale, promotional purposes or
creation of new works, can be
obtained from Permissions Officer,
Duke University Press,
Box 90660, Durham NC 27708
(fax: 919-688-3524).

Subscriptions
Subscription rates for New Series
Volume 6 (1996; issues 69–72)
are $24 for individuals and $54
for institutions; please add $12 for
subscriptions outside the U.S.
Single copies and back issues are
$10 for individuals and $15 for
institutions; please add an
additional $3 for the first copy and
$1 for each additional copy for
shipments outside the U.S.
Subscription requests and change-
of-address notifications should be
directed to the Journals Fulfillment
Department, Duke University
Press, Box 90660, Durham NC
27708-0660. For phone orders
using a credit card, call
919-687-3614, Monday–Friday,
8 A.M.–4:30 P.M., EST.
http://www.duke.edu/web/dupress/

Postmaster: Send address changes to
Transition, *Journals Fulfillment*
Department, Duke University
Press, 905 West Main Street, Suite
18-B, Durham NC 27701.
Second-class postage pending
at Cambridge, MA, and additional
mailing offices.

Transition *is printed on acid-free*
paper that meets the minimum
requirements of ANSI Standard
Z39.48-1984 (Permanence
of Paper), beginning with Issue 51
(New Series V1N1).

Home and Harem:
Nation, Gender, Empire, and the Cultures of Travel

Inderpal Grewal
"A stunning account of the complex interactions between England and India, the women's movements and imperialism in the former and the anti-imperialist (and often anti-feminist) nationalist movements of the latter."—Mary N. Layoun, University of Wisconsin at Madison
288 pages, paper $15.95, library cloth edition $45.95
Post-Contemporary Interventions

Displacement, Diaspora, and Geographies of Identity

Smadar Lavie
and Ted Swedenburg, editors
"Displacement, Diaspora, and Geographies of Identity is informed not only by detailed attention to specific case studies or theoretical analyses, but also by an awareness of theoretical work in several fields which allows the highlighting of points and circuits of connections across disciplines and areas. This collection succeeds in ways which are thought provoking and likely to lead to vital discussions across disciplines."
— David Lloyd, University of California at Berkeley
344 pages, 6 b&w photographs, paper $16.95, library cloth edition $49.95

DUKE UNIVERSITY PRESS   BOX 90660 DURHAM, NORTH CAROLINA 27708-0660
http://www.duke.edu /web/dupress/

Lifebuoy Men, Lux Women

*Commodification, Consumption, and Cleanliness
in Modern Zimbabwe*
Timothy Burke
"Well researched, highly intelligent, well written, and
markedly original—there is nothing like it in the
literature of East, Central, and Southern Africa."
—Terence Ranger, Oxford University
328 pages, 20 b&w photographs, paper $17.95,
library cloth edition $49.95

The Making and Unmaking of the Haya Lived World

*Consumption, Commoditization,
and Everyday Practice*
Brad Weiss
"This is an important ethnography, beautifully
written and tightly conceived. . . . Weiss establishes
the value of a person-centered, historically situated
African ethnography and sets a new standard for
clarity of exposition of complex contemporary issues
on these terms."—Debbora Battaglia, Mount
Holyoke College
264 pages, 9 b&w photographs, paper $17.95,
library cloth edition $49.95

Clothing and Difference

*Embodied Identities in Colonial
and Post-Colonial Africa*
Hildi Hendrickson, editor
"An excellent book. *Clothing and Difference* will
contribute to knowledge about Africa as well as to
the general topic of the communication process
involved in dressing the body."—Joanne B. Eicher,
University of Minnesota
304 pages, 22 b&w photographs, paper $16.95,
library cloth edition $49.95

Duke University Press
Box 90660 Durham, NC 27708-0660
http://web.duke.edu/web/dupress

New from Duke

Pop Out: Queer Warhol
Jennifer Doyle, Jonathan Flatley,
& José Esteban Muñoz, editors
280 pages, 53 illustrations, paper $16.95,
library cloth edition $49.95
Series Q

Guilty Pleasures:
Feminist Camp from Mae West
to Madonna
Pamela Robertson
216 pages, 10 b&w photographs,
paper $15.95, library cloth edition $45.95

Fatal Advice:
How Safe-Sex Education
Went Wrong
Elaine K. Ginsberg, editor
296 pages, 6 illustrations,
paper $16.95, library cloth edition $45.95
New Americanists

What the Body Told
Rafael Campo
132 pages, paper $12.95,
library cloth edition $35.95

Passing and the Fictions
of Identity
Cindy Patton
200 pages, 10 illustrations,
paper $15.95, library cloth edition $45.95
Series Q

Duke University Press
Box 90660 Durham
North Carolina 27708-0660
http://www.duke.edu/web/dupress/

MELUS

Forthcoming in
Volume 21

Ethnic Humor

Varieties of Ethnic Criticism

Poetry and Politics ·

Other Americas

Published quarterly, *MELUS* features articles, interviews, and reviews reflecting the multi-ethnic scope of American literature. Lively, informative, and thought-provoking, *MELUS* is a valuable resource for teachers and students interested in African American, Hispanic, Asian and Pacific American, Native American, and ethnically specific Euro-American works, their authors, and their cultural contexts.

INDIVIDUAL SUBSCRIBERS become members of The Society for the Study of the Multi-Ethnic Literature of the United States. To subscribe, send a check (payable to *MELUS*) to: Arlene A. Elder, Treasurer, *MELUS*, Dept. of English, University of Cincinnati, Cincinnati, OH 45219. Regular, $35.00; students & retirees, $20.00; overseas, add $5.00 postage.

INSTITUTIONS Colleges, universities and libraries should send requests for rates and subscription orders to the Editorial Office at: *MELUS*, Dept. of English, 272 Bartlett Hall, University of Massachusetts, Amherst, MA 01003.

The Journal of the Society for the Study of the Multi-Ethnic Literature of the United States